Bird in a Cage

Rebecca Roher

Library and Archives Canada Cataloguing in Publication

Roher, Rebecca, author, illustrator

   Bird in a Cage / Rebecca Roher.

ISBN 978-1-77262-005-4 (paperback)

   1. Graphic novels. I. Title.

PN6733.R64B57 2016   741.5'971   C2016-900824-X

First Edition
Printed in Gatineau, Quebec by Gauvin

Conundrum Press
Wolfville, Nova Scotia, Canada
www.conundrumpress.com

Conundrum Press acknowledges the financial support of the
Canada Council for the Arts and the government of Canada
through the Canada Book Fund toward its publishing activities.

Canada Council   Conseil des Arts
for the Arts   du Canada

Bird in a Cage

Rebecca Roher

Dedicated to the Memory of
Grandma Wylie,
Jim Campbell
& Sheila

For mom, Dad, Jessica, Sophie, Christine, Rachel, Jamie, Rose, Rollo, Tancred, Alban, the Allens, Litherlands, Armstrongs, Campbells, Stinsons & Rohers. Thank you for your love & encouragement.

Thank you to Jonathan Rotsztain for editing help & support, & Ilana, Alison, Jean, Mary, Michelle, Kira, Bethany, Hannah, Sarah V, Sarah GT, CFOS, Daniel & Natalie. What would I do without you?

Thanks to James Sturm, Michelle Ollie, Jason Lutes, Steve Bisette, Jon Chad, Sophie Yanow, Nicole J. Georges, the Rainbow Goth Club & extended CCS tribe.

Thank you to Andy, Joe, Meags & Dakota.

And to Maura & Pete, & my new friends at AGP.

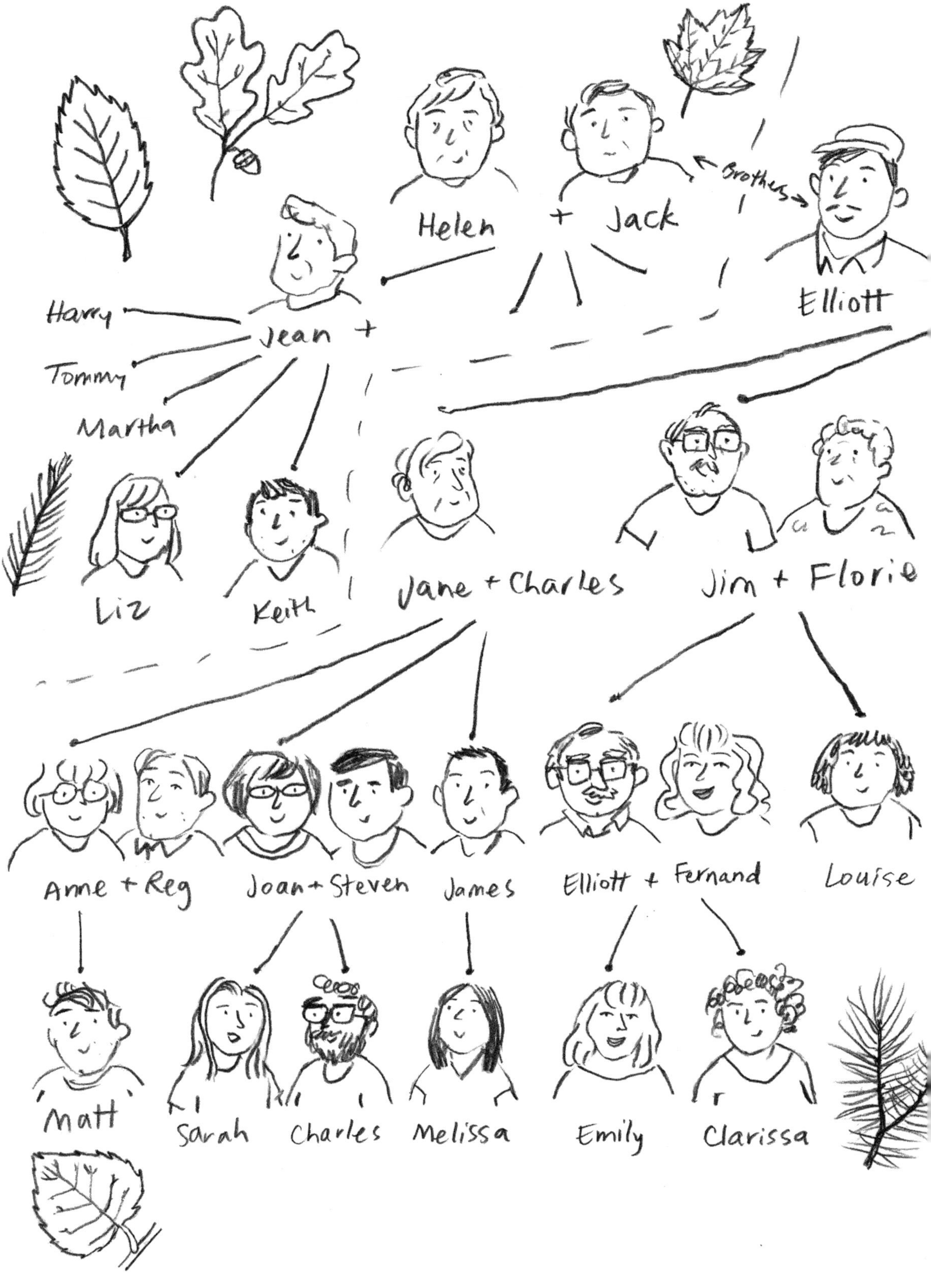

brothers
Helen + Jack
Elliott
Harry
Jean +
Tommy
Martha
Liz
Keith
Jane + Charles
Jim + Florie
Anne + Reg
Joan + Steven
James
Elliott + Fernand
Louise
Matt
Sarah
Charles
Melissa
Emily
Clarissa

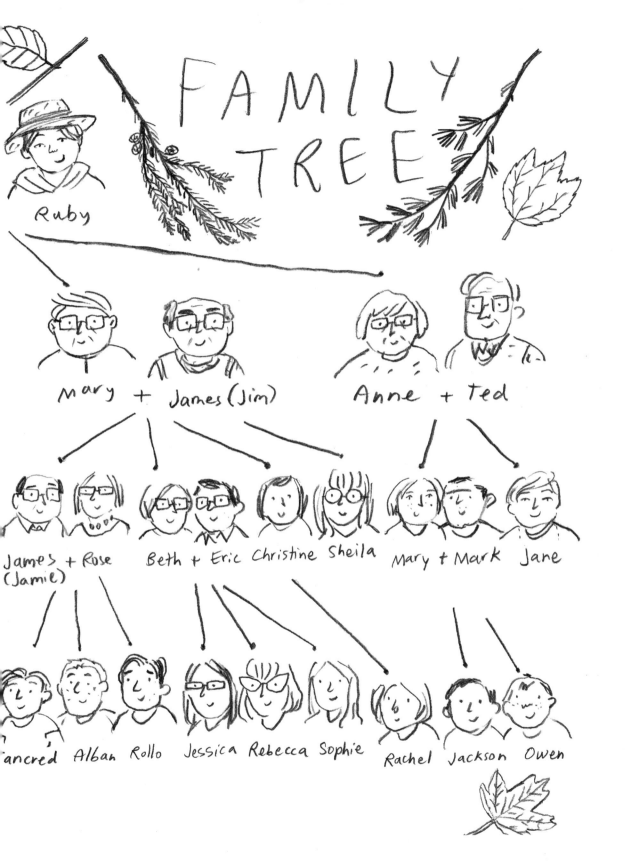

FAMILY TREE

Ruby

Mary + James (Jim)   Anne + Ted

James + Rose   Beth + Eric   Christine   Sheila   Mary + Mark   Jane
(Jamie)

ancred   Alban   Rollo   Jessica   Rebecca   Sophie   Rachel   Jackson   Owen

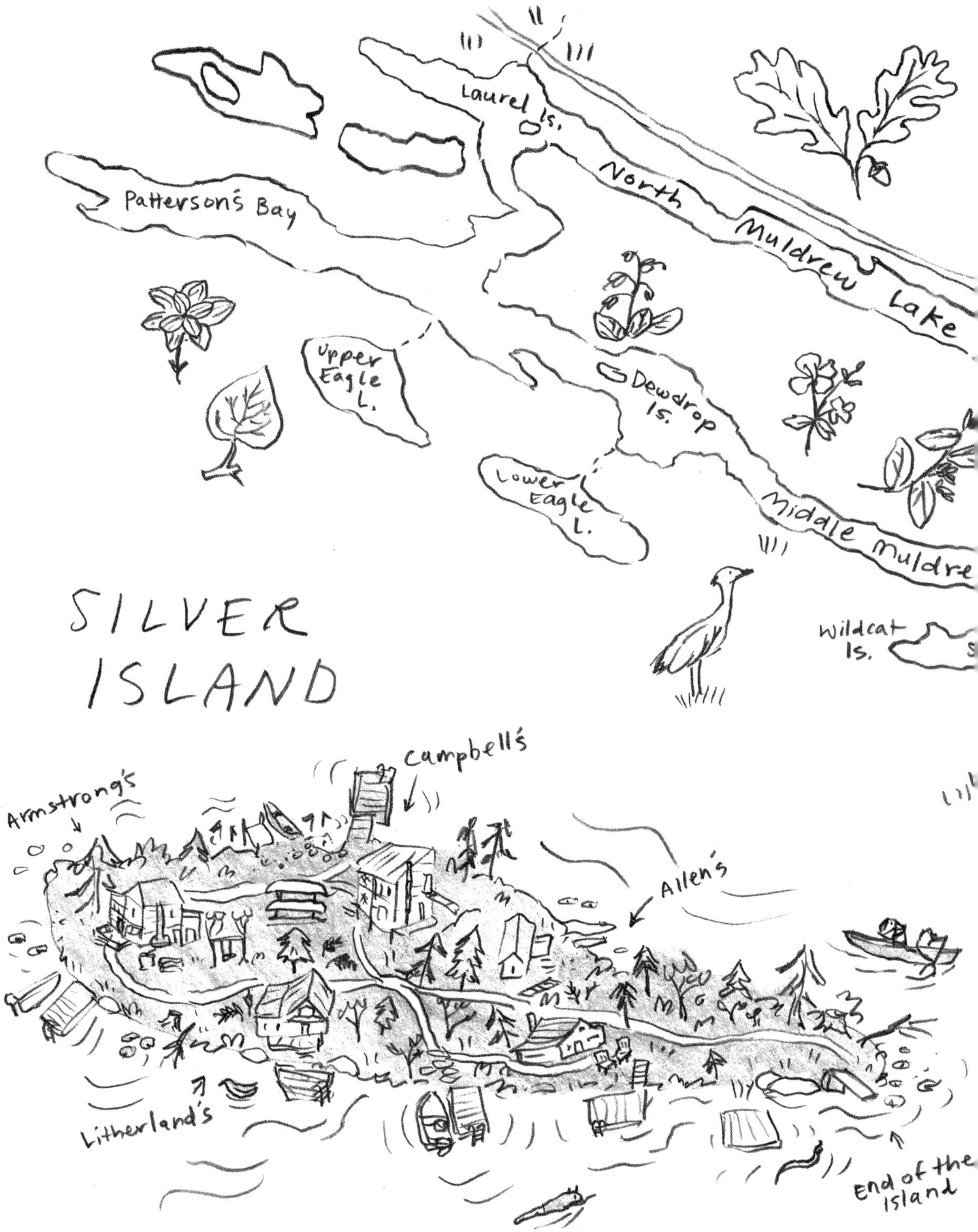

Laurel Is.
Patterson's Bay
North Muldrew Lake
Upper Eagle L.
Dewdrop Is.
Lower Eagle L.
Middle Muldre
SILVER ISLAND
Wildcat Is.
Campbell's
Armstrong's
Allen's
Litherland's
End of the Island

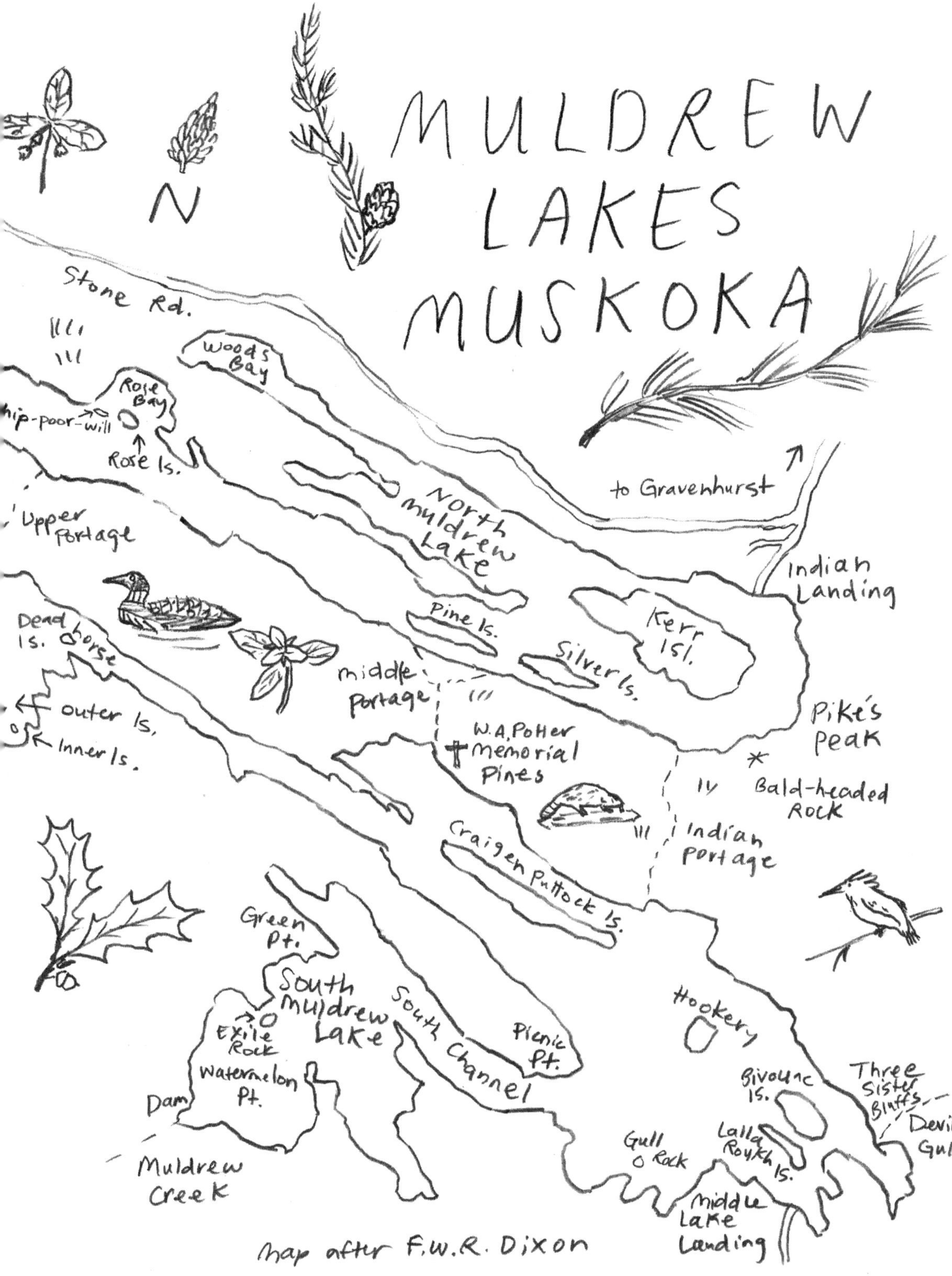
MULDREW LAKES MUSKOKA
N
Stone Rd.
Woods Bay
Rose Bay
hip-poor-will
Rose Is.
Upper Portage
North Muldrew Lake
to Gravenhurst
Indian Landing
Kerr Isl.
Pine Is.
Silver Is.
Dead horse Is.
middle portage
outer Is.
Inner Is.
W.A. Potter Memorial Pines
Pike's Peak
Bald-headed Rock
Indian Portage
Craigen Puttock Is.
Green Pt.
South Muldrew Lake
South Channel
Exile Rock
Picnic Pt.
Watermelon Pt.
Dam
Hookery
Bivouac Is.
Three Sisters Bluffs
Devils Gulch
Gull Rock
Lalla Roukh Is.
Muldrew Creek
Middle Lake Landing
map after F.W.R. Dixon

This book is a work of memory & may not
reflect the recollections of others

PART I

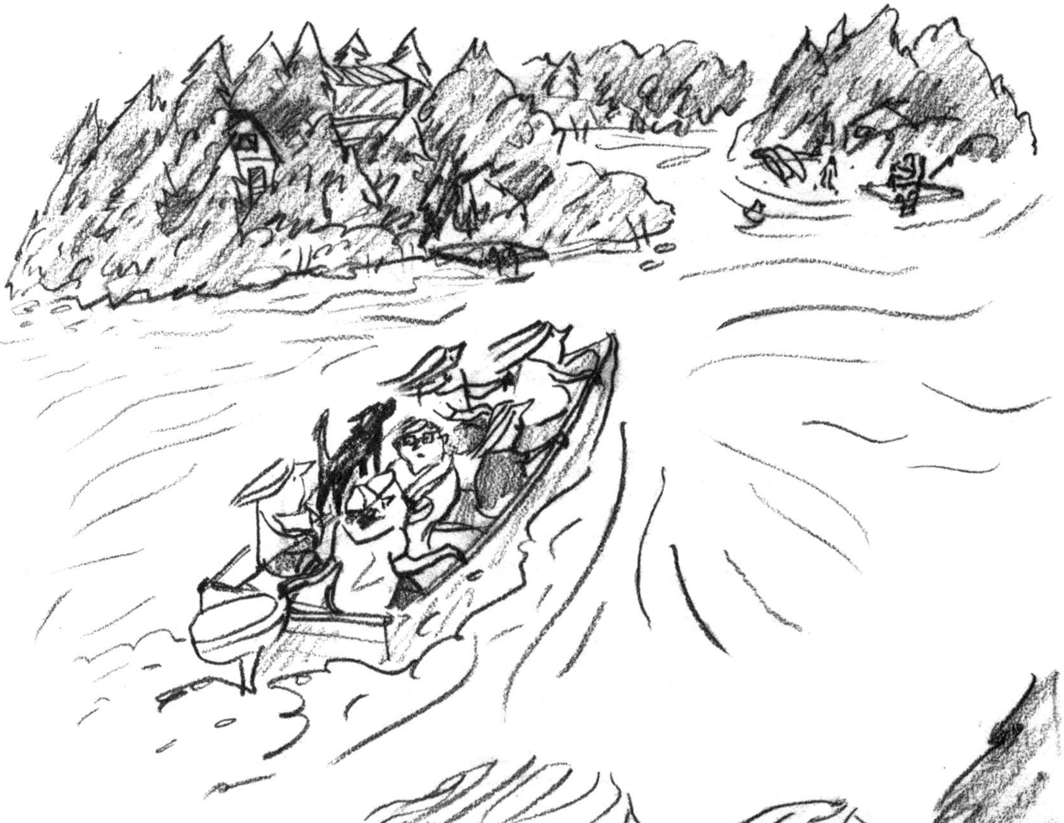

It was the weekend of the family sing-song

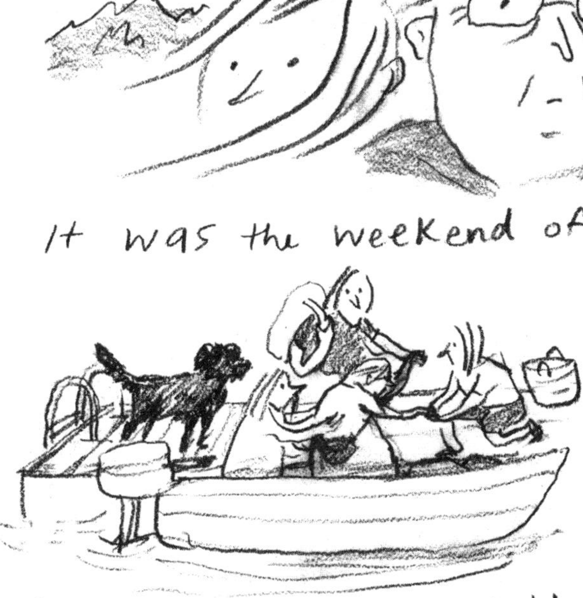

& the last time we would take grandma to the cottage

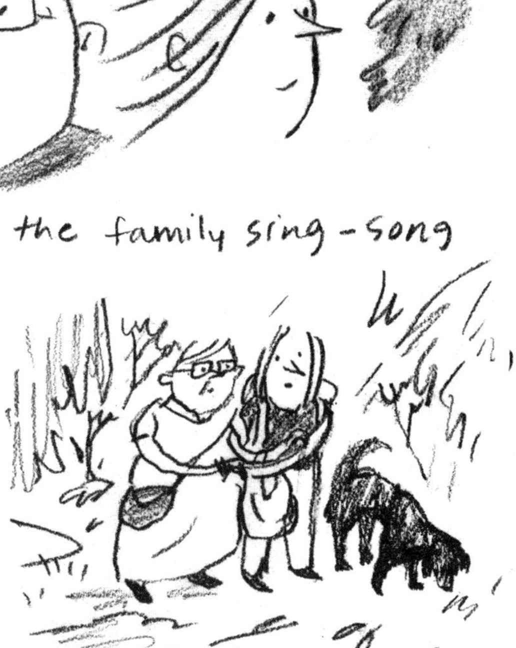

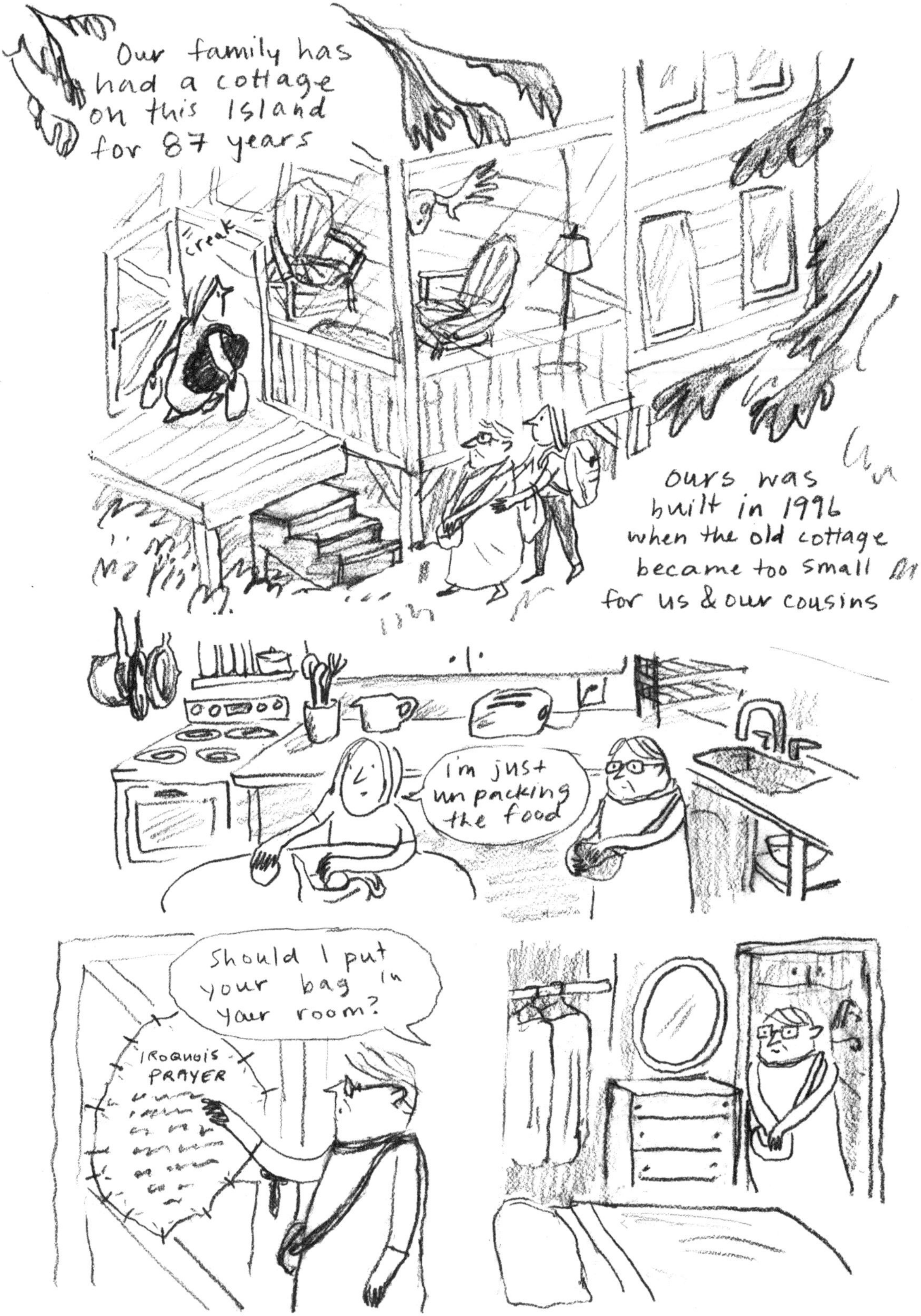
Our family has had a cottage on this Island for 87 years
creak
ours was built in 1996 when the old cottage became too small for us & our cousins
I'm just unpacking the food
Should I put your bag in your room?
IROQUOIS PRAYER

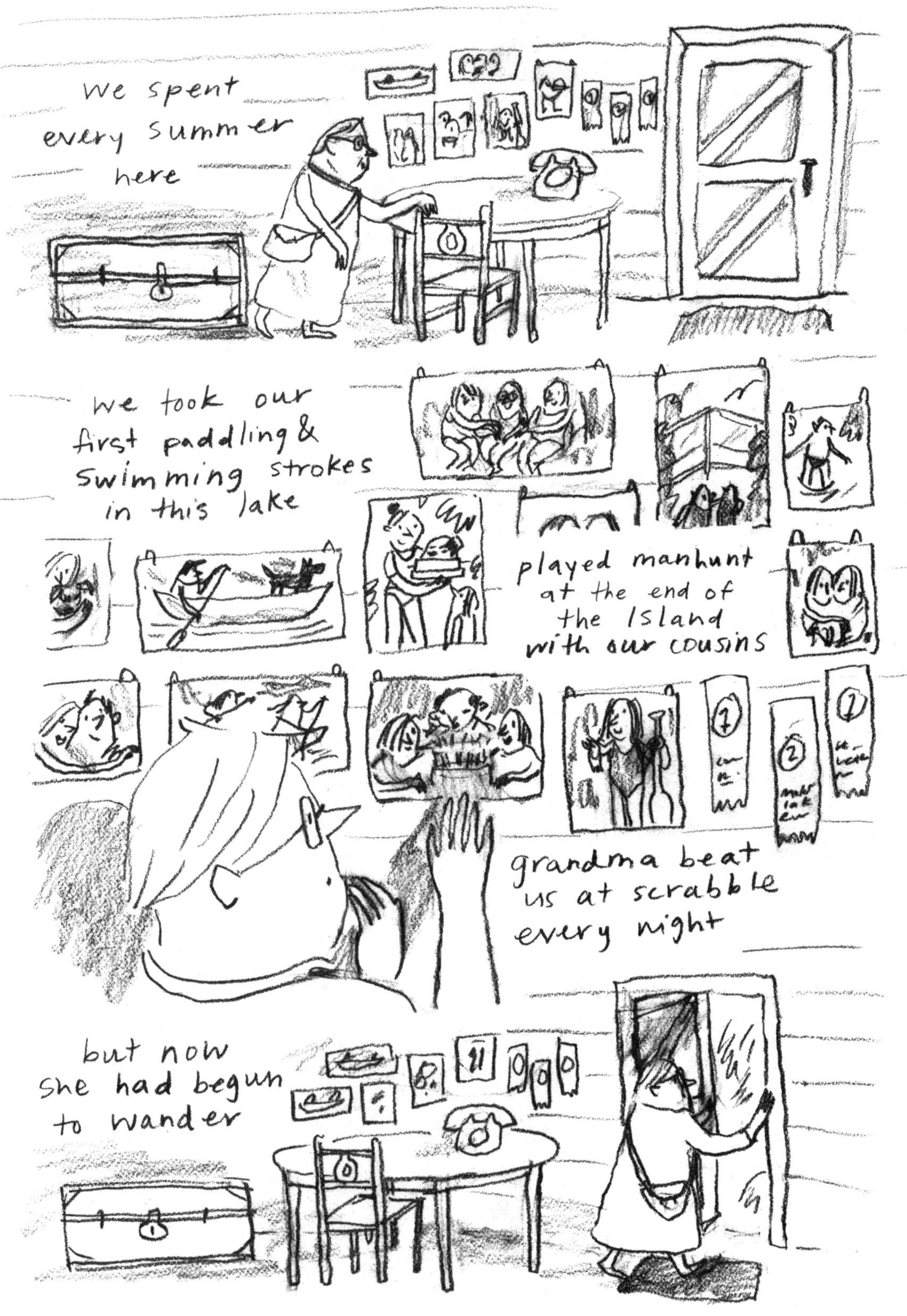
we spent every summer here
we took our first paddling & swimming strokes in this lake
played manhunt at the end of the Island with our cousins
grandma beat us at scrabble every night
but now she had begun to wander

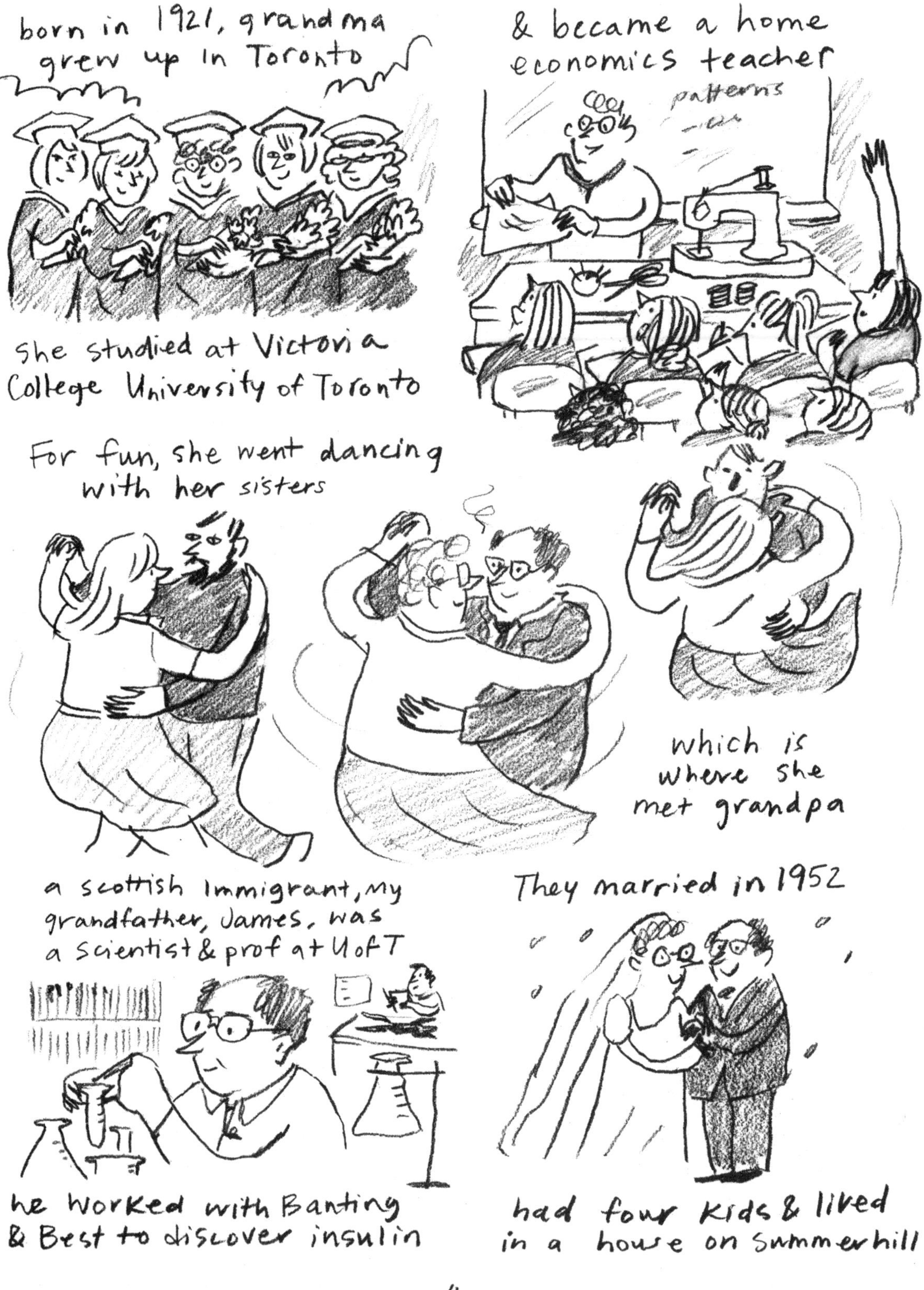
born in 1921, grandma grew up in Toronto
she studied at Victoria College University of Toronto
& became a home economics teacher
patterns
For fun, she went dancing with her sisters
which is where she met grandpa
a scottish immigrant, my grandfather, James, was a scientist & prof at UofT
he worked with Banting & Best to discover insulin
They married in 1952
had four kids & lived in a house on Summerhill

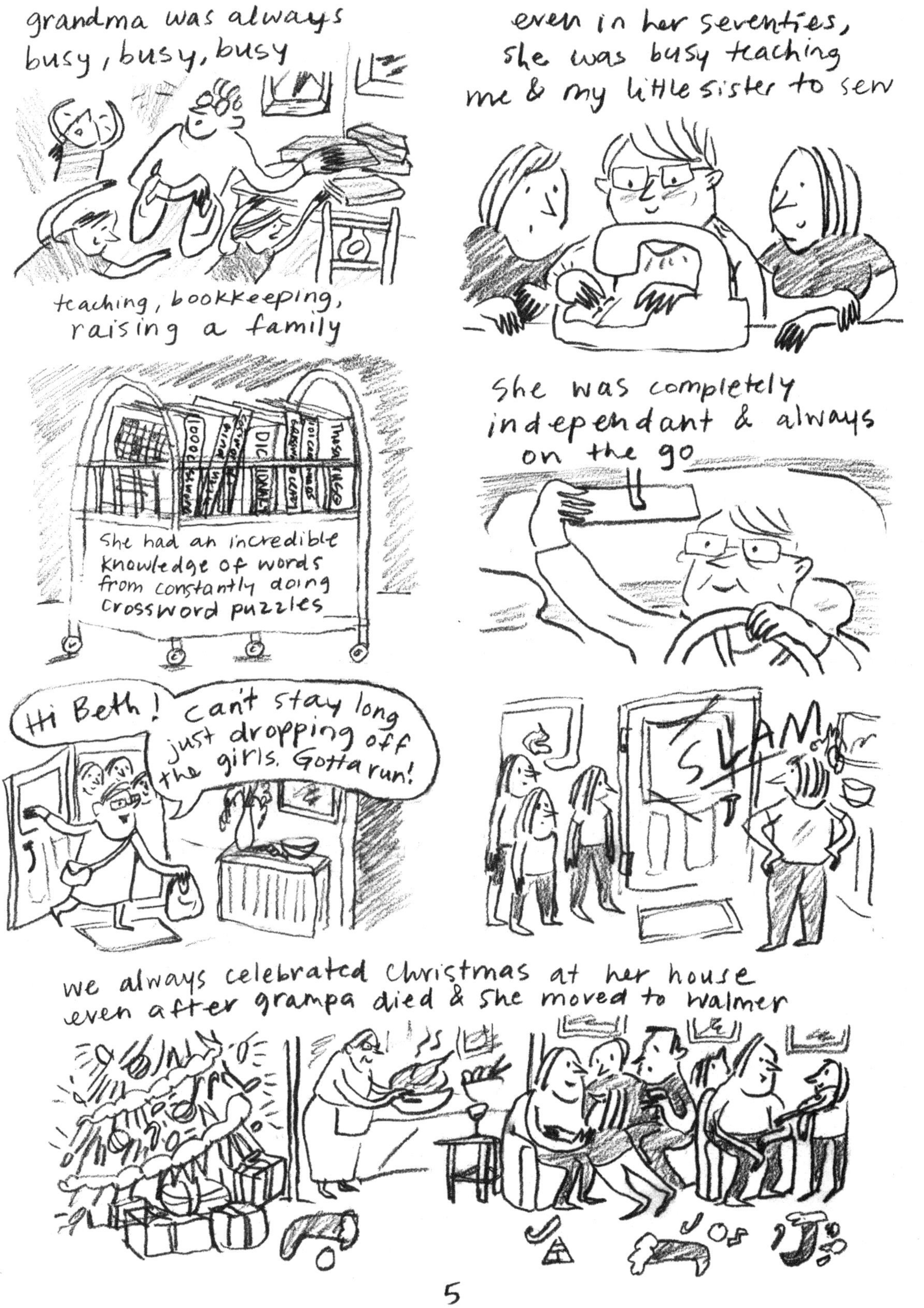
grandma was always busy, busy, busy
teaching, bookkeeping, raising a family
even in her seventies, she was busy teaching me & my little sister to sew
She had an incredible knowledge of words from constantly doing crossword puzzles
She was completely independant & always on the go
Hi Beth!
Can't stay long just dropping off the girls. Gotta run!
SLAM
we always celebrated Christmas at her house even after grampa died & she moved to walmer

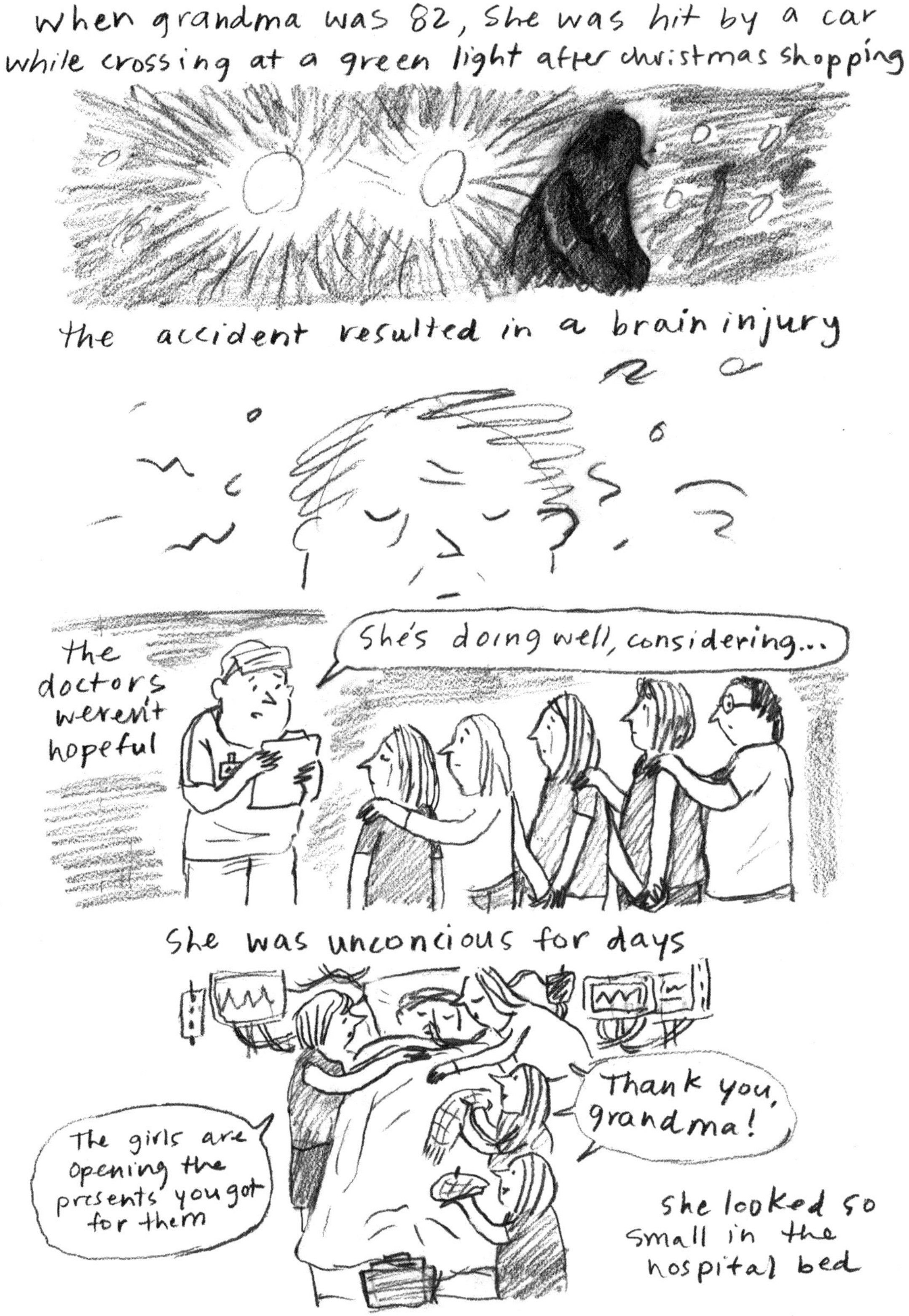
when grandma was 82, she was hit by a car while crossing at a green light after christmas shopping
the accident resulted in a brain injury
the doctors weren't hopeful
She's doing well, considering...
She was unconcious for days
The girls are opening the presents you got for them
Thank you, grandma!
she looked so small in the hospital bed

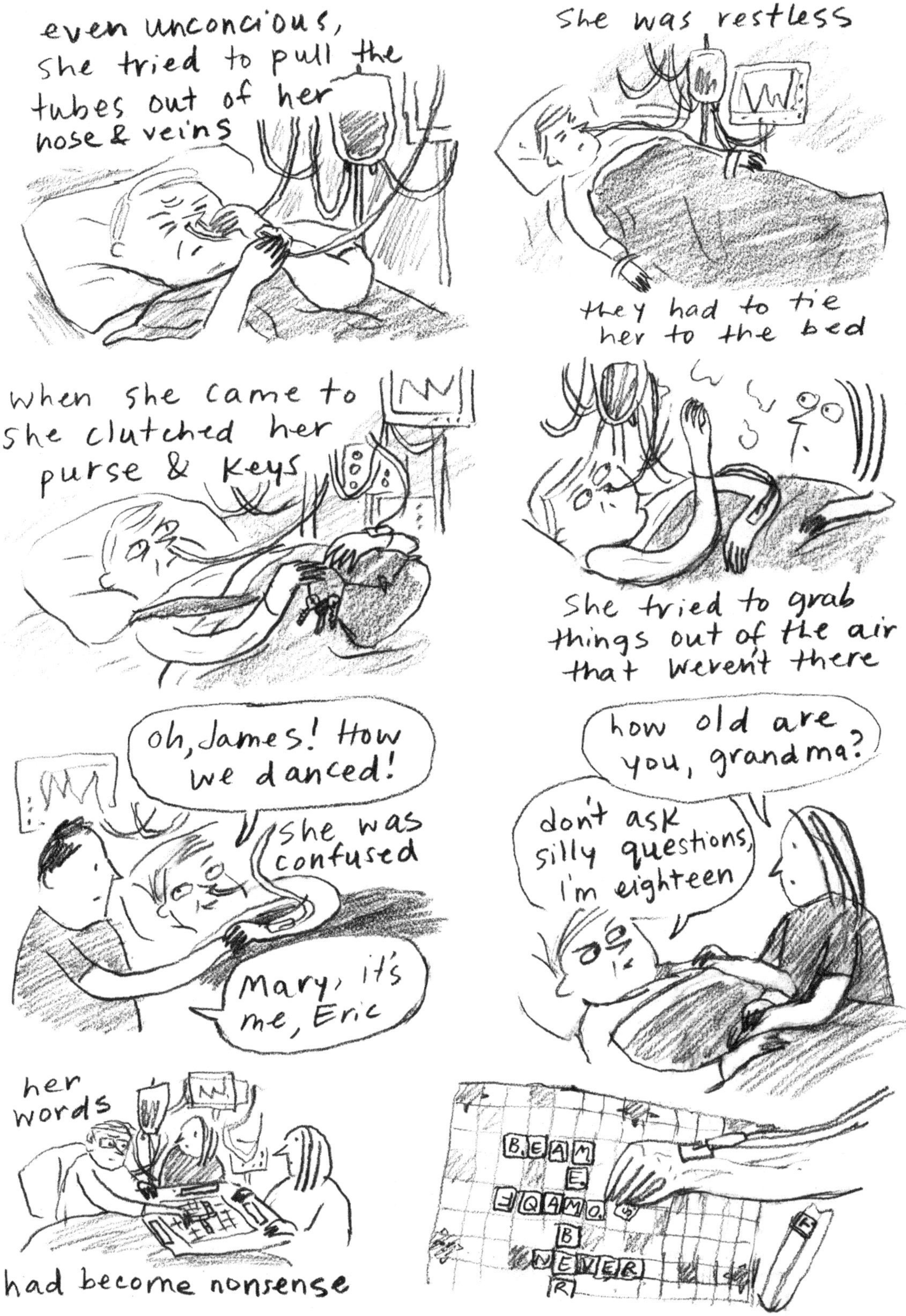

even unconcious, she tried to pull the tubes out of her nose & veins
she was restless
they had to tie her to the bed
when she came to she clutched her purse & keys
she tried to grab things out of the air that weren't there
oh, James! How we danced!
she was confused
Mary, it's me, Eric
how old are you, grandma?
don't ask silly questions, I'm eighteen
her words
had become nonsense
BEAM
EQAMO
NEVER

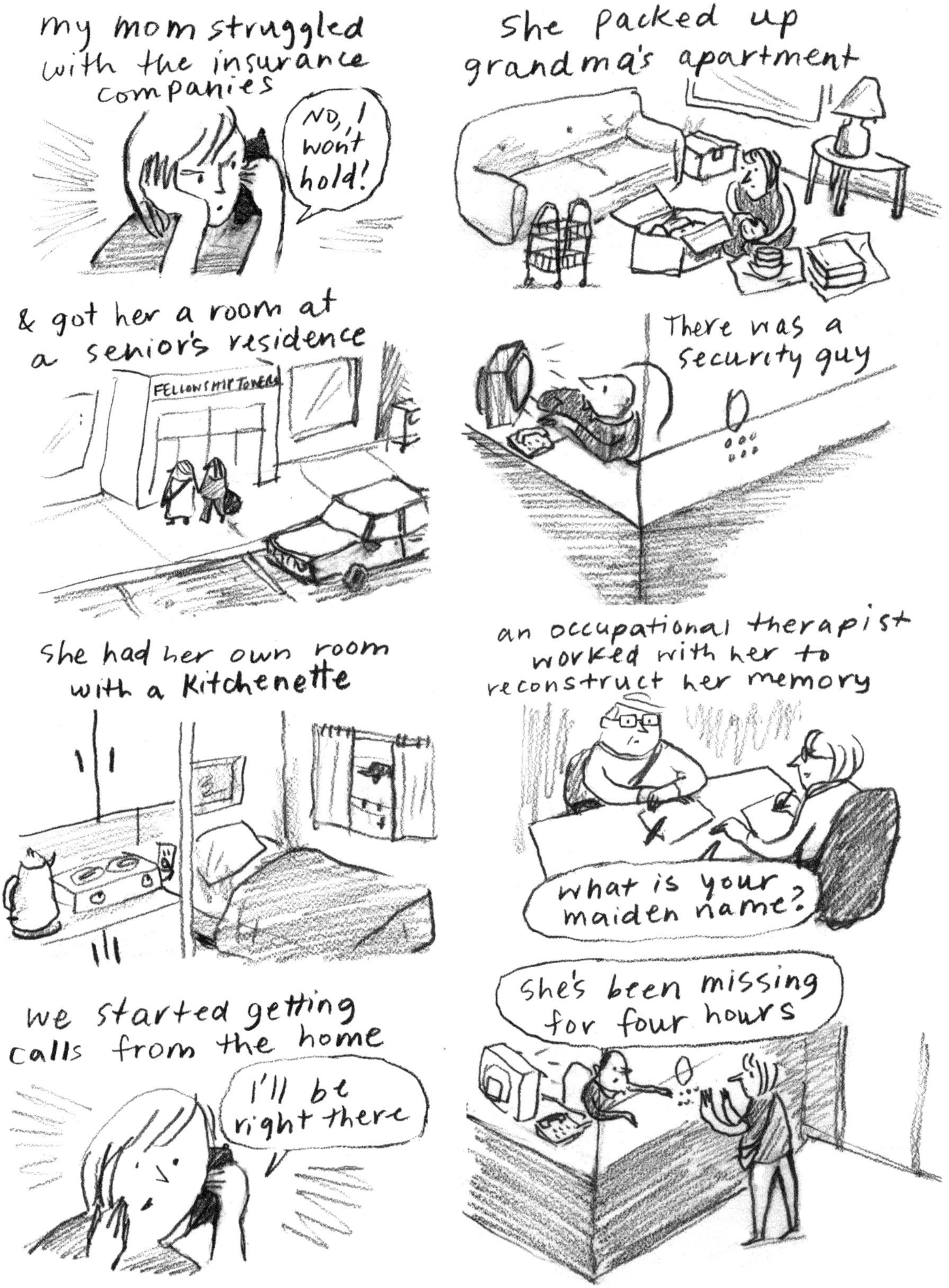
my mom struggled with the insurance companies
No, I won't hold!
She packed up grandma's apartment
& got her a room at a senior's residence
FELLOWSHIP TOWERS
There was a security guy
she had her own room with a kitchenette
an occupational therapist worked with her to reconstruct her memory
what is your maiden name?
we started getting calls from the home
I'll be right there
She's been missing for four hours

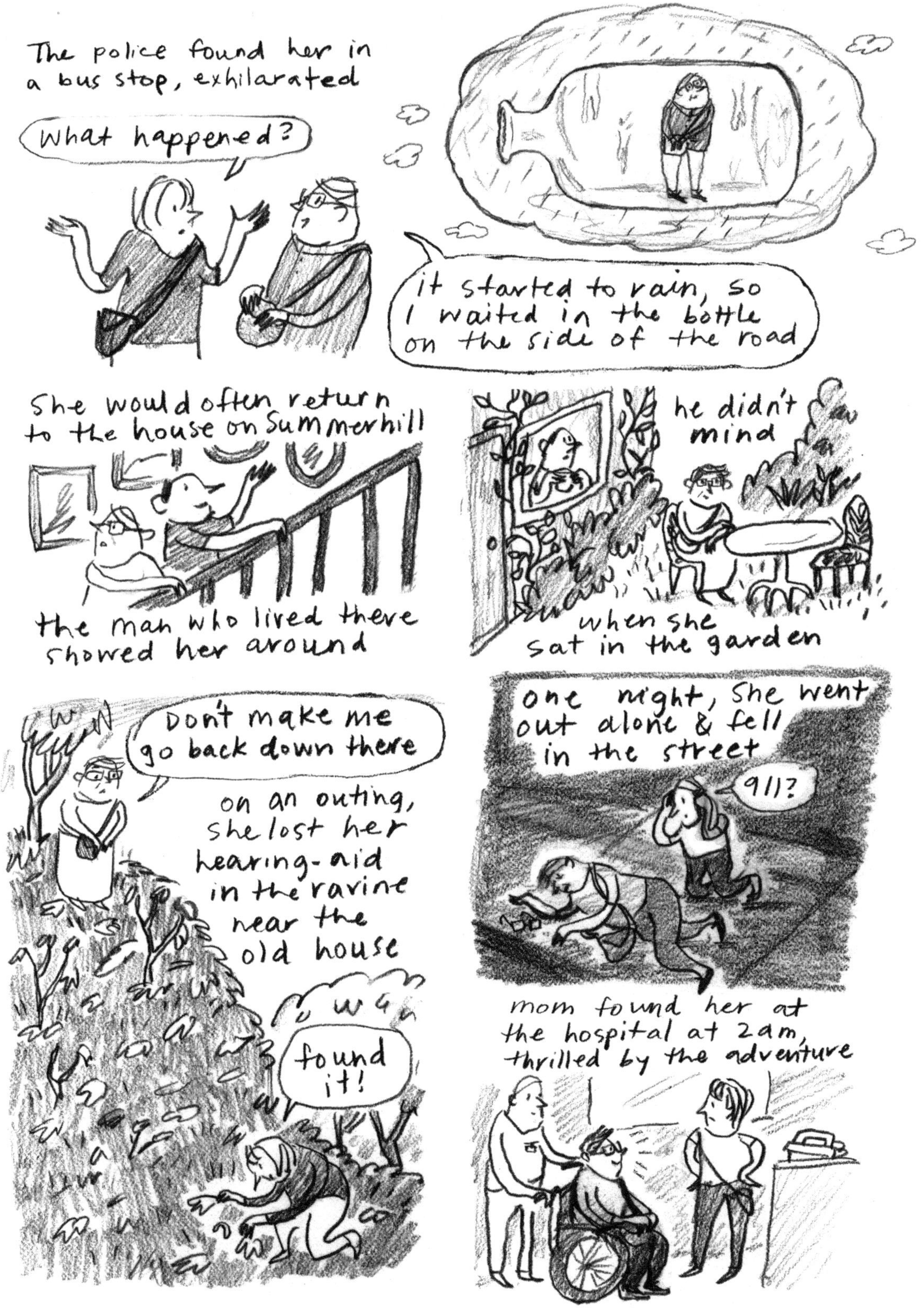
The police found her in a bus stop, exhilarated
What happened?
it started to rain, so I waited in the bottle on the side of the road
She would often return to the house on Summerhill
the man who lived there showed her around
he didn't mind
when she sat in the garden
Don't make me go back down there
on an outing, she lost her hearing-aid in the ravine near the old house
found it!
one night, she went out alone & fell in the street
911?
mom found her at the hospital at 2am, thrilled by the adventure

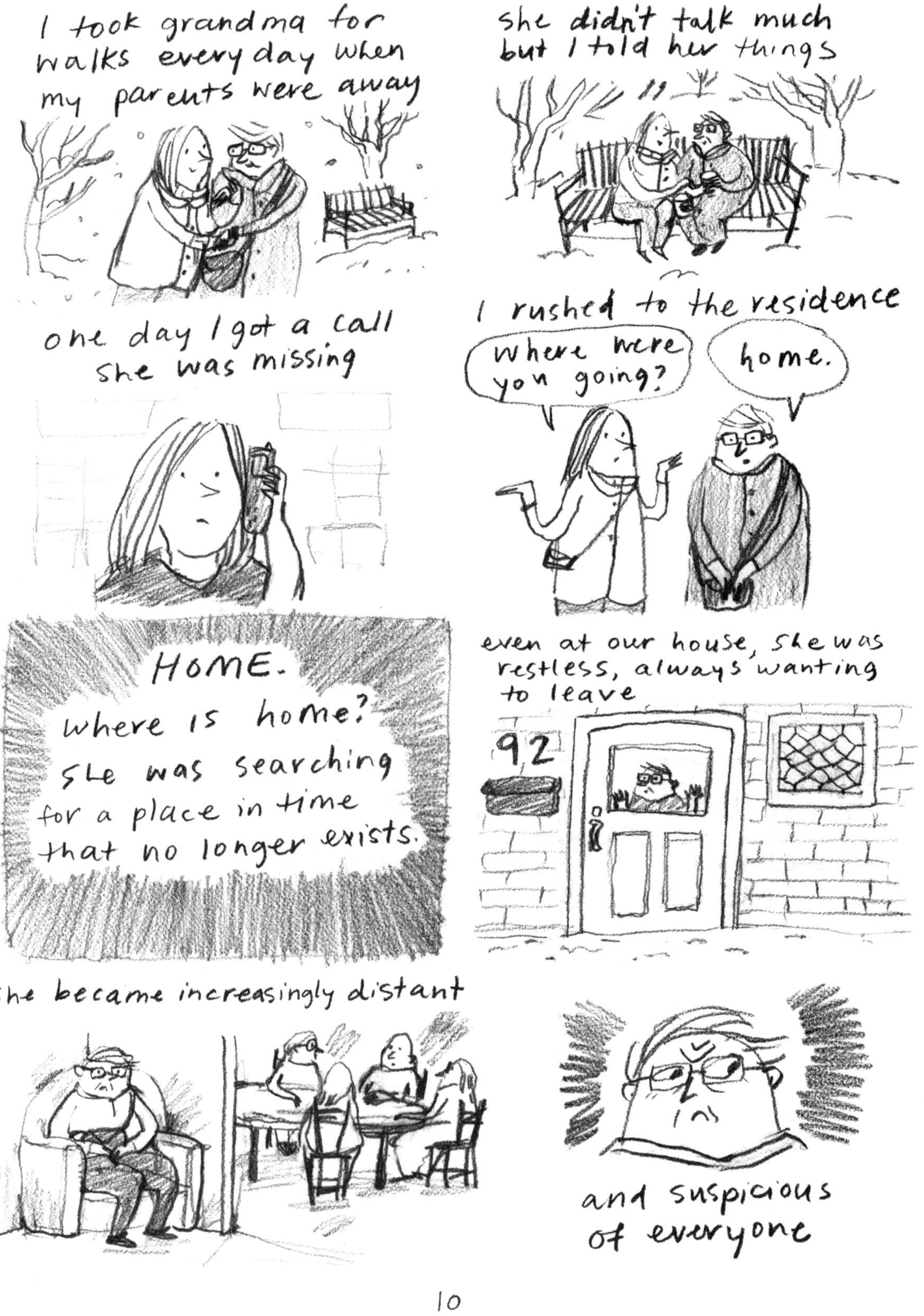
I took grandma for walks every day when my parents were away
she didn't talk much but I told her things
one day I got a call she was missing
I rushed to the residence
where were you going?
home.
HOME.
where is home?
she was searching for a place in time that no longer exists.
even at our house, she was restless, always wanting to leave
92
she became increasingly distant
and suspicious of everyone

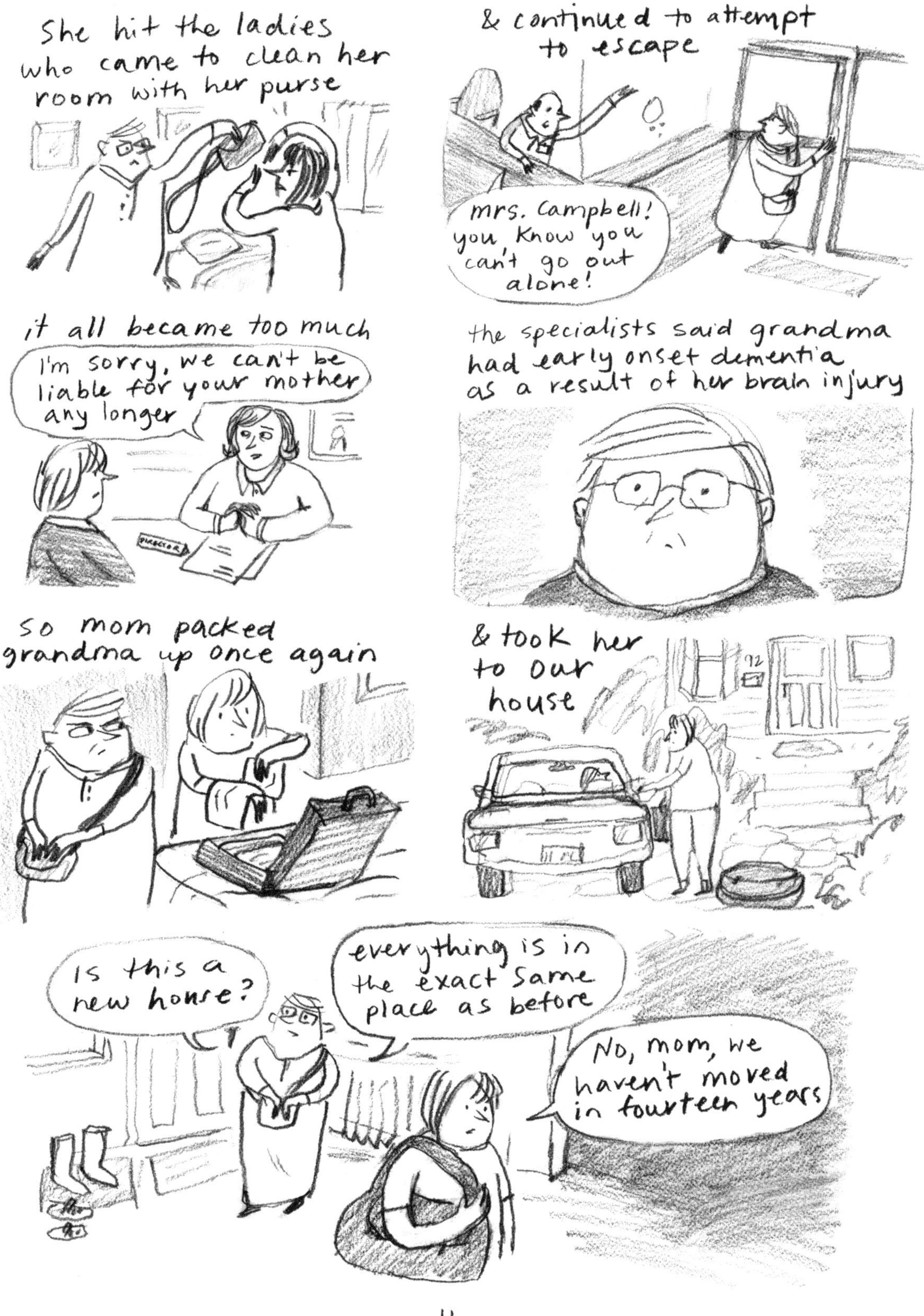

She hit the ladies who came to clean her room with her purse
& continued to attempt to escape
mrs. Campbell! you know you can't go out alone!
it all became too much
I'm sorry, we can't be liable for your mother any longer
DIRECTOR
the specialists said grandma had early onset dementia as a result of her brain injury
so mom packed grandma up once again
& took her to our house
92
Is this a new house?
everything is in the exact same place as before
No, mom, we haven't moved in fourteen years

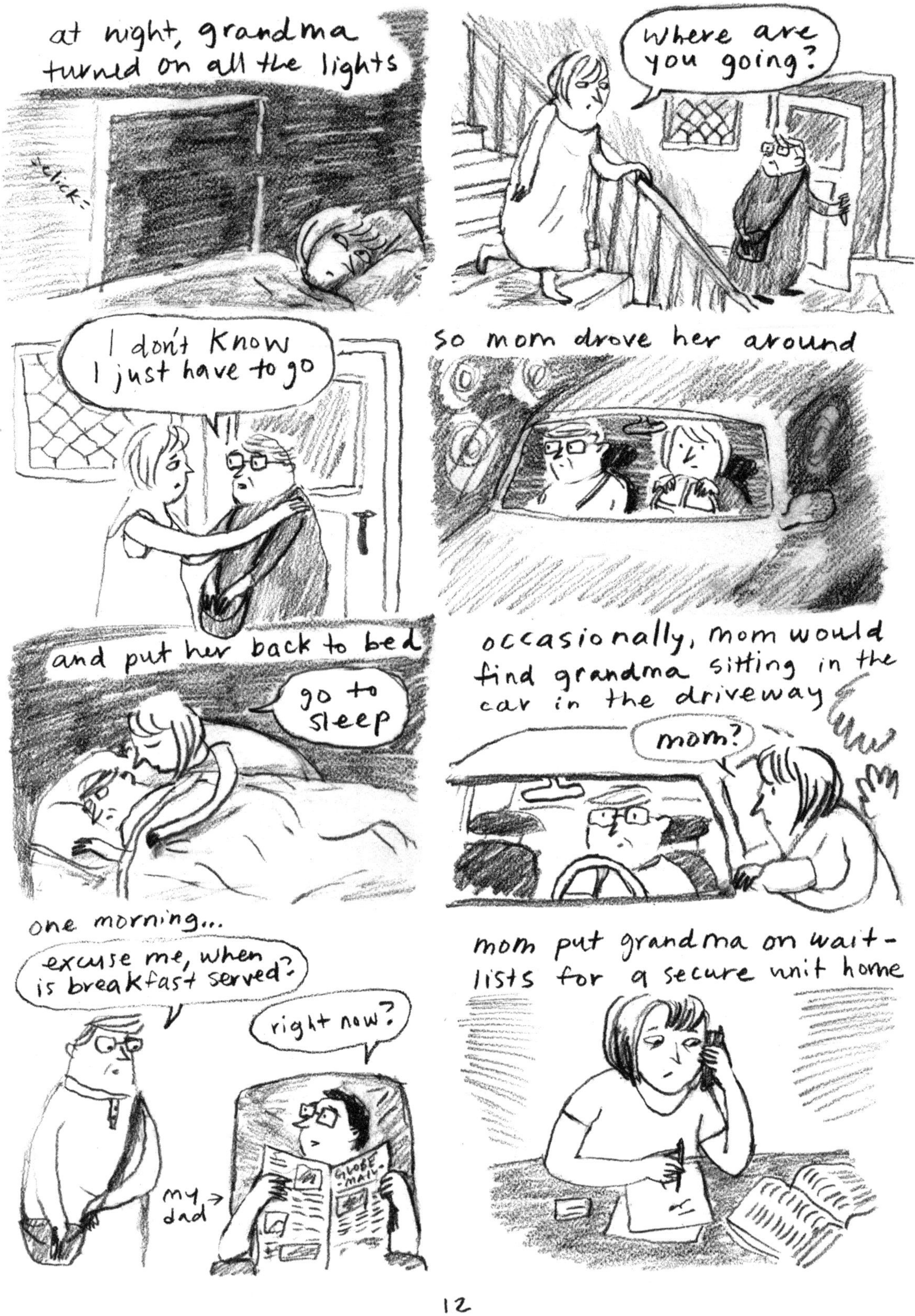
at night, grandma turned on all the lights
click
where are you going?
I don't know I just have to go
so mom drove her around
and put her back to bed
go to sleep
occasionally, mom would find grandma sitting in the car in the driveway
mom?
one morning...
excuse me, when is breakfast served?
right now?
my dad
GLOBE MAIL
mom put grandma on wait-lists for a secure unit home

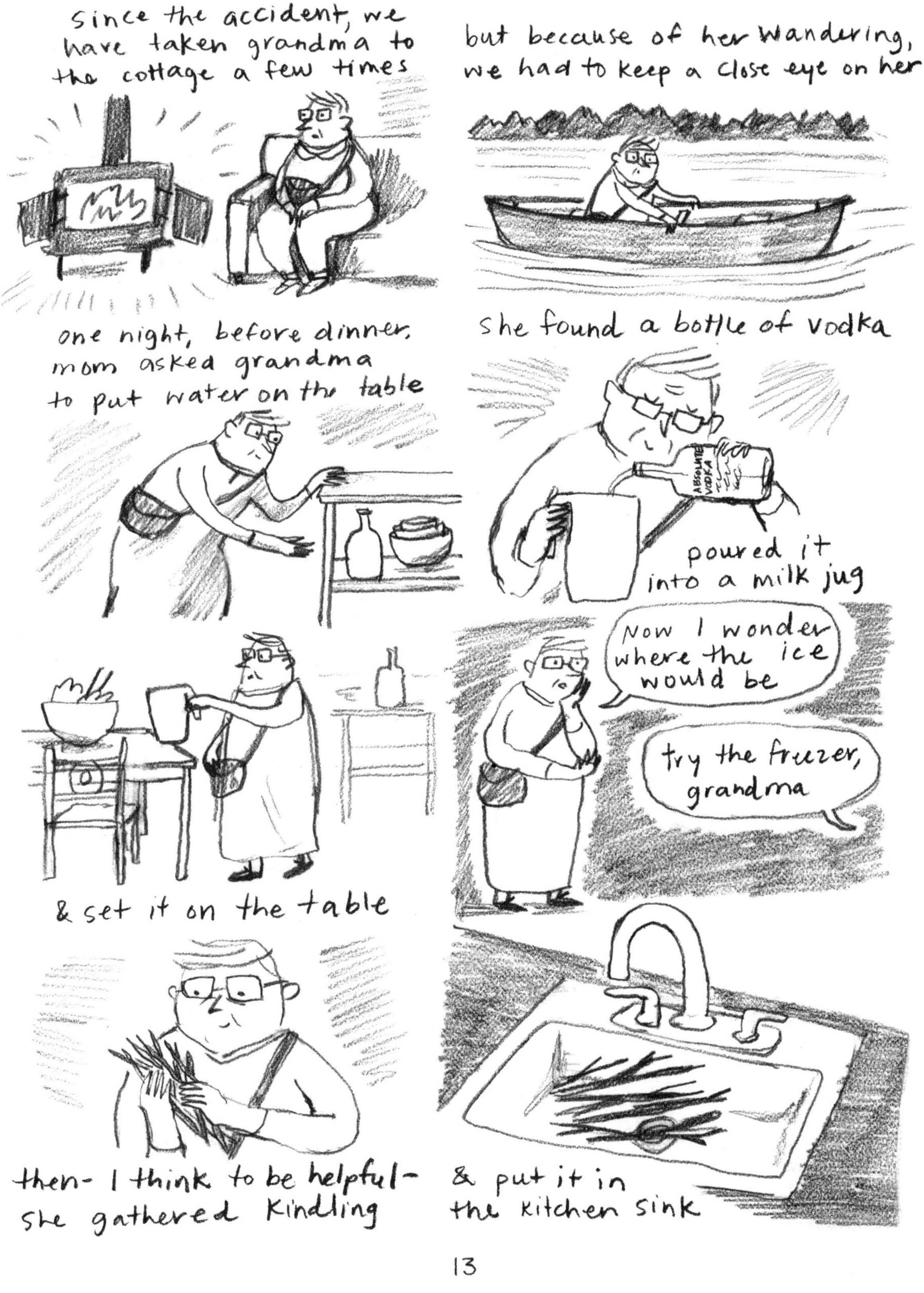
since the accident, we have taken grandma to the cottage a few times
but because of her wandering, we had to keep a close eye on her
one night, before dinner, mom asked grandma to put water on the table
she found a bottle of vodka
ABSOLUTE VODKA
poured it into a milk jug
& set it on the table
Now I wonder where the ice would be
try the freezer, grandma
then- I think to be helpful- she gathered kindling
& put it in the kitchen sink

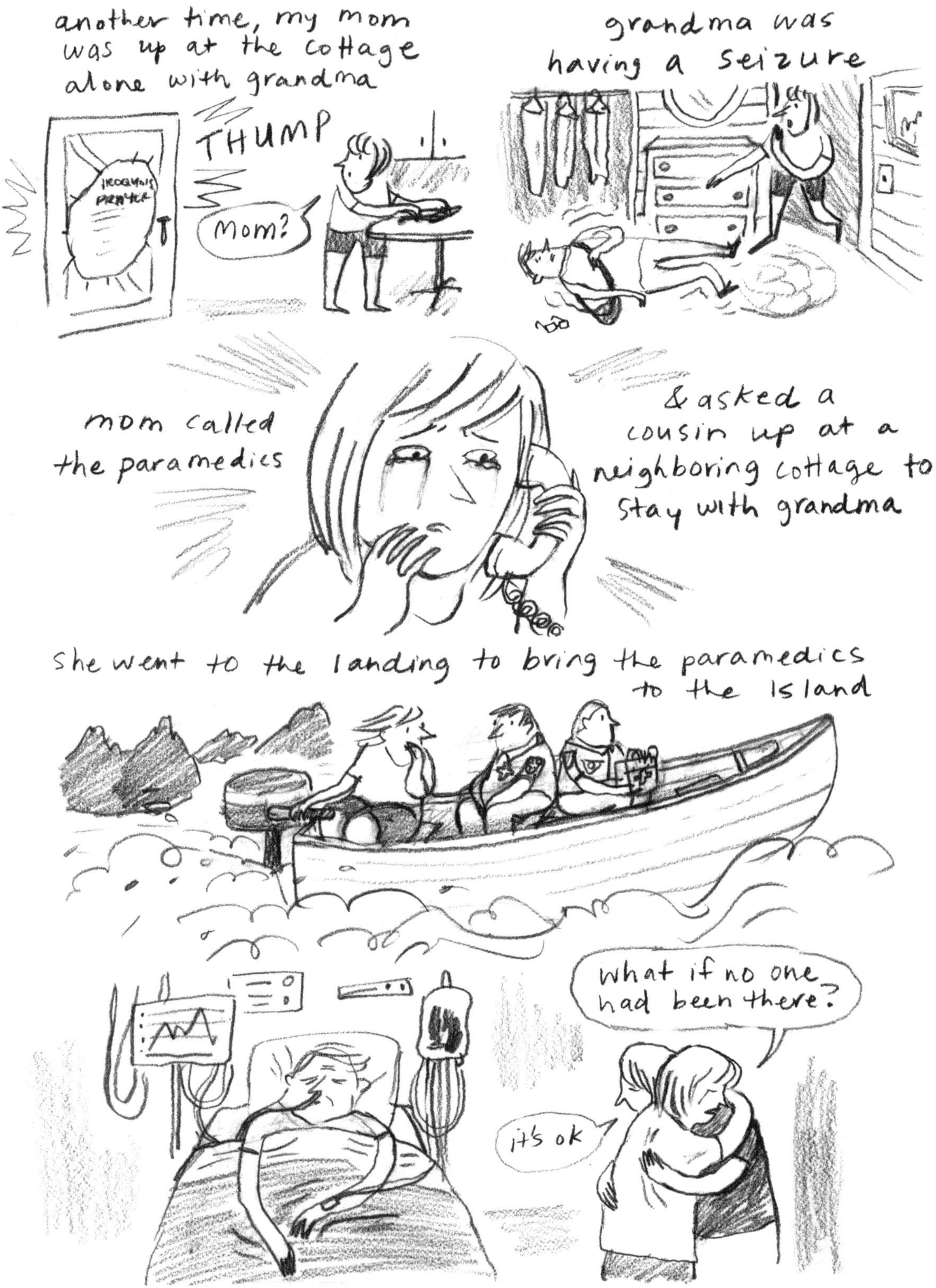

another time, my mom was up at the cottage alone with grandma
THUMP
Mom?
grandma was having a seizure
mom called the paramedics
& asked a cousin up at a neighboring cottage to stay with grandma
she went to the landing to bring the paramedics to the island
what if no one had been there?
it's ok

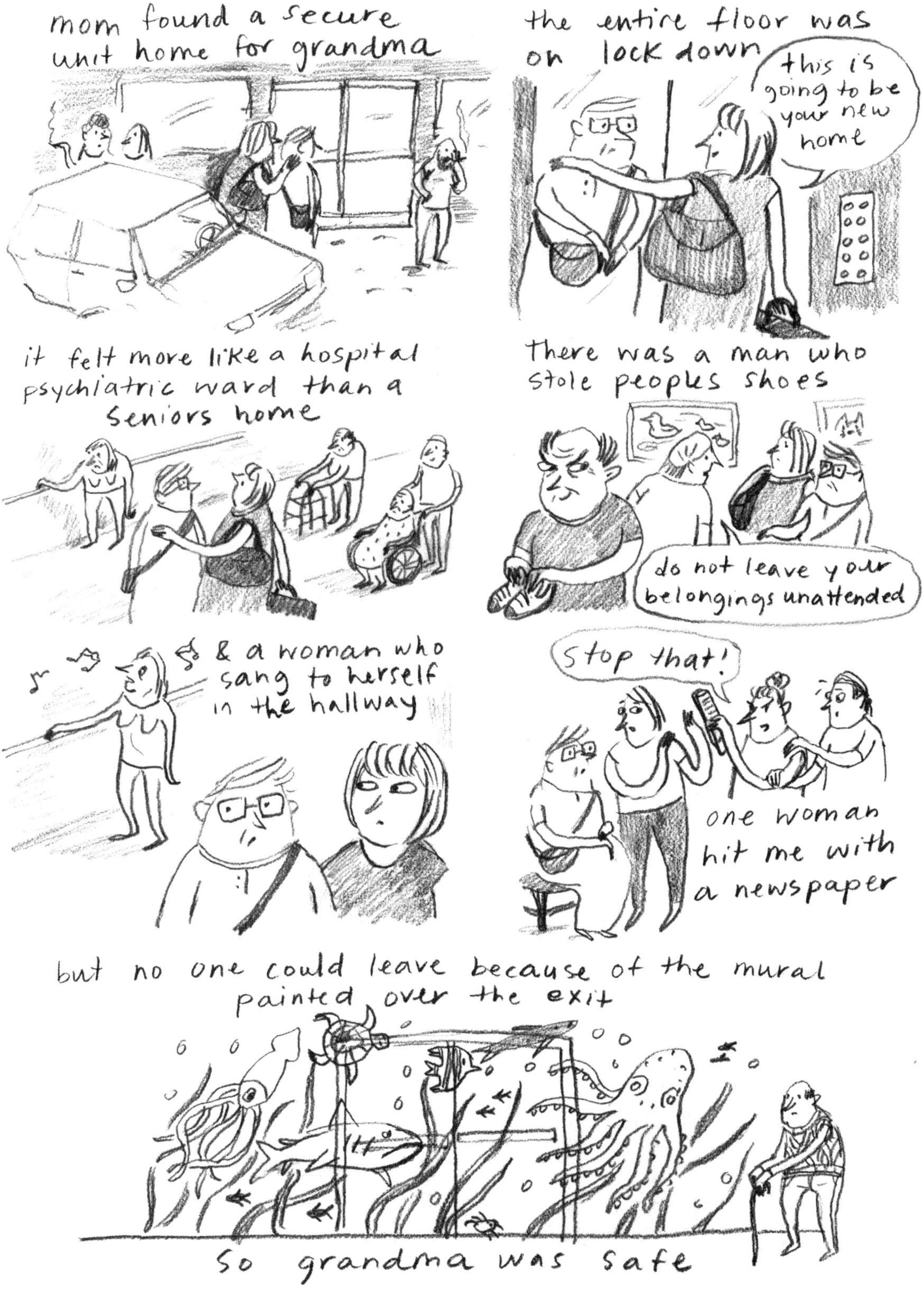
mom found a secure unit home for grandma
the entire floor was on lock down
this is going to be your new home
it felt more like a hospital psychiatric ward than a seniors home
There was a man who stole peoples shoes
do not leave your belongings unattended
& a woman who sang to herself in the hallway
Stop that!
one woman hit me with a newspaper
but no one could leave because of the mural painted over the exit
so grandma was safe

mom finally got grandma a spot in a great residence

it was in a fun neighborhood, close to our house with clean facilities and kind attendants

you're going to like it here

but she was still restless

they put a bracelet on her wrist that would set off an alarm if she got out

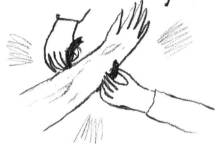

but she still managed to get it off & escape always coming back exhilarated

they had to change all their codes & security procedures

my mom came up with a brilliant plan

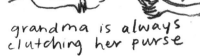

we'll put it in her purse!

grandma is always clutching her purse

wooo wooo woooo

works every time

16

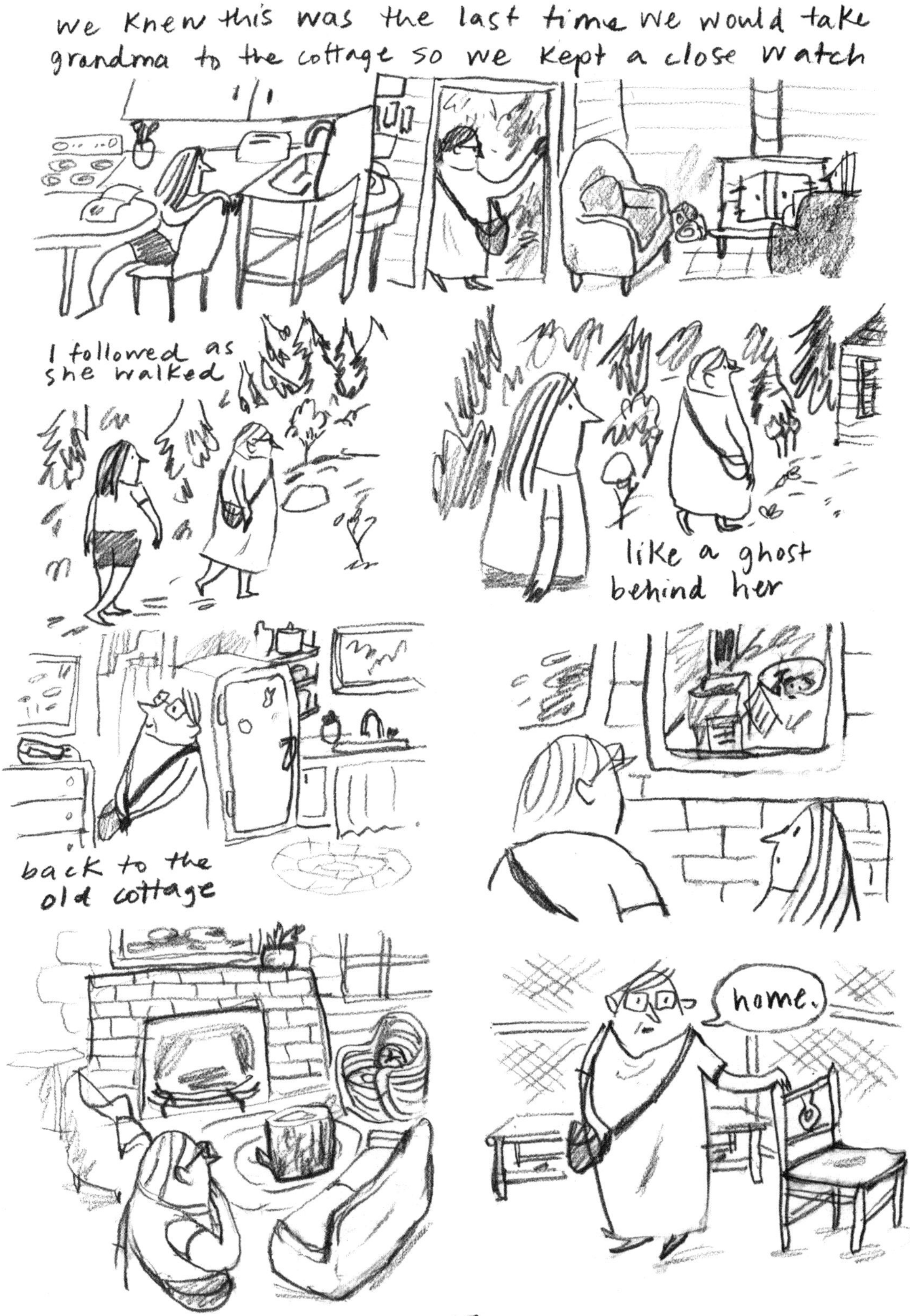
we knew this was the last time we would take grandma to the cottage so we kept a close watch
I followed as she walked
like a ghost behind her
back to the old cottage
home.

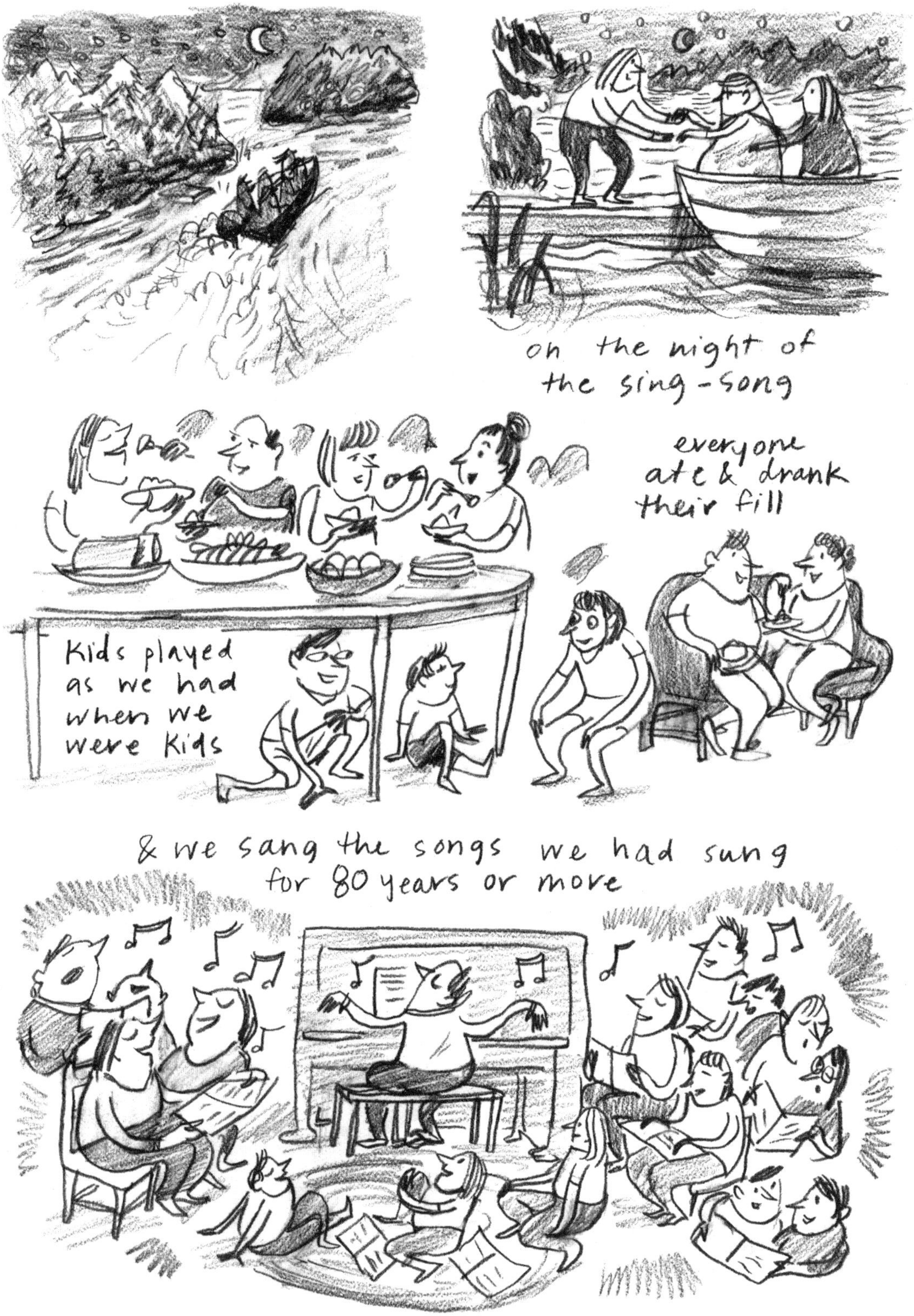
on the night of
the sing-song
everyone
ate & drank
their fill
Kids played
as we had
when we
were kids
& we sang the songs we had sung
for 80 years or more

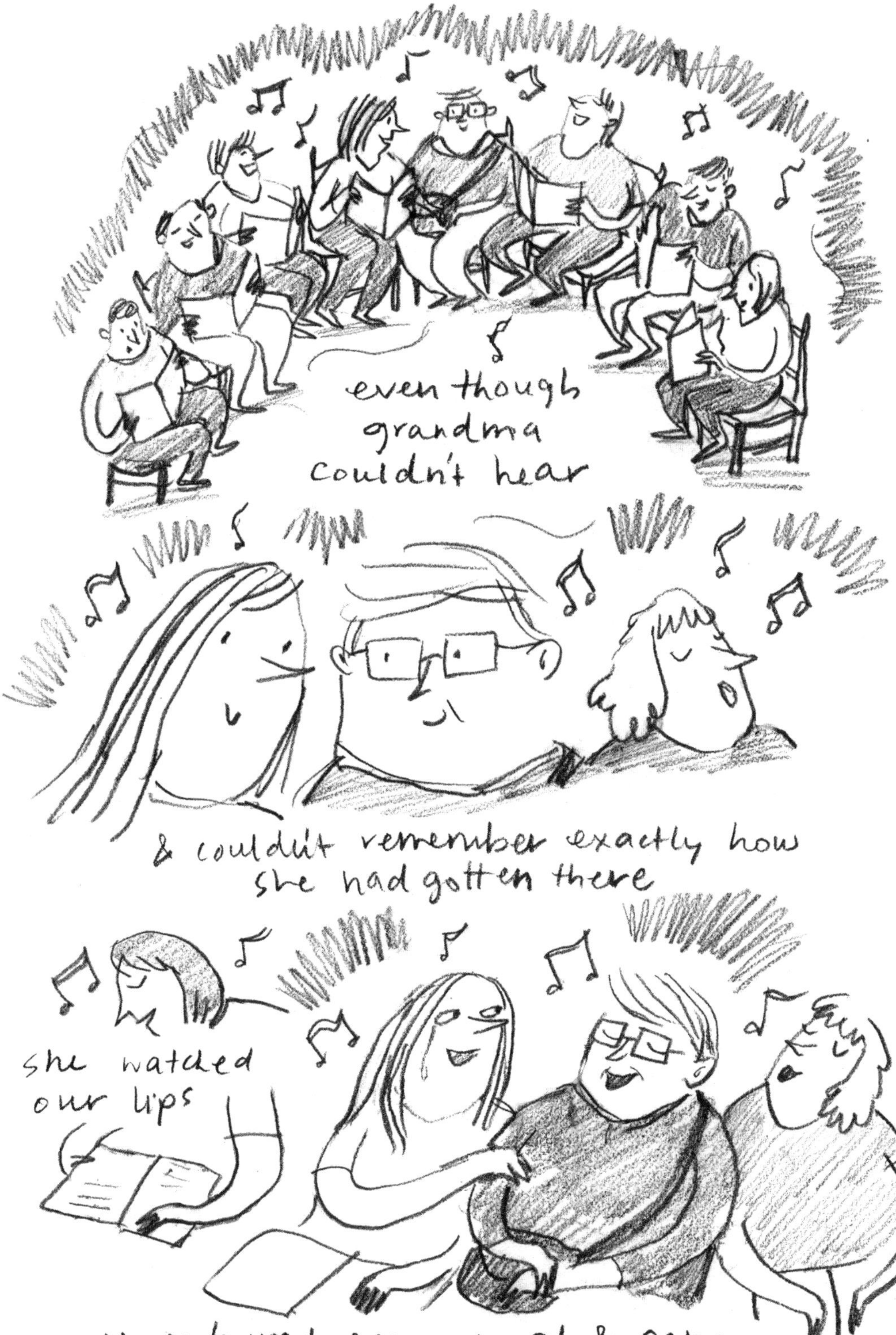
even though grandma couldn't hear
& couldn't remember exactly how she had gotten there
she watched our lips
remembered every word & sang

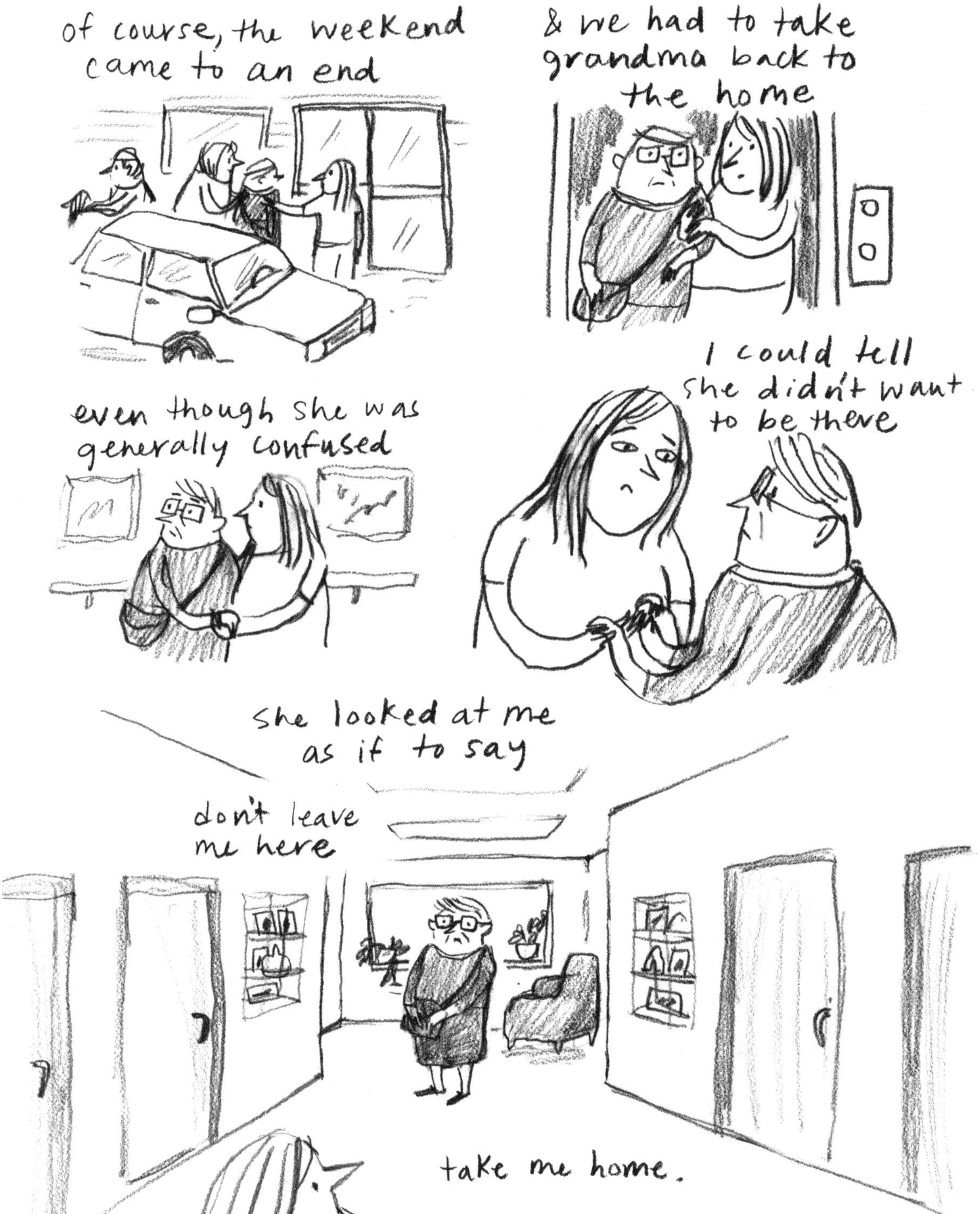
of course, the weekend came to an end
& we had to take grandma back to the home
even though she was generally confused
I could tell she didn't want to be there
she looked at me as if to say
don't leave me here
take me home.

PART II

Grandma stayed at the long term facility for many years

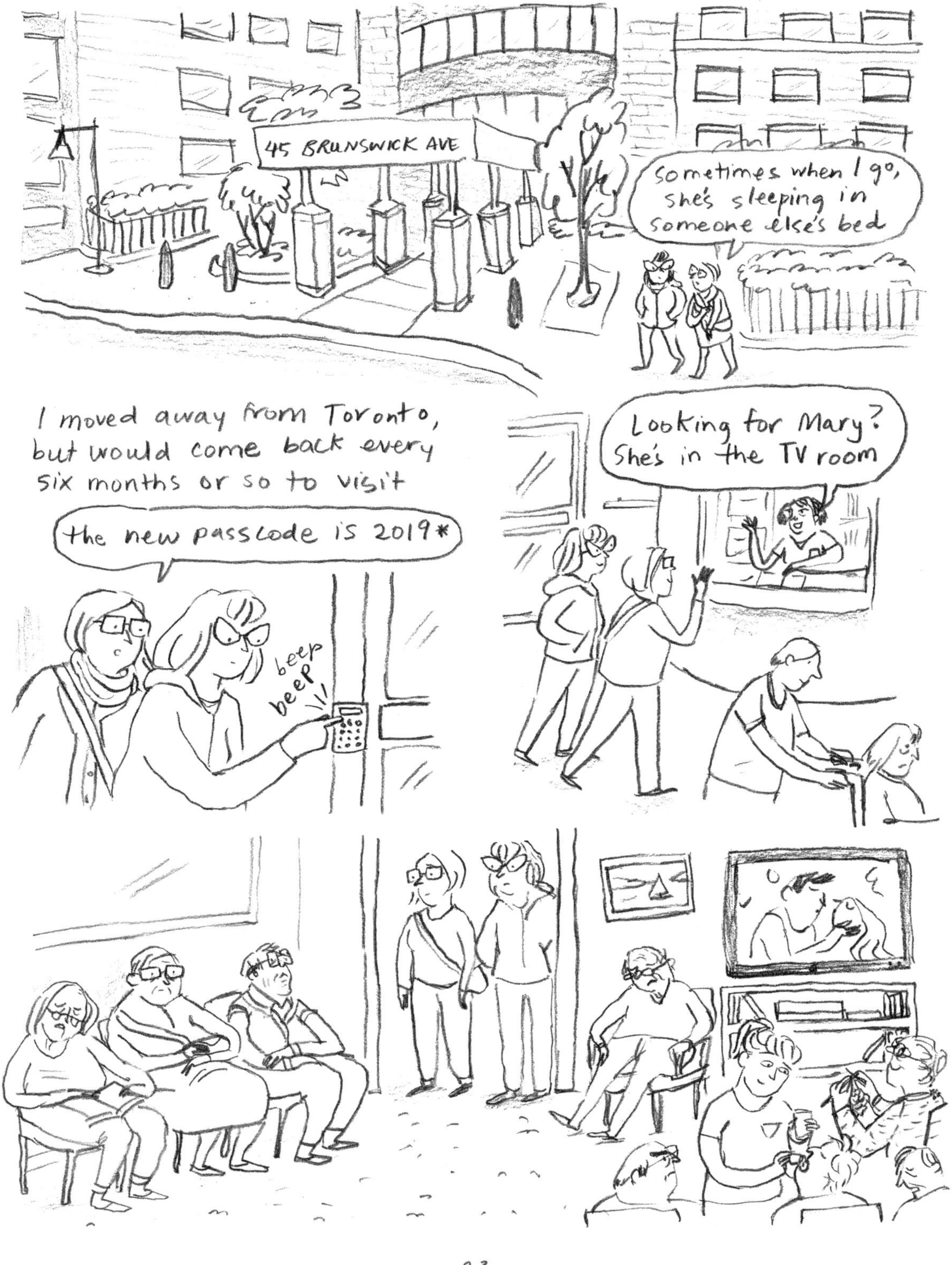
45 BRUNSWICK AVE
Sometimes when I go, she's sleeping in someone else's bed
I moved away from Toronto, but would come back every six months or so to visit
the new passcode is 2019*
beep beep
Looking for Mary? She's in the TV room

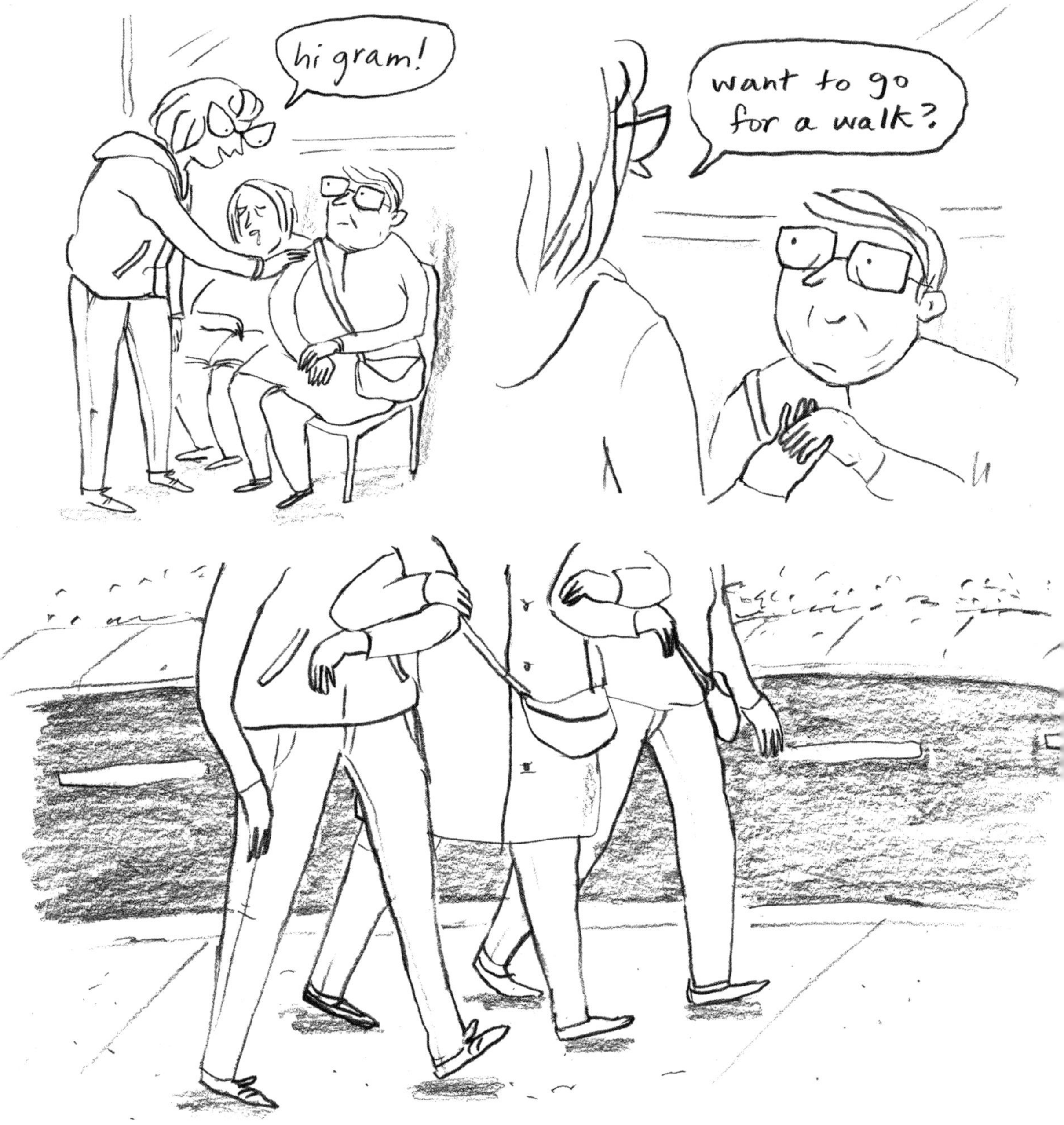
hi gram!
want to go for a walk?

She had this way of matching our steps when we walked.

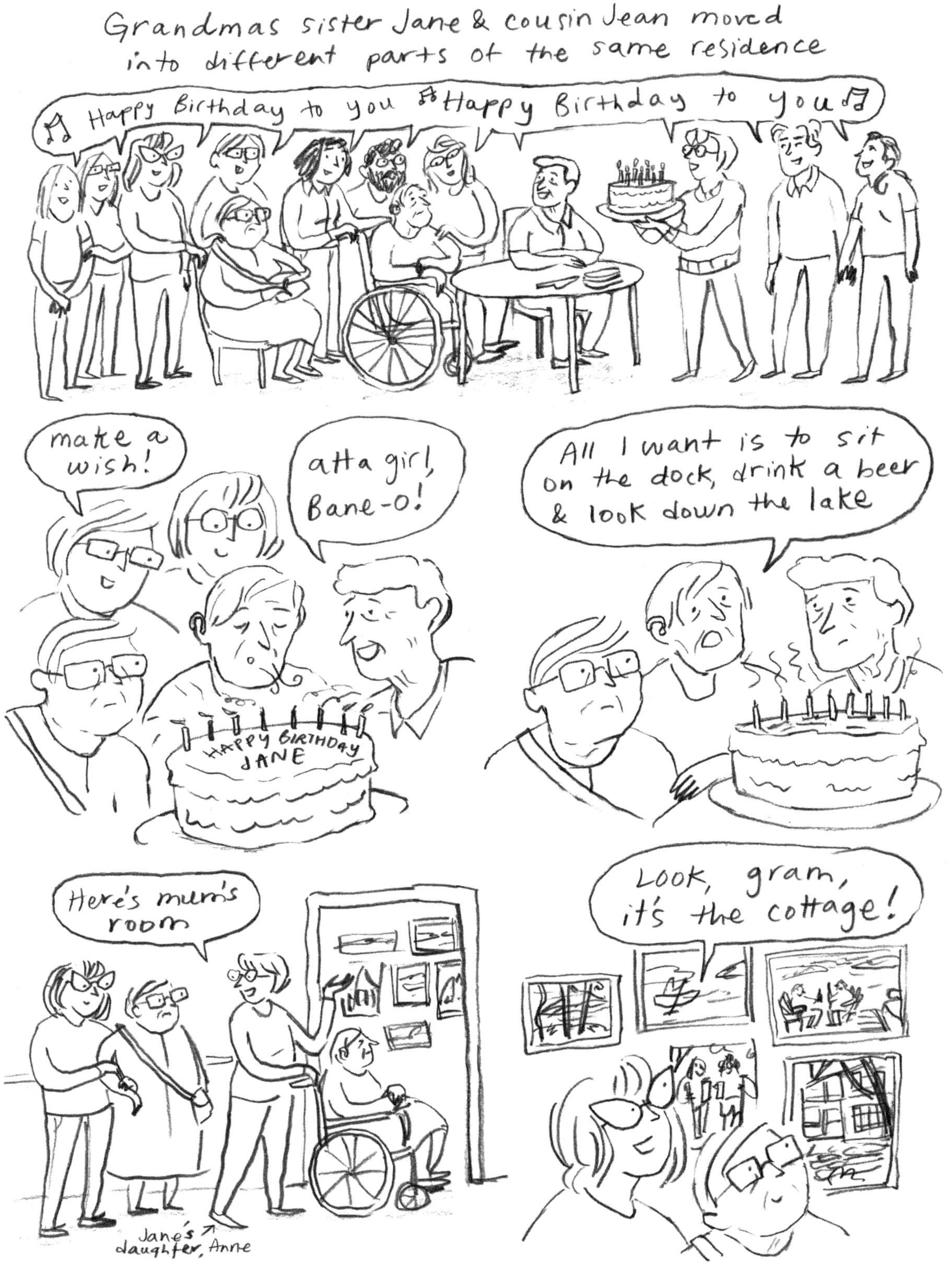
Grandmas sister Jane & cousin Jean moved into different parts of the same residence
Happy Birthday to you Happy Birthday to you
make a wish!
atta girl, Bane-o!
HAPPY BIRTHDAY JANE
All I want is to sit on the dock, drink a beer & look down the lake
Here's mum's room
Jane's daughter, Anne
Look, gram, it's the cottage!

Mary, Jane & Jean grew up on Muldrew Lake together

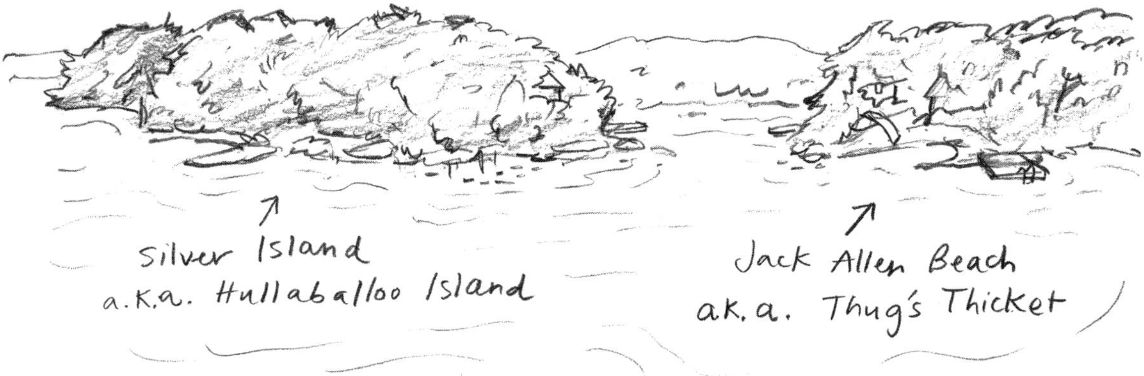
Silver Island
a.k.a. Hullaballoo Island
Jack Allen Beach
a.k.a. Thug's Thicket

Grandma's father, Elliott Allen, bought the Northwest half of Silver Island in 1929

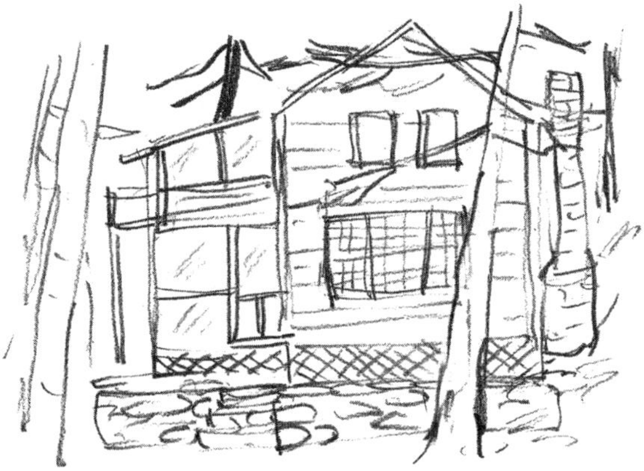

unable to bear the thought of sharing it, he bought the other half the following year

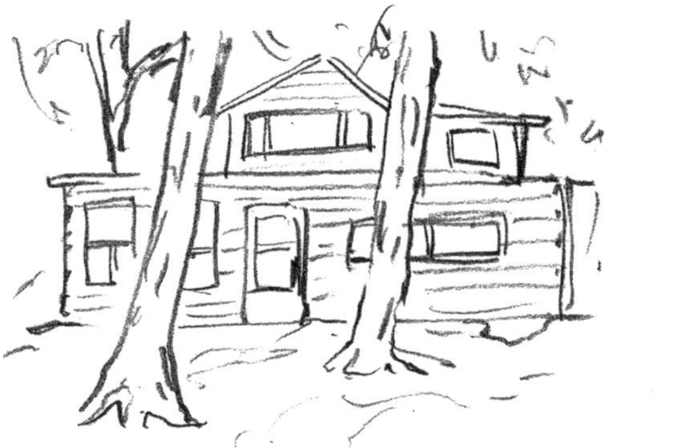

It was the depression & the threat of war was looming, but grandma, her siblings (Jane, Jim & Anne) & their cousins were all happily unaware

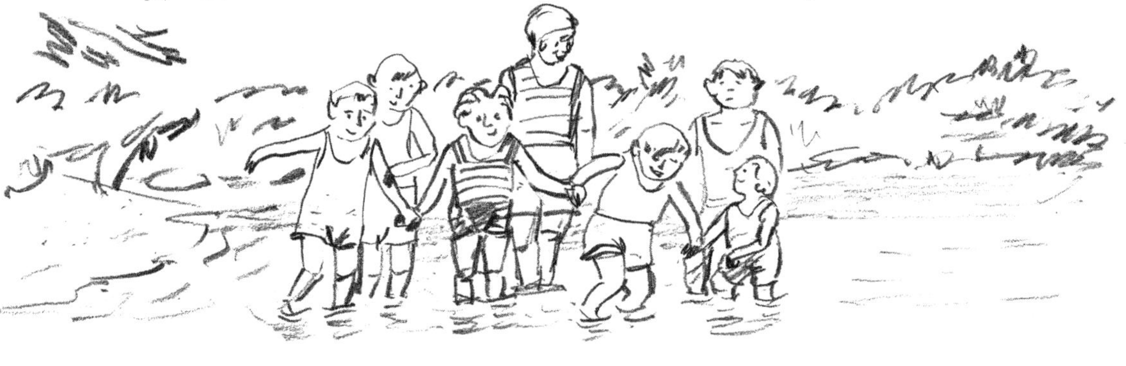

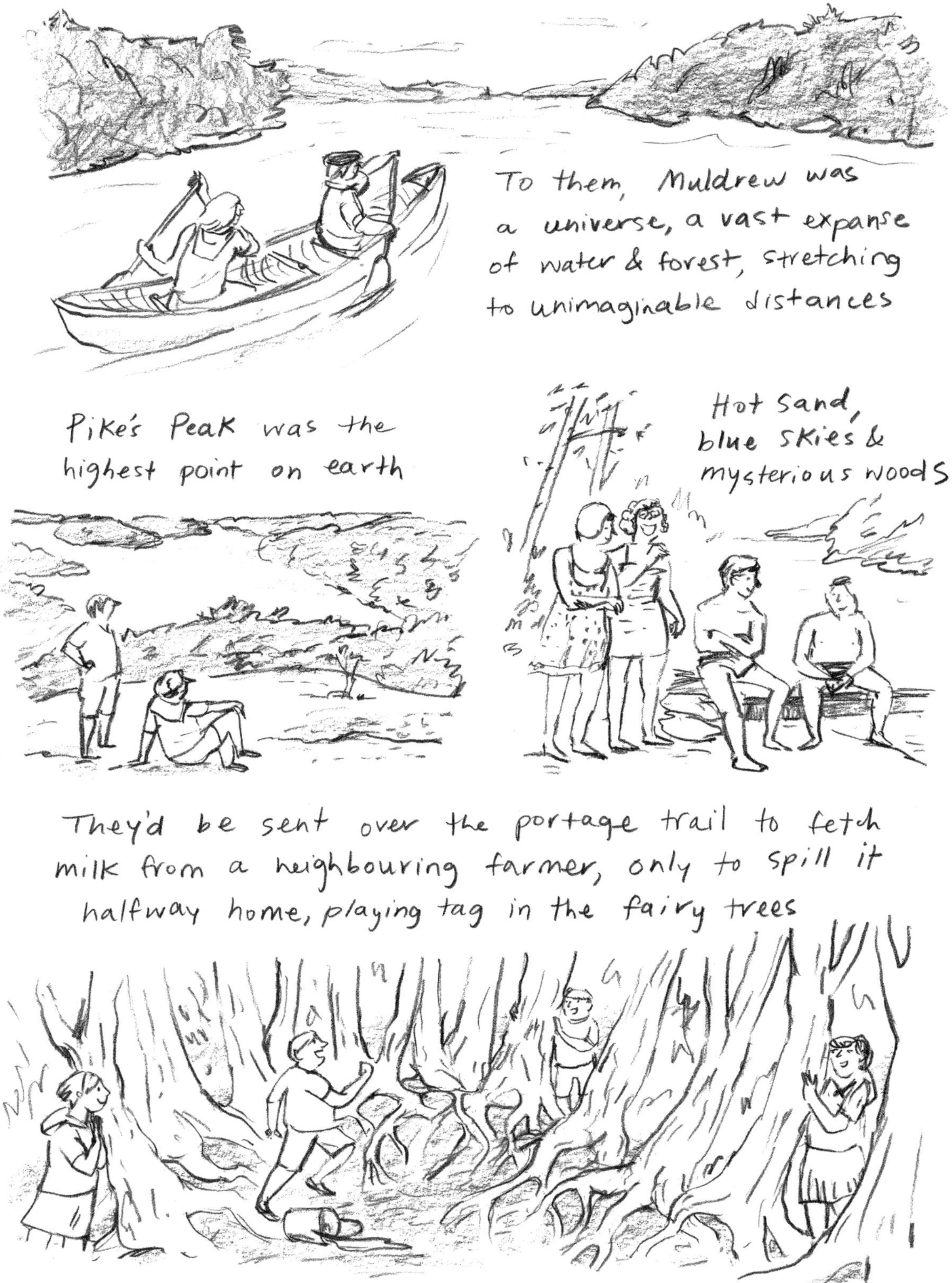
To them, Muldrew was a universe, a vast expanse of water & forest, stretching to unimaginable distances
Pike's Peak was the highest point on earth
Hot sand, blue skies & mysterious woods
They'd be sent over the portage trail to fetch milk from a neighbouring farmer, only to spill it halfway home, playing tag in the fairy trees

They played sardines in the woods on Silver Island

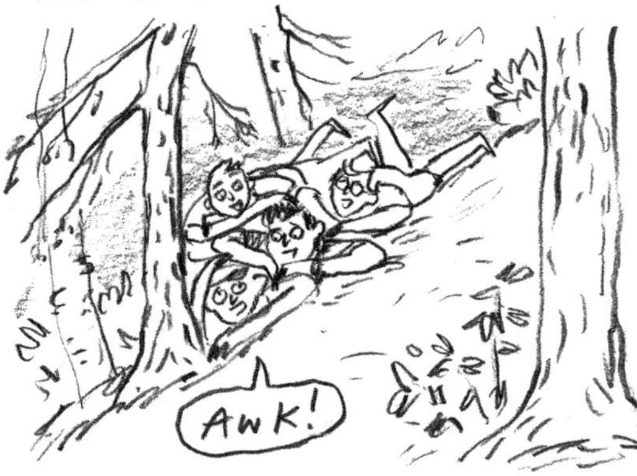
AWK!

The shores teemed with wildlife

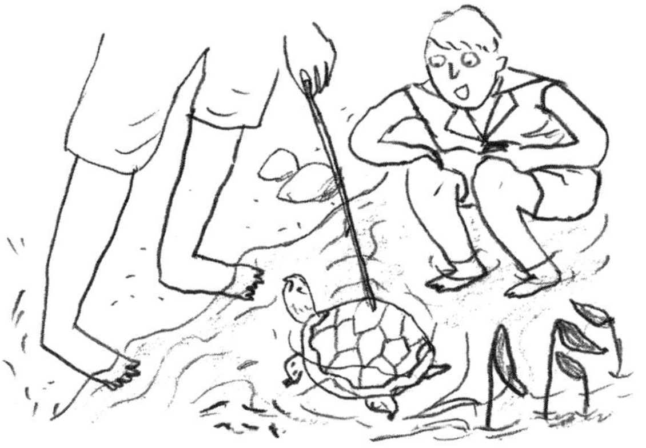

On Sundays, they attended church at Memorial pines & sang hymns

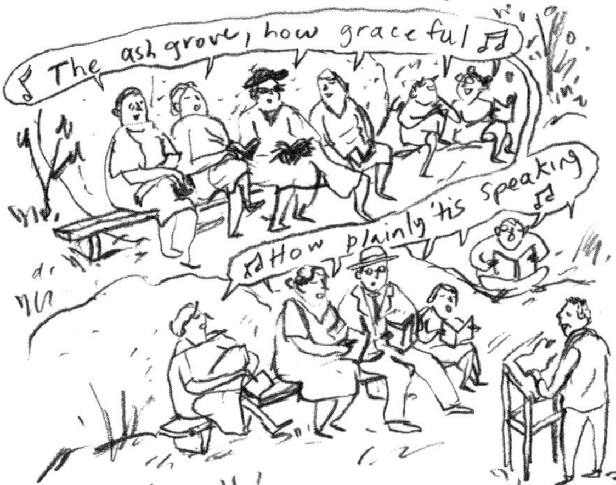
♪ The ash grove, how graceful ♫
♫ How plainly 'tis speaking ♫

Afterwards, they'd go swimming off Big Rock

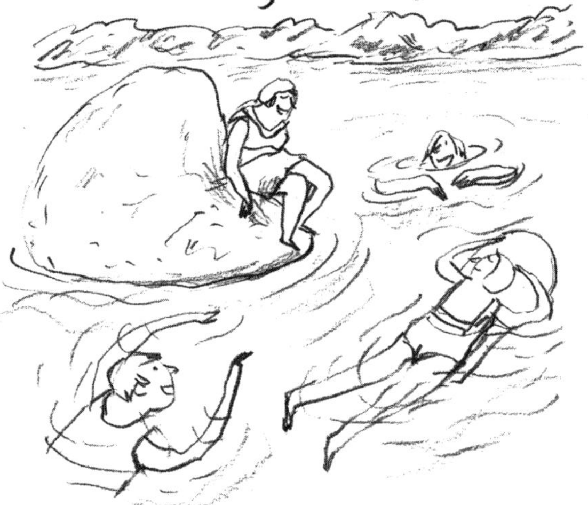

At the annual Regatta, everyone competed in every race & were sunstruck by sunset

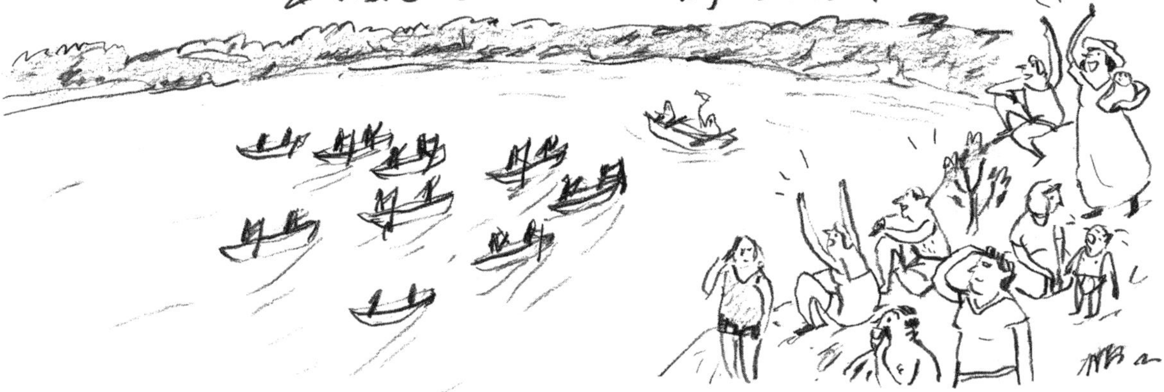

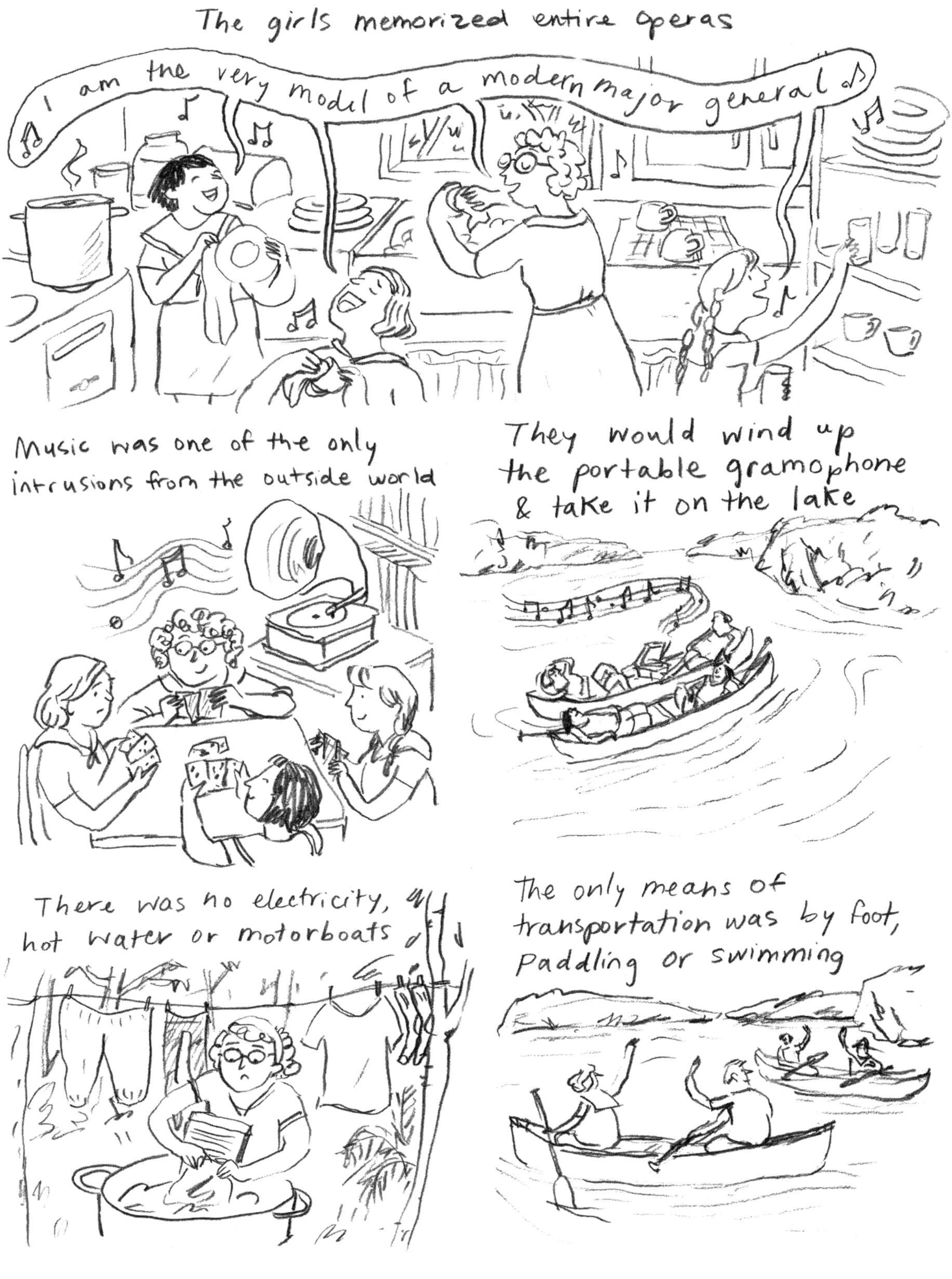
The girls memorized entire operas
I am the very model of a modern major general
Music was one of the only intrusions from the outside world
They would wind up the portable gramophone & take it on the lake
There was no electricity, hot water or motorboats
The only means of transportation was by foot, paddling or swimming

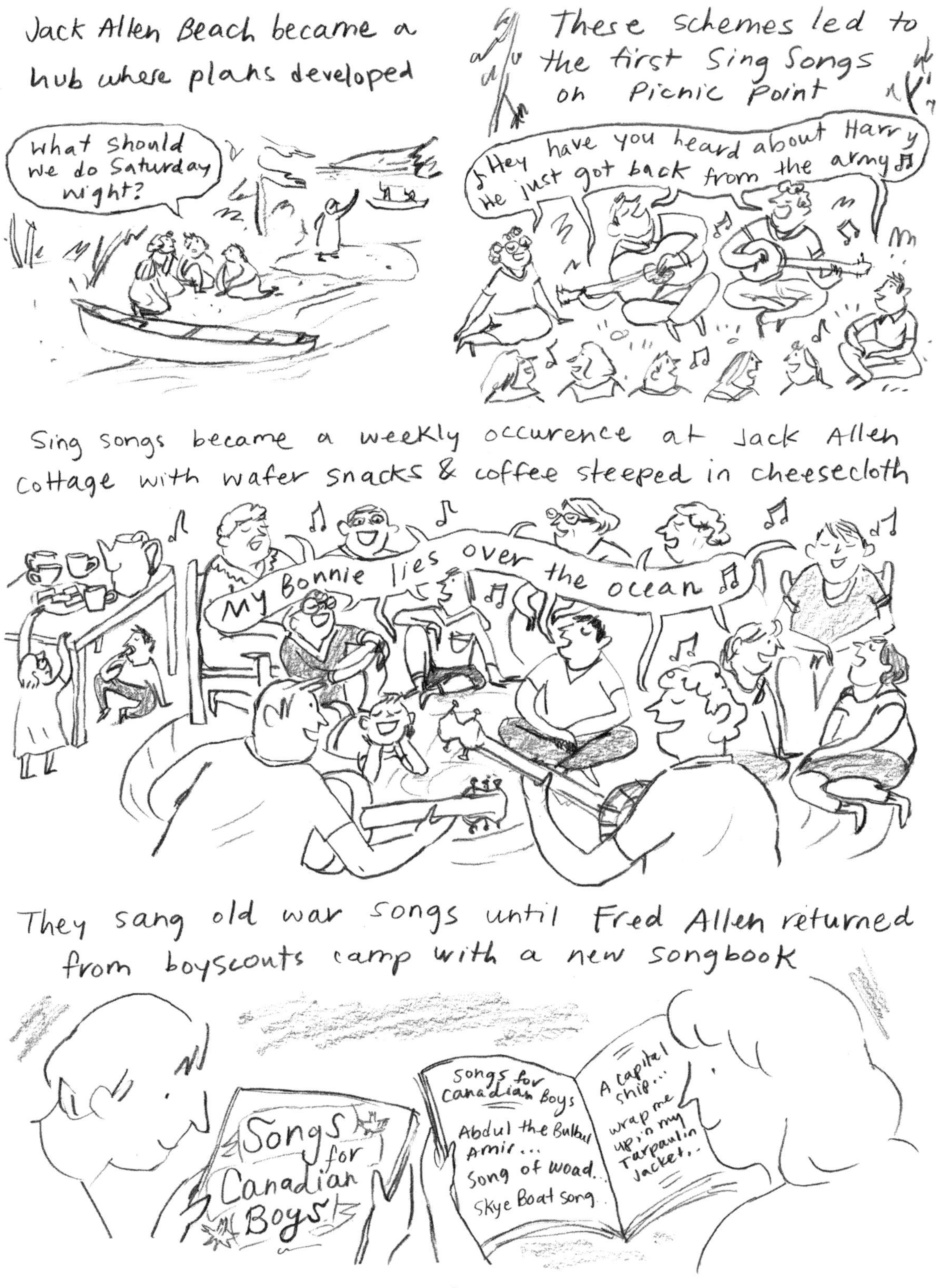
Jack Allen Beach became a hub where plans developed
What should we do Saturday night?
These schemes led to the first Sing Songs on Picnic Point
Hey have you heard about Harry He just got back from the army
Sing songs became a weekly occurence at Jack Allen cottage with wafer snacks & coffee steeped in cheesecloth
My Bonnie lies over the ocean
They sang old war songs until Fred Allen returned from boyscouts camp with a new songbook
Songs for Canadian Boys
Songs for Canadian Boys
Abdul the Bulbul Amir...
Song of Woad...
Skye Boat song
A capital ship...
wrap me up in my Tarpaulin Jacket..

Designed for young boys' voices, the notes were too high for the Muldrew crowd, but they suffered through it

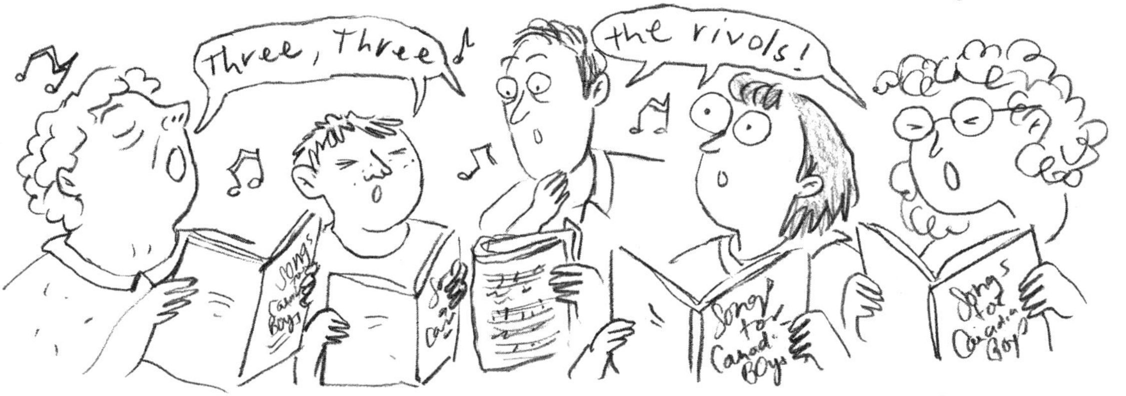
Three, Three
the rivols!

There was one summer in 1938 when a Mr. Jackson arrived at Muldrew

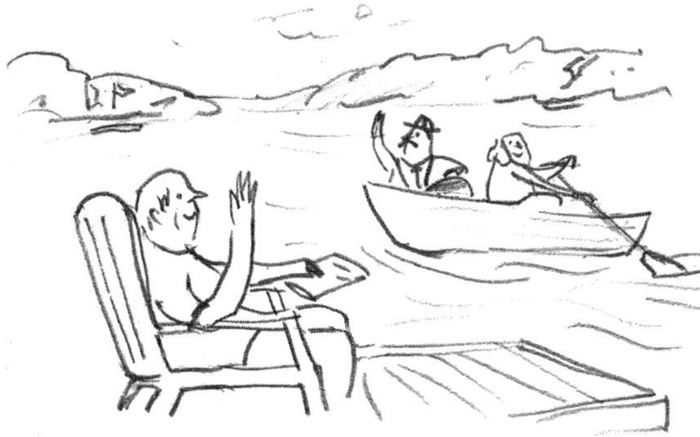

News travelled fast that he was a soloist with the D'oyle Carte Company

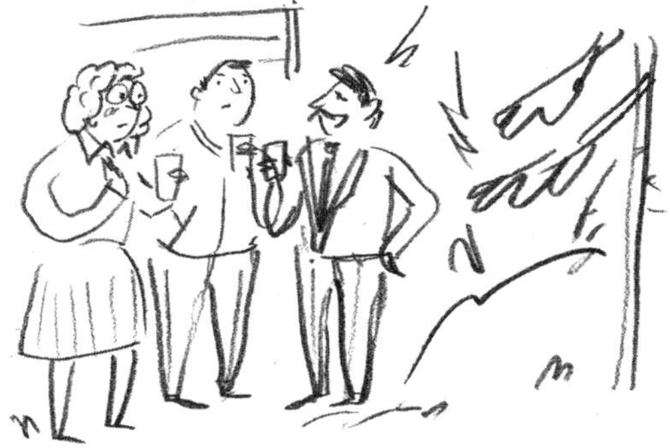

This would not have been more exhilarating than if, a generation later, Paul McCartney sang at the Sing Song

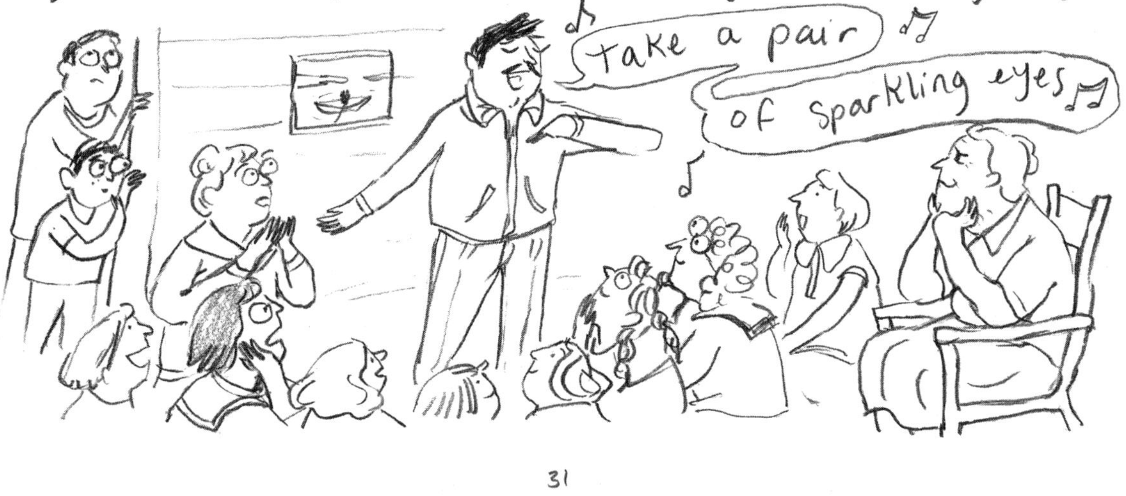
Take a pair
of sparkling eyes

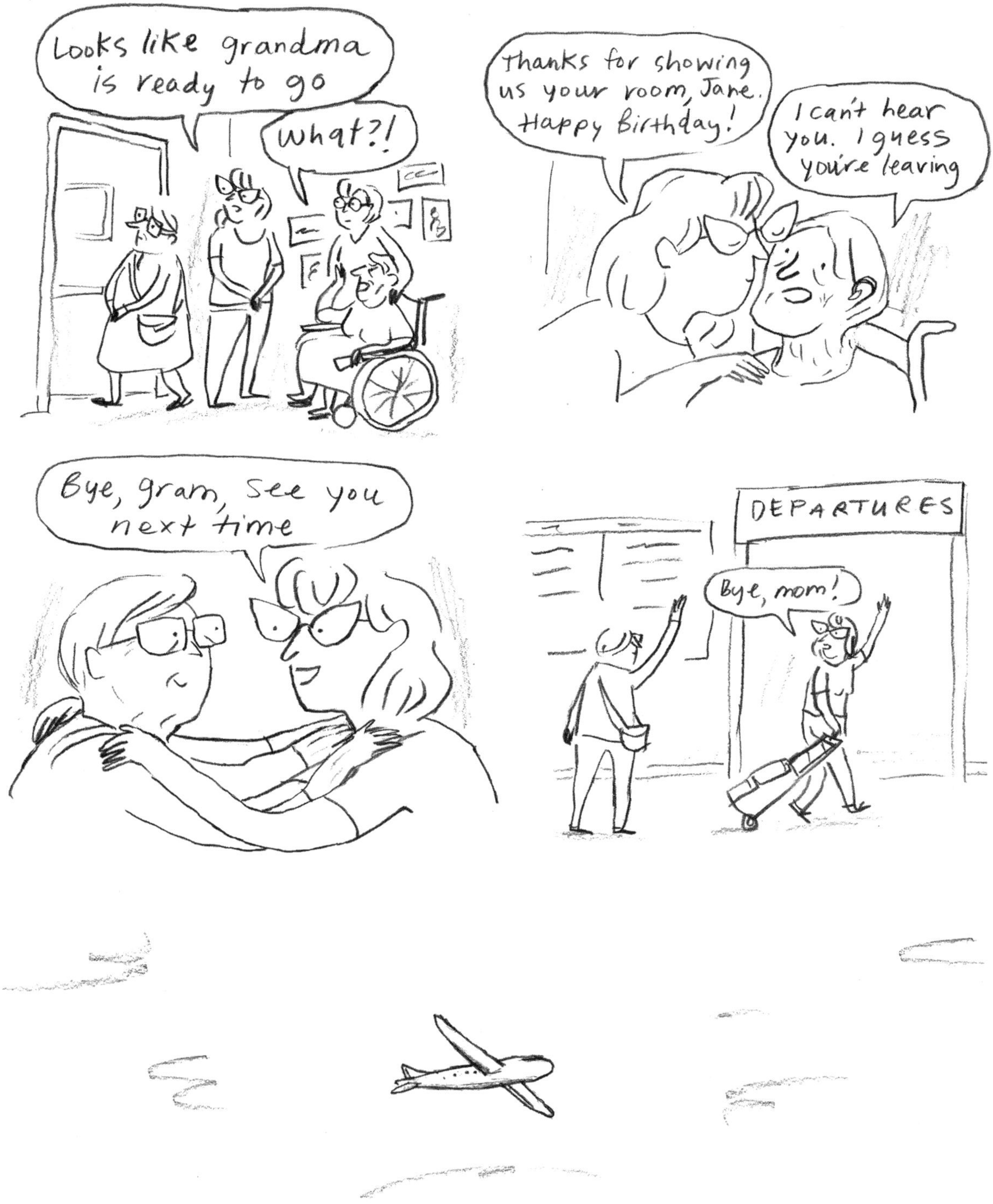
Looks like grandma is ready to go
What?!
Thanks for showing us your room, Jane. Happy Birthday!
I can't hear you. I guess you're leaving
Bye, gram, see you next time
DEPARTURES
Bye, mom!

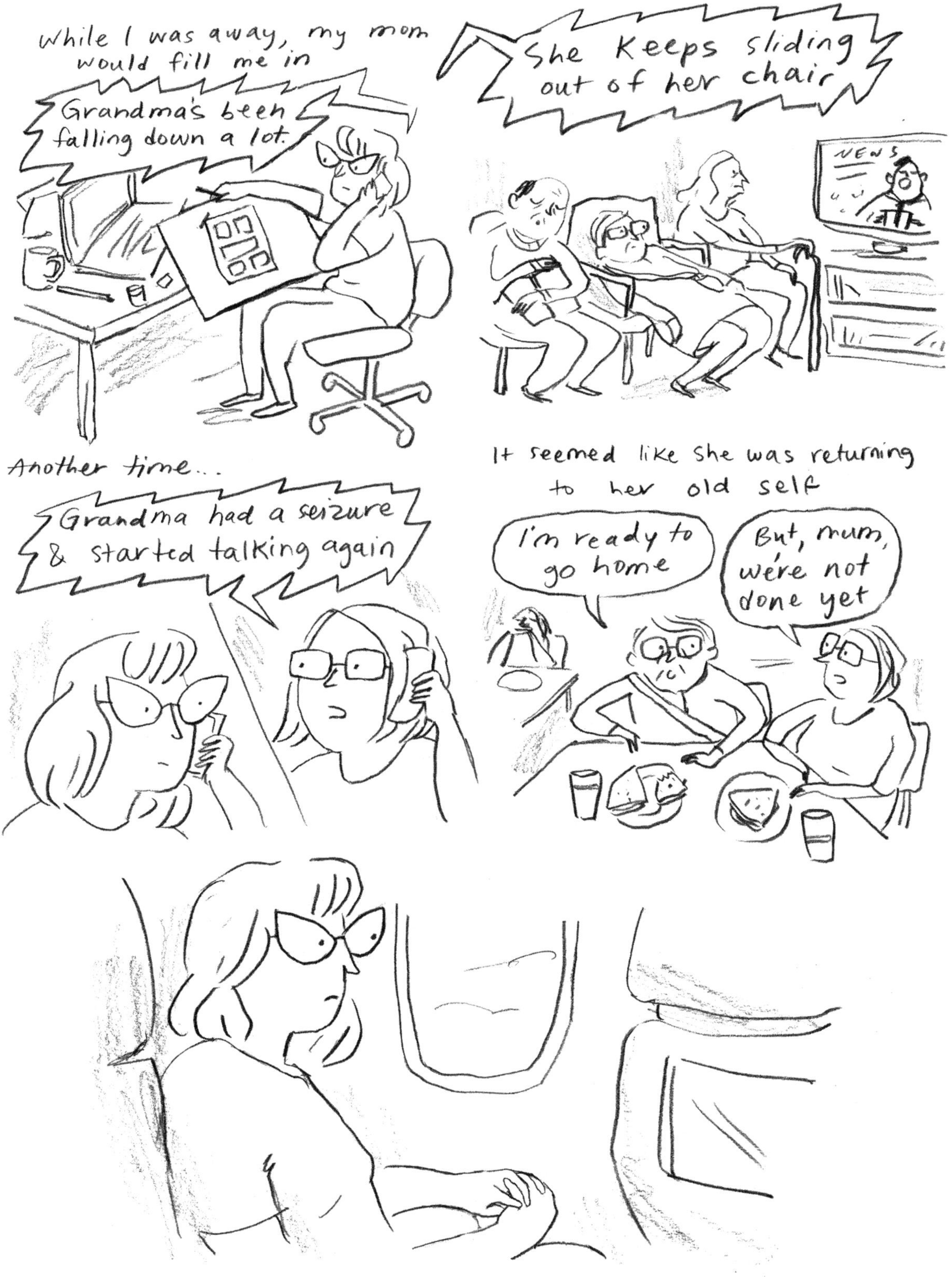
While I was away, my mom would fill me in
Grandma's been falling down a lot.
She keeps sliding out of her chair
NEWS
Another time...
Grandma had a seizure & started talking again
It seemed like she was returning to her old self
I'm ready to go home
But, mum, we're not done yet

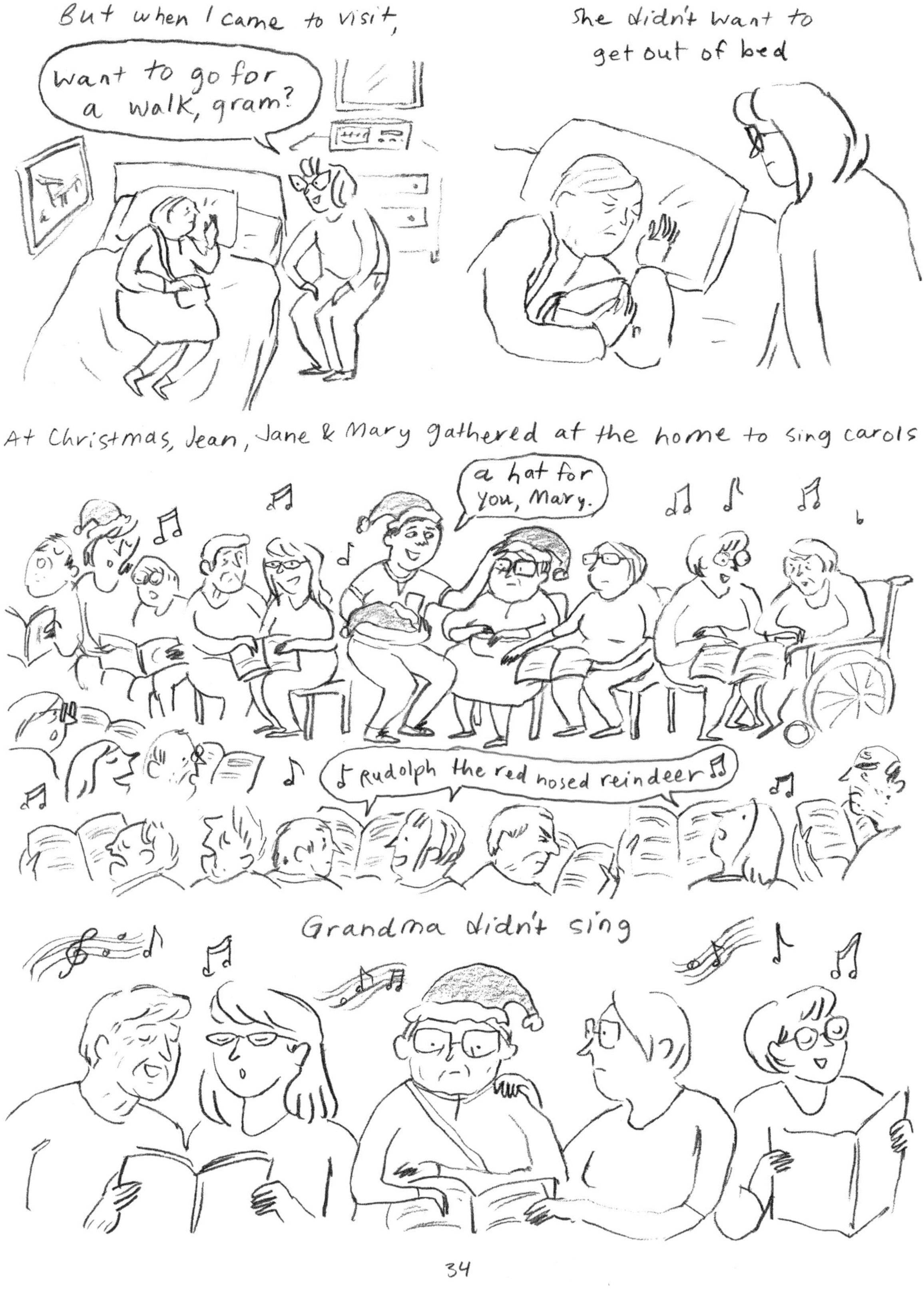
But when I came to visit,
want to go for a walk, gram?
She didn't want to get out of bed
At Christmas, Jean, Jane & Mary gathered at the home to sing carols
a hat for you, Mary.
Rudolph the red nosed reindeer
Grandma didn't sing

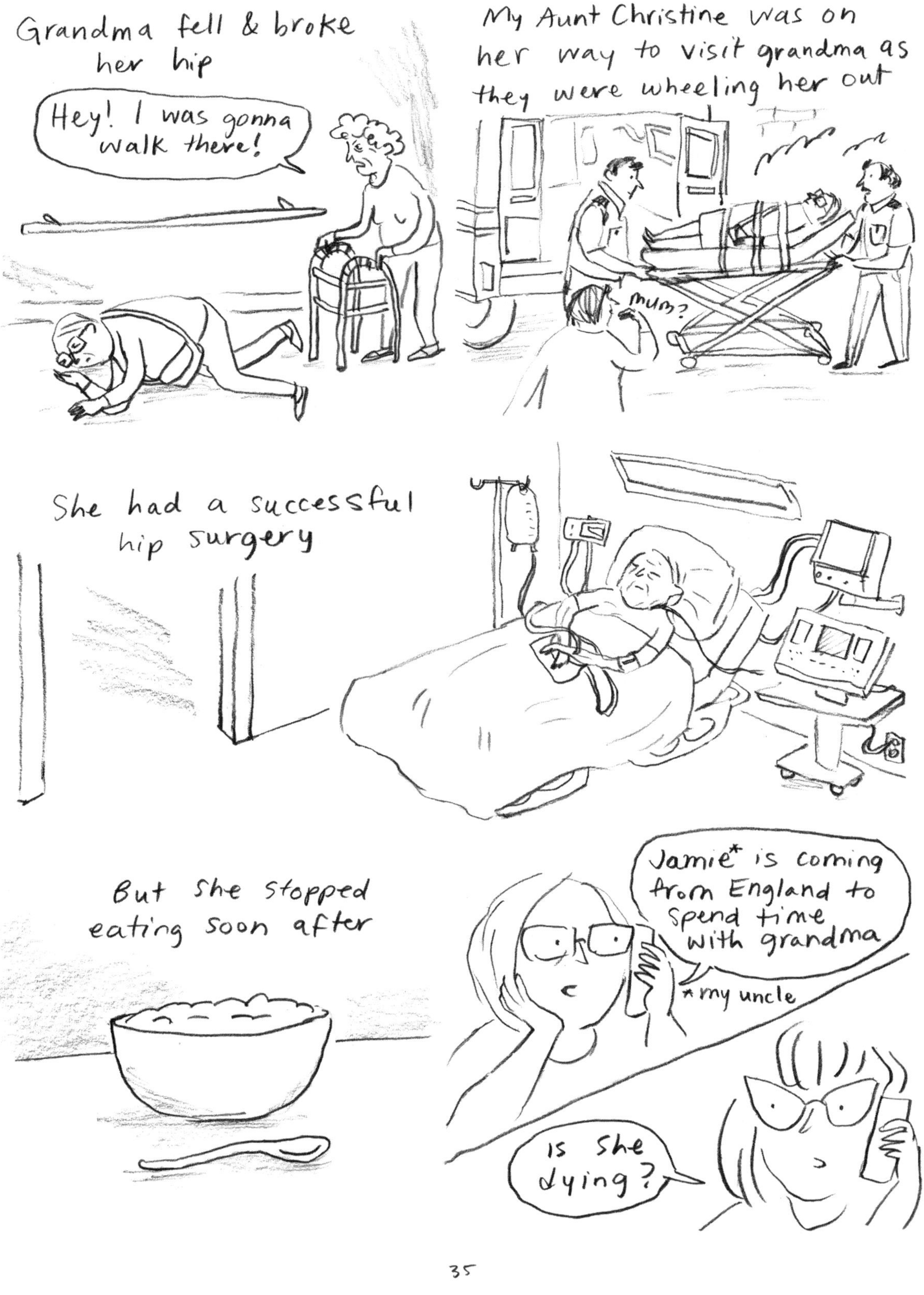
Grandma fell & broke her hip
Hey! I was gonna walk there!
My Aunt Christine was on her way to visit grandma as they were wheeling her out
mum?
She had a successful hip surgery
But she stopped eating soon after
Jamie* is coming from England to spend time with grandma
*my uncle
Is she dying?

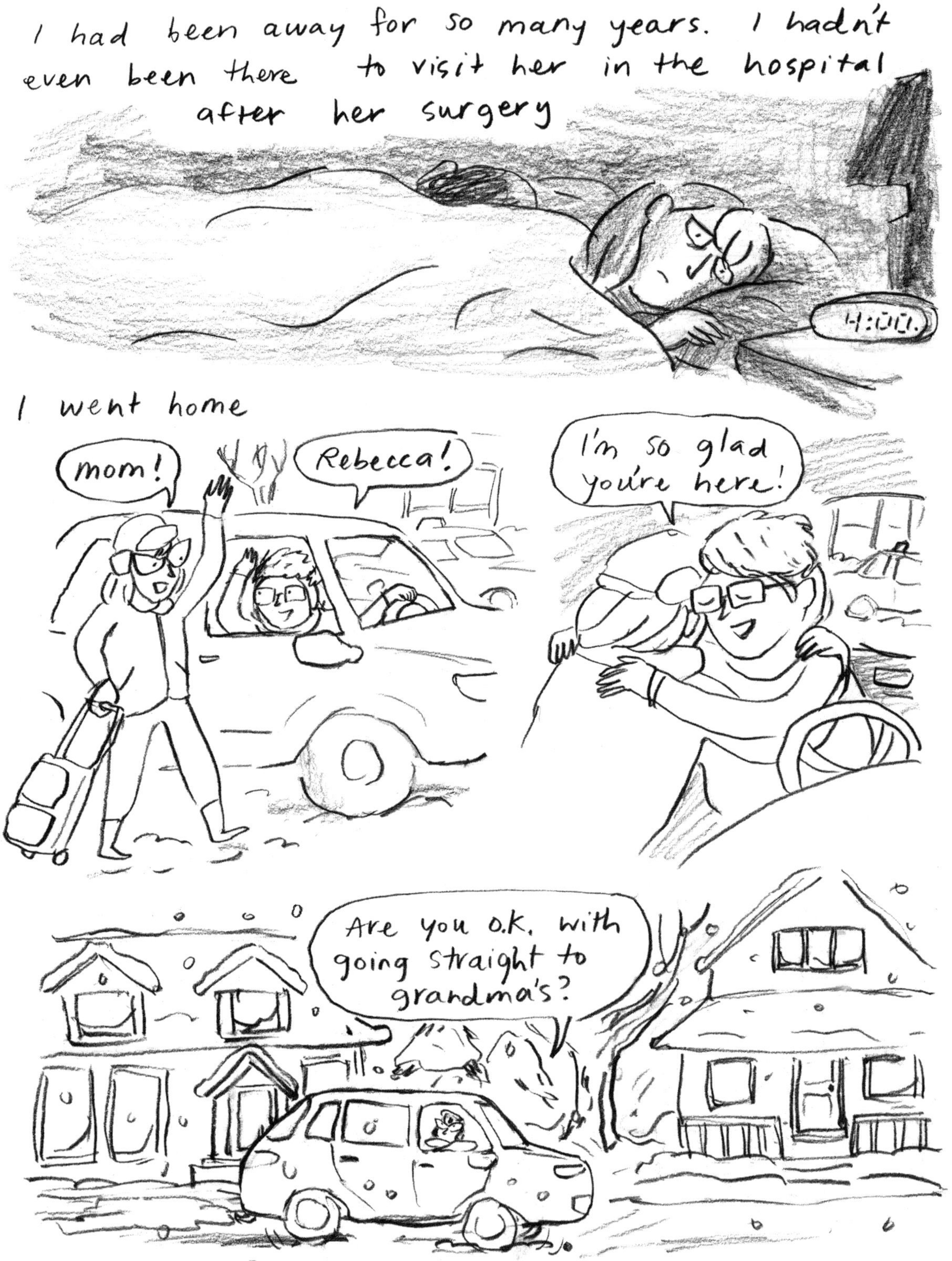
I had been away for so many years. I hadn't even been there to visit her in the hospital after her surgery
4:00.
I went home
mom!
Rebecca!
I'm so glad you're here!
Are you O.K. with going straight to grandma's?

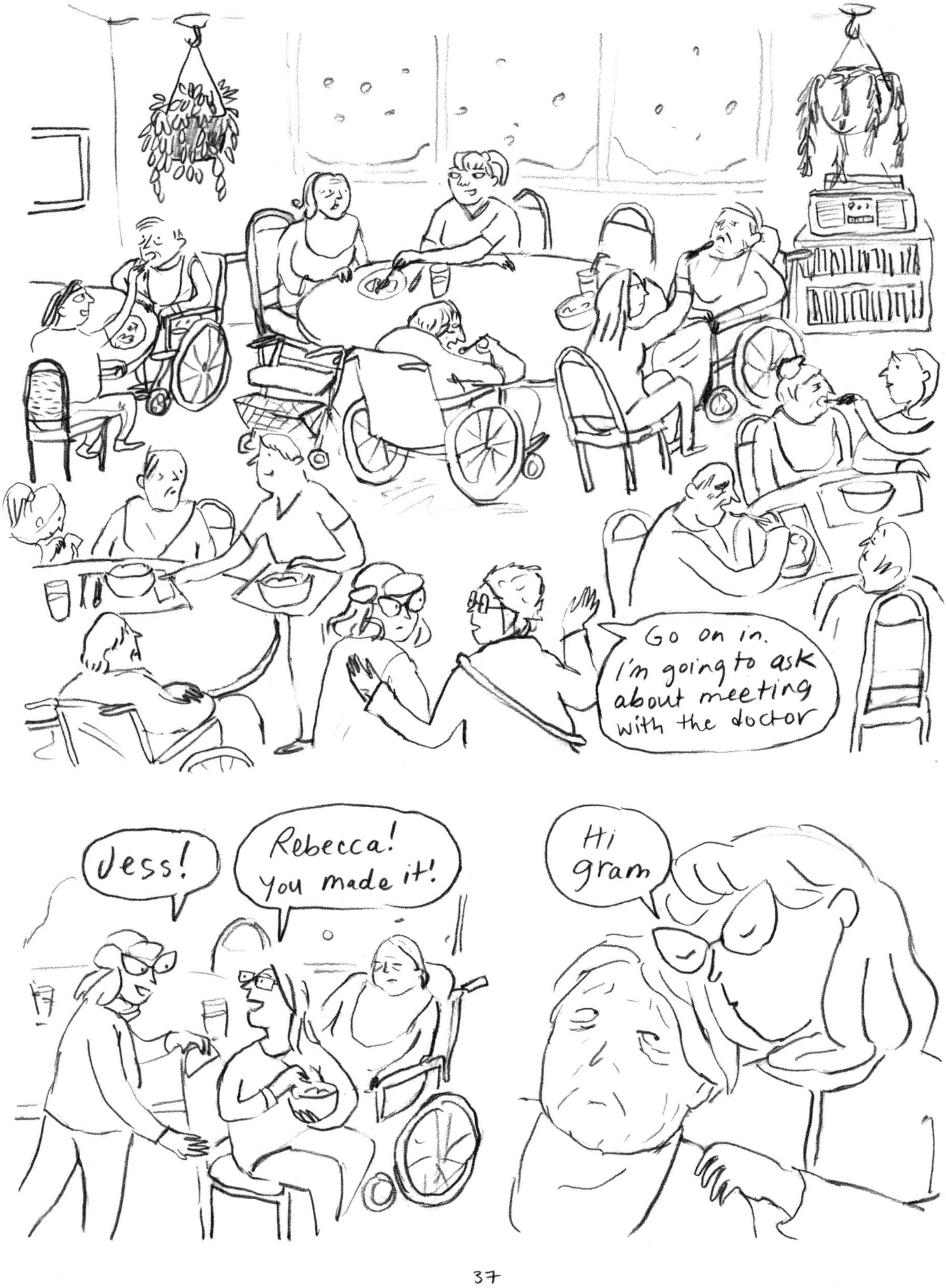
Go on in. I'm going to ask about meeting with the doctor
Jess!
Rebecca! You made it!
Hi gram

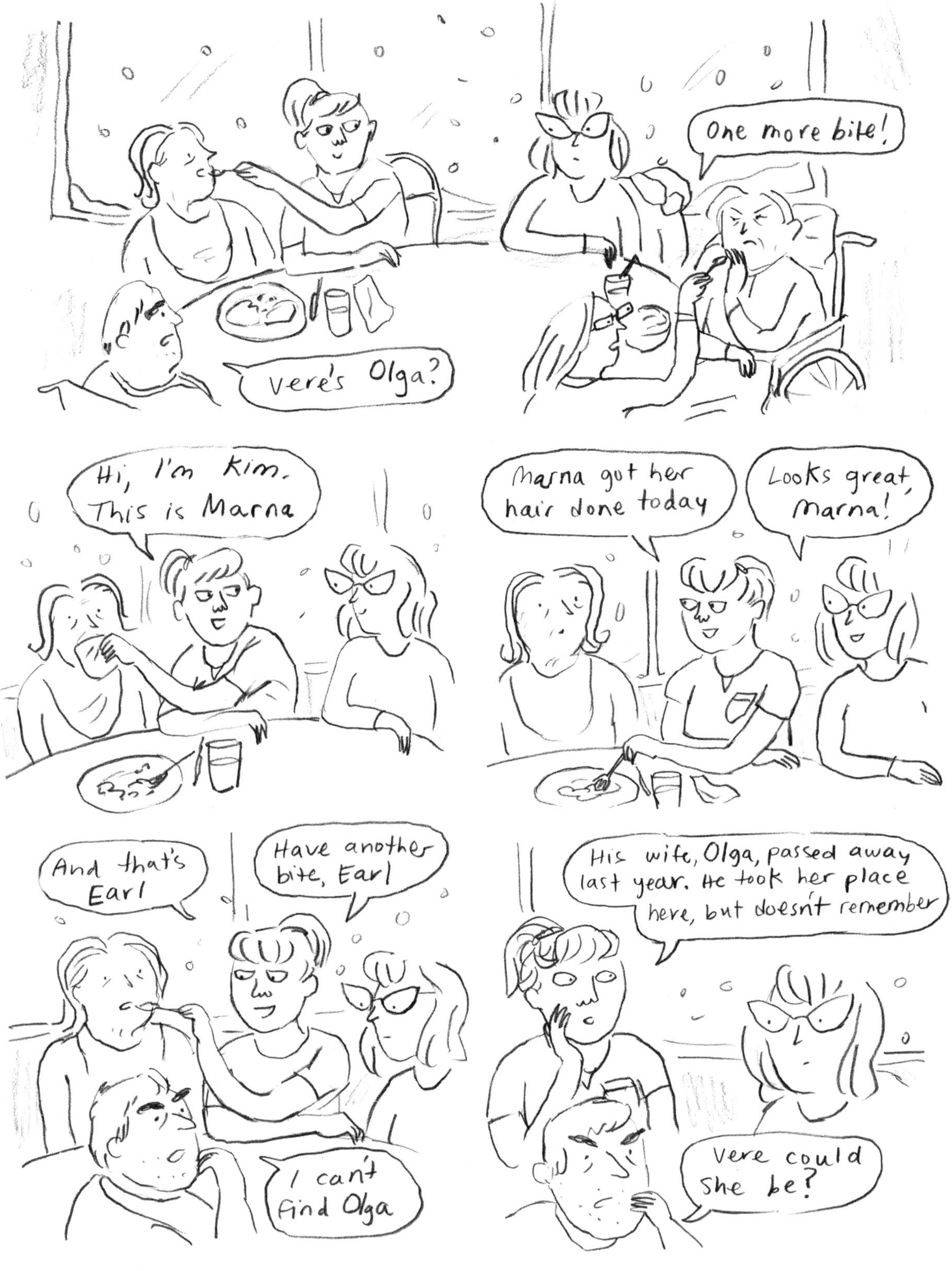
Vere's Olga?
One more bite!
Hi, I'm Kim. This is Marna
Marna got her hair done today
Looks great, Marna!
And that's Earl
Have another bite, Earl
I can't find Olga
His wife, Olga, passed away last year. He took her place here, but doesn't remember
Vere could she be?

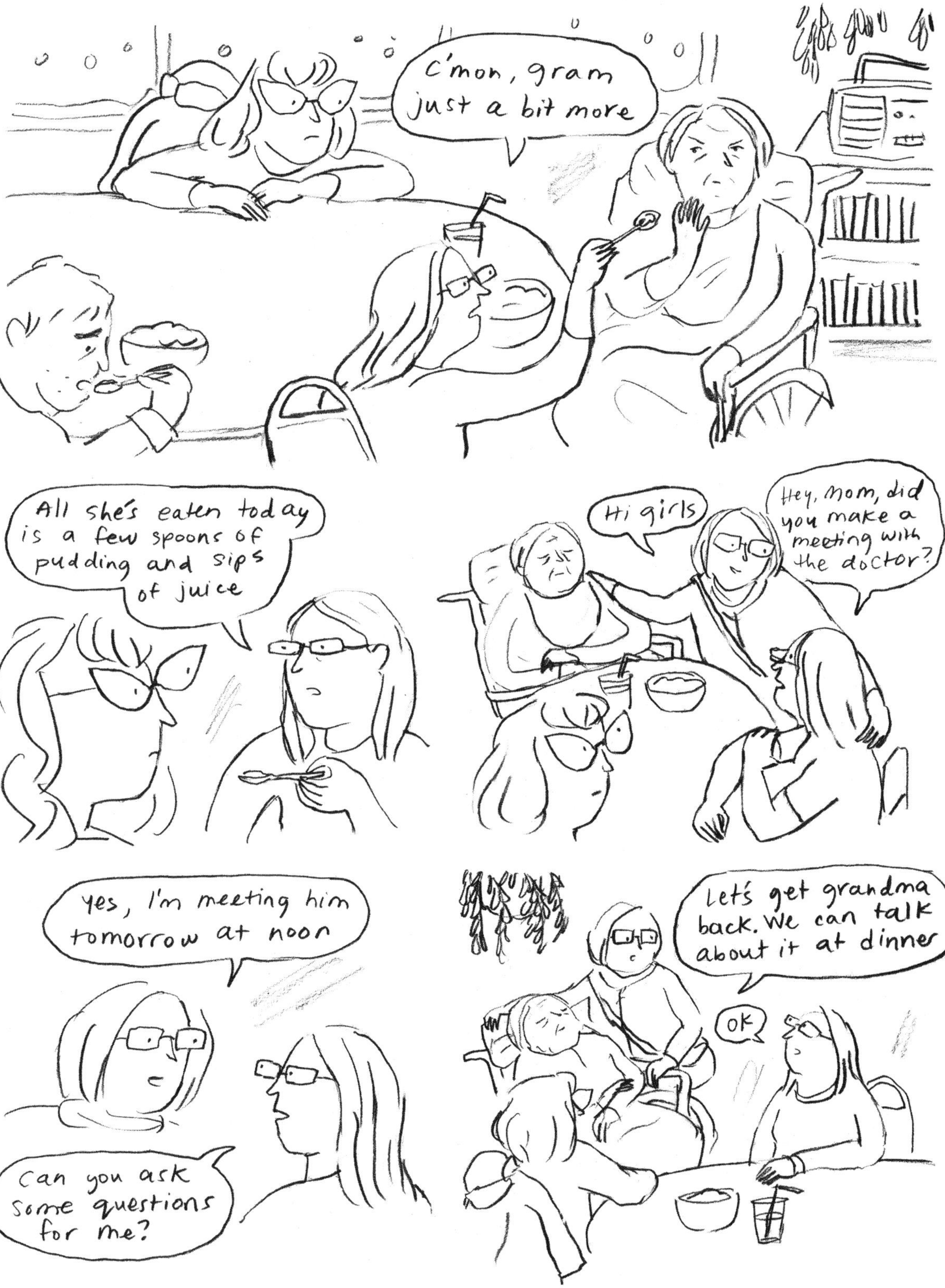
C'mon, gram
just a bit more
All she's eaten today is a few spoons of pudding and sips of juice
Hi girls
Hey, mom, did you make a meeting with the doctor?
Yes, I'm meeting him tomorrow at noon
Can you ask some questions for me?
Let's get grandma back. We can talk about it at dinner
OK

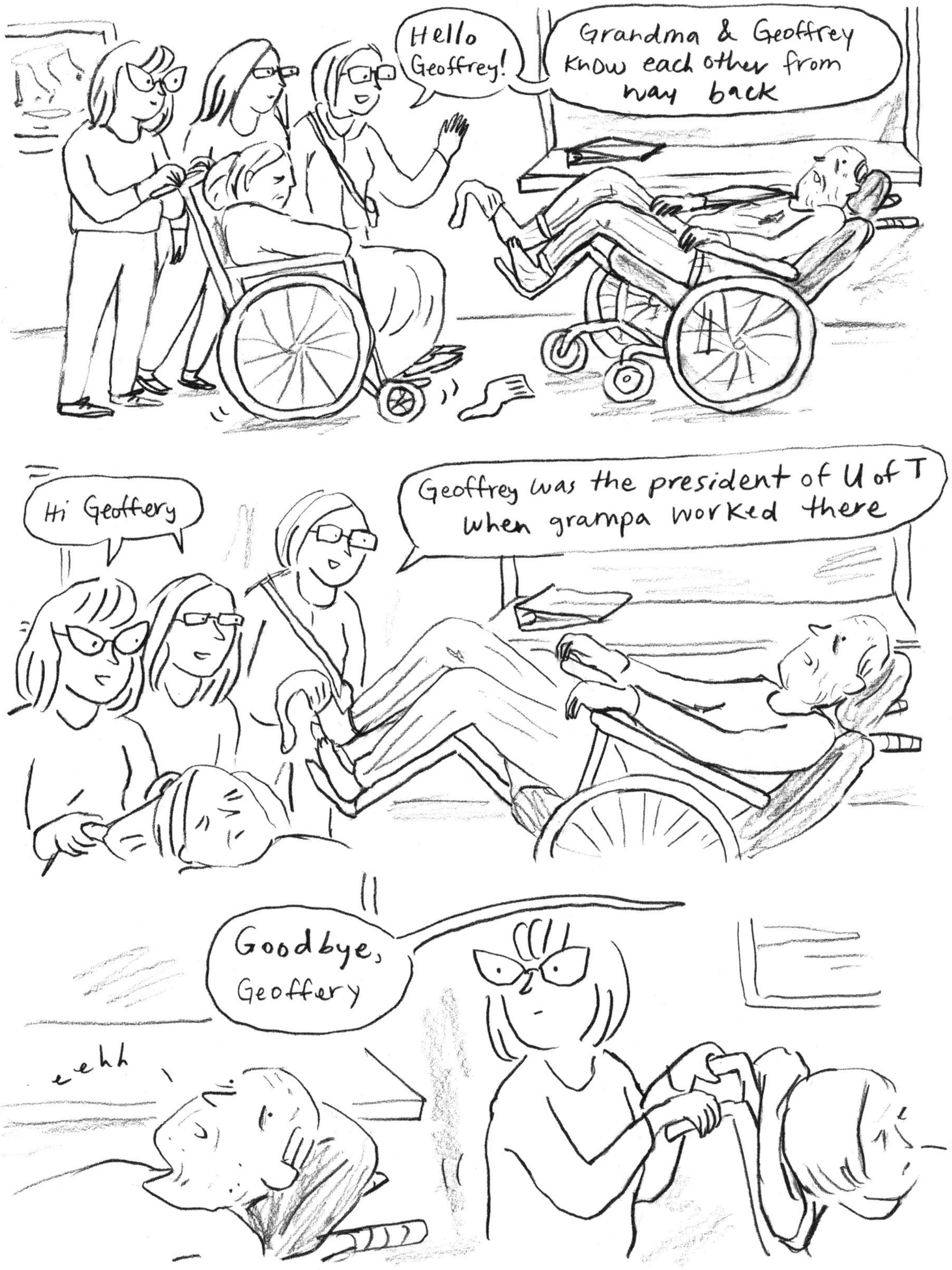
Hello Geoffrey!
Grandma & Geoffrey know each other from way back
Hi Geoffery
Geoffrey was the president of U of T when grampa worked there
Goodbye, Geoffery
eehh

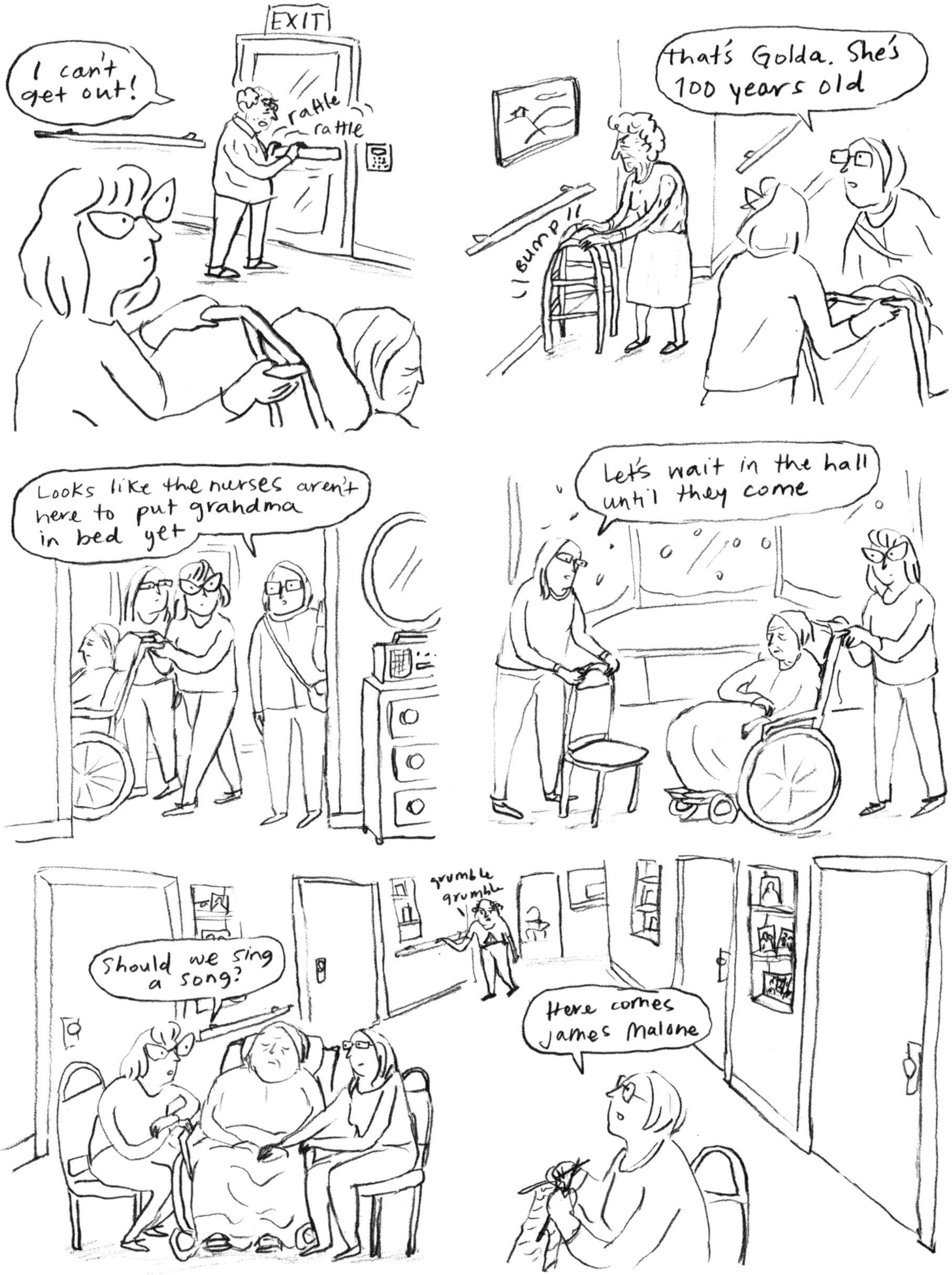
EXIT
I can't get out!
rattle rattle
that's Golda. She's 100 years old
bump!!
Looks like the nurses aren't here to put grandma in bed yet
Let's wait in the hall until they come
Should we sing a song?
grumble grumble
Here comes James Malone

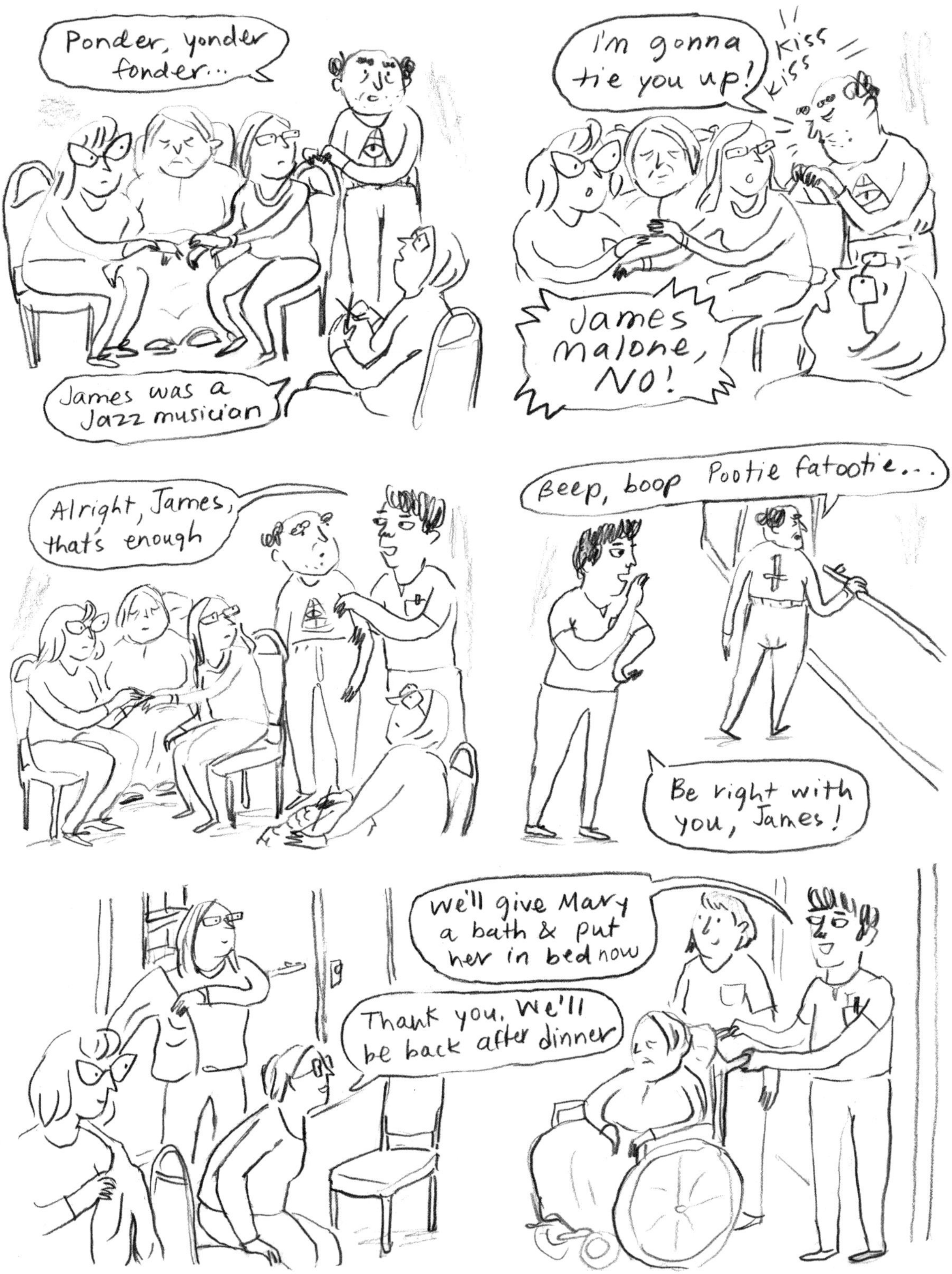
Ponder, yonder fonder...
James was a Jazz musician
I'm gonna tie you up!
Kiss Kiss
James Malone, NO!
Alright, James, that's enough
Beep, boop Pootie fatootie...
Be right with you, James!
We'll give Mary a bath & put her in bed now
Thank you. We'll be back after dinner

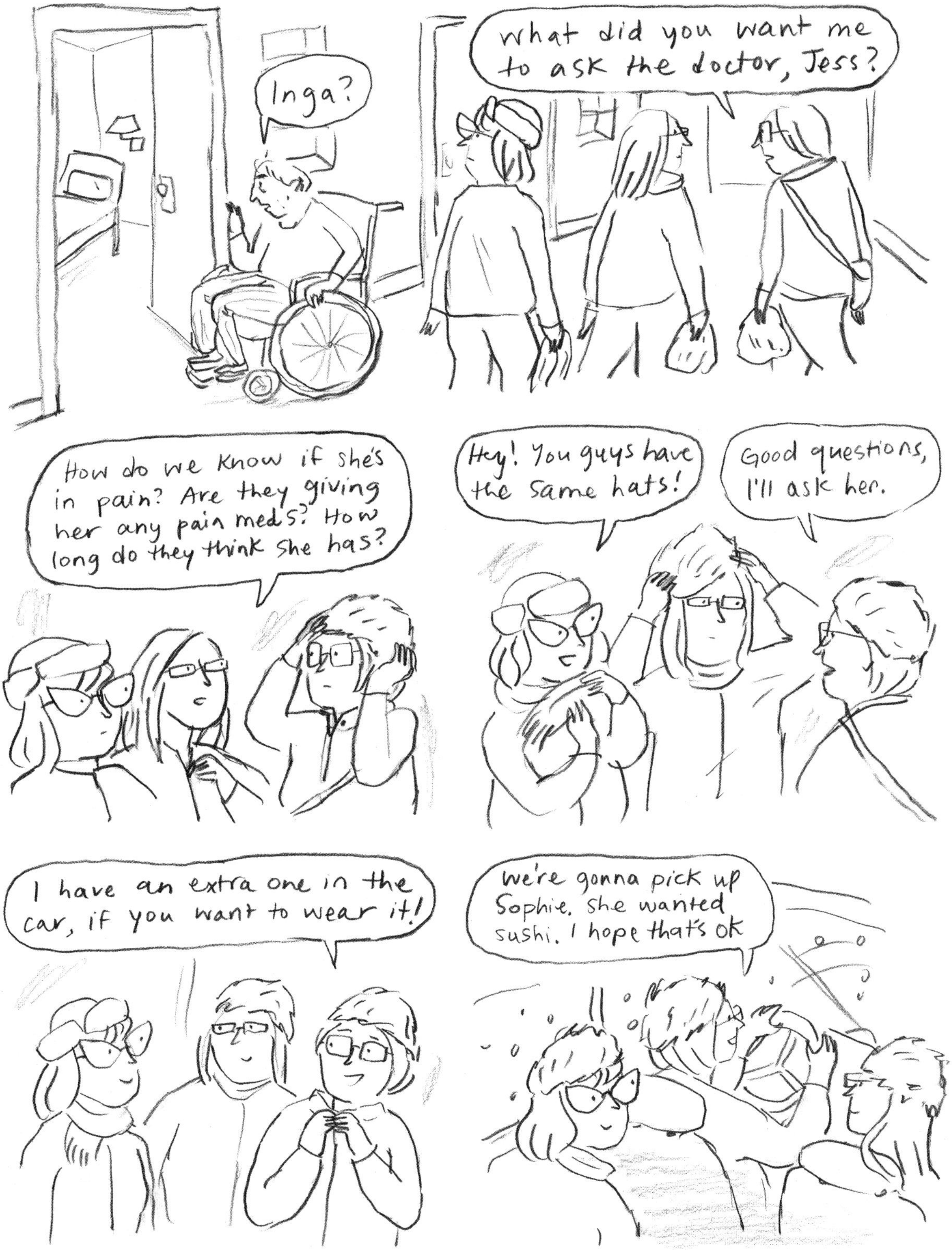
Inga?
What did you want me to ask the doctor, Jess?
How do we know if she's in pain? Are they giving her any pain meds? How long do they think she has?
Hey! You guys have the same hats!
Good questions, I'll ask her.
I have an extra one in the car, if you want to wear it!
We're gonna pick up Sophie. She wanted sushi. I hope that's ok

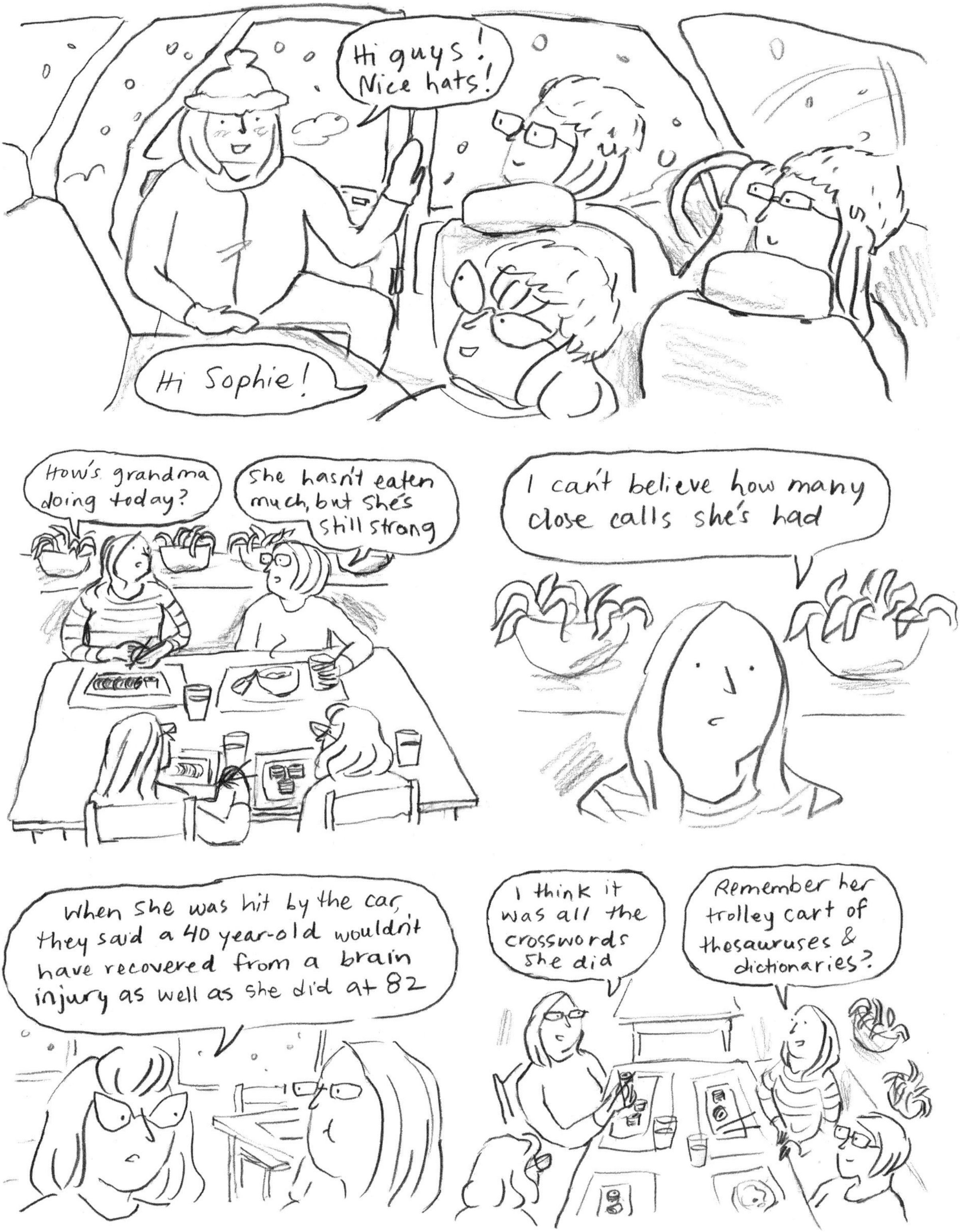
Hi guys! Nice hats!
Hi Sophie!
How's grandma doing today?
She hasn't eaten much, but she's still strong
I can't believe how many close calls she's had
When she was hit by the car, they said a 40 year-old wouldn't have recovered from a brain injury as well as she did at 82
I think it was all the crosswords she did
Remember her trolley cart of thesauruses & dictionaries?

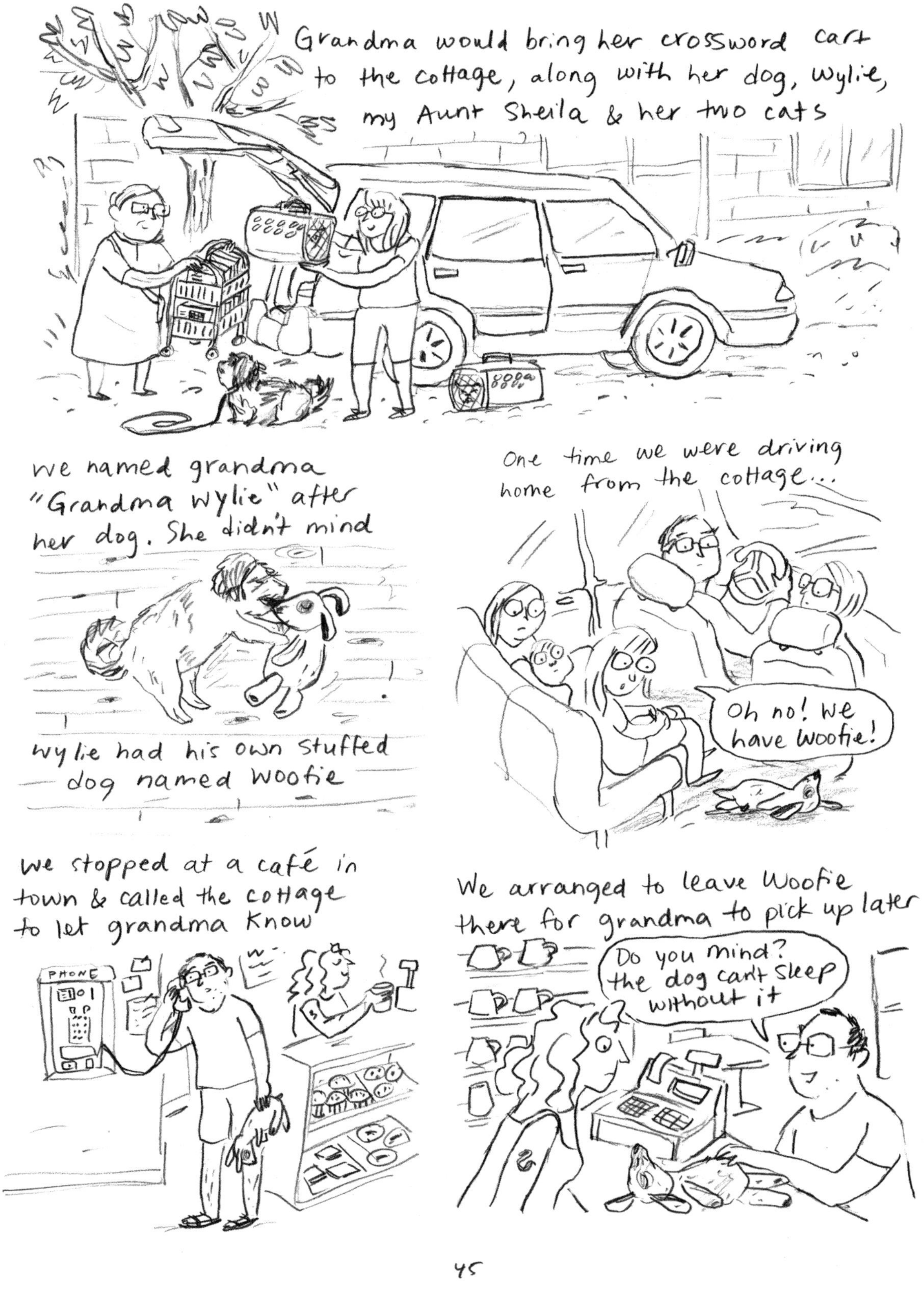
Grandma would bring her crossword cart to the cottage, along with her dog, Wylie, my Aunt Sheila & her two cats
We named grandma "Grandma Wylie" after her dog. She didn't mind
Wylie had his own stuffed dog named Woofie
One time we were driving home from the cottage...
Oh no! We have Woofie!
We stopped at a café in town & called the cottage to let grandma know
PHONE
We arranged to leave Woofie there for grandma to pick up later
Do you mind? the dog can't sleep without it

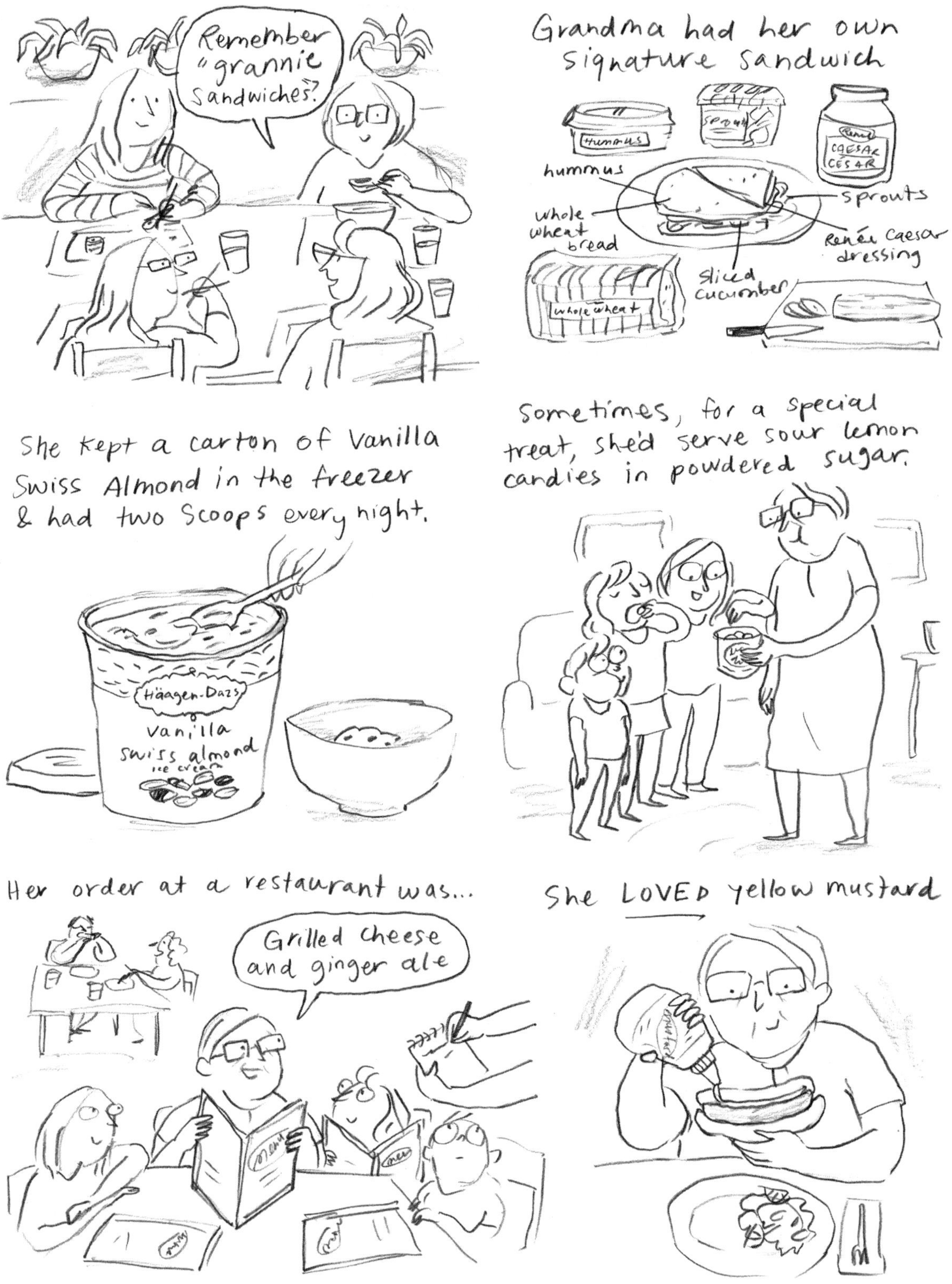
Remember "grannie sandwiches"?
Grandma had her own signature sandwich
Hummus
Sprouts
Renée
CAESAR
CÉSAR
hummus
whole wheat bread
sprouts
Renée Caesar dressing
sliced cucumber
whole wheat
She kept a carton of Vanilla Swiss Almond in the freezer & had two scoops every night.
Häagen-Dazs
vanilla swiss almond
ice cream
Sometimes, for a special treat, she'd serve sour lemon candies in powdered sugar.
Her order at a restaurant was...
Grilled cheese and ginger ale
menu
menu
She LOVED yellow mustard
mustard

When grandma moved to her Walmer Road apartment, we spent lots of time there after school & on weekends

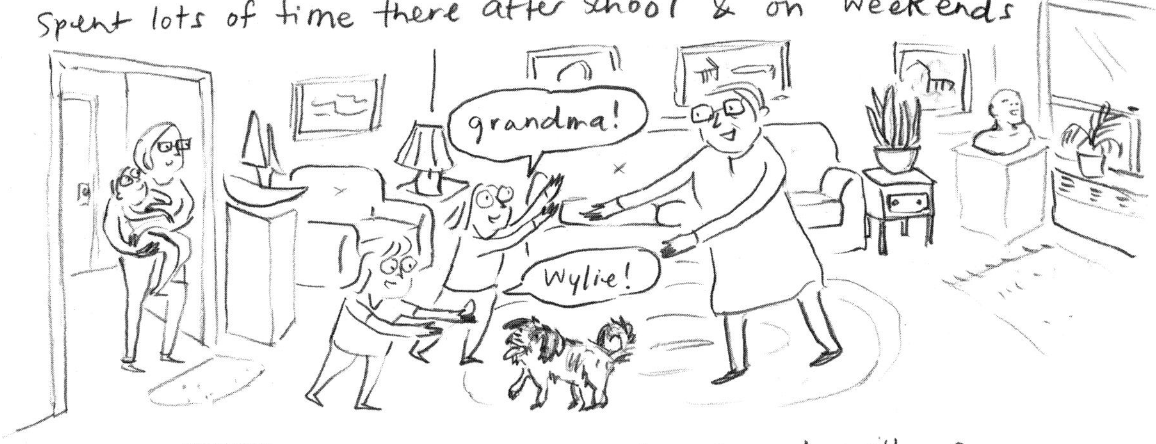
grandma!
Wylie!

We played with a purse full of lipsticks & her electric typewriter

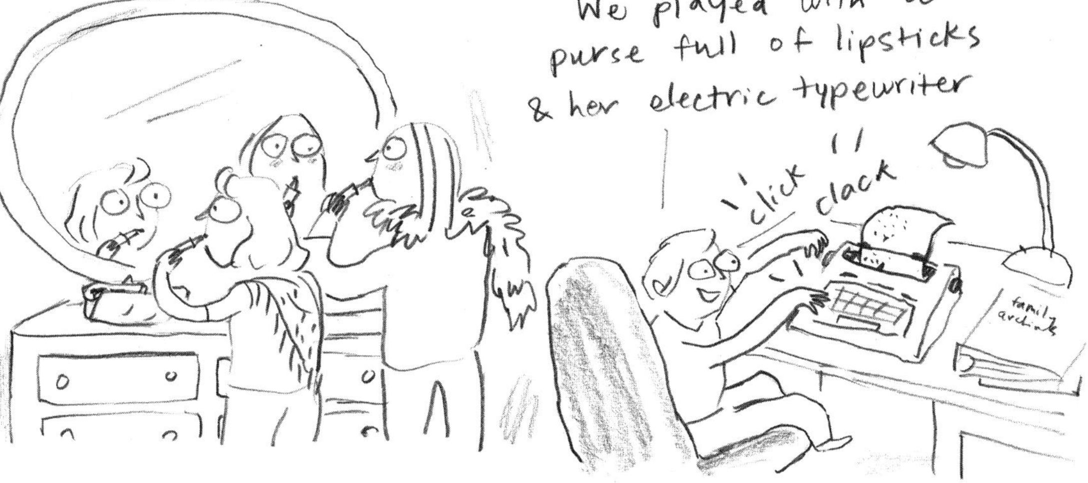
click
clack

My family was brought up Jewish, but we would celebrate Christmas at grandma's, sleeping over the night before to decorate every plant in the apartment

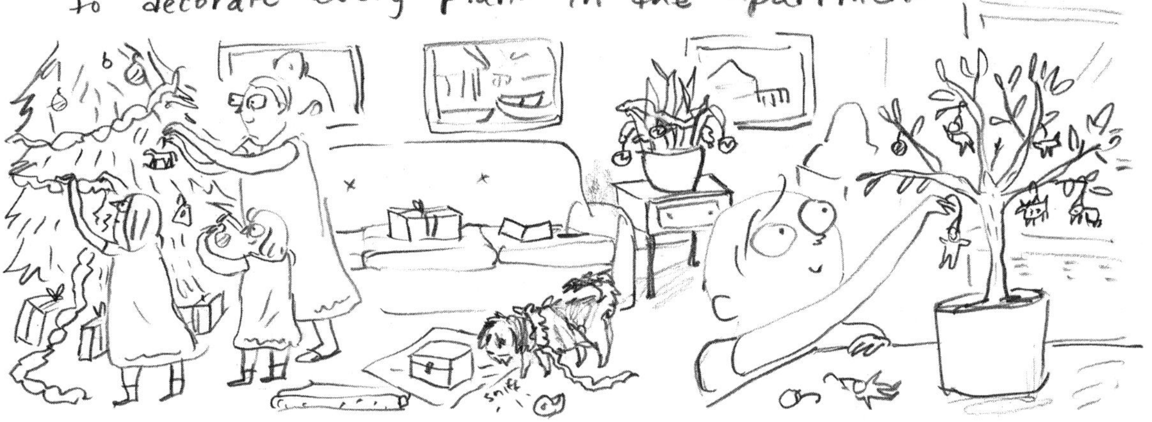

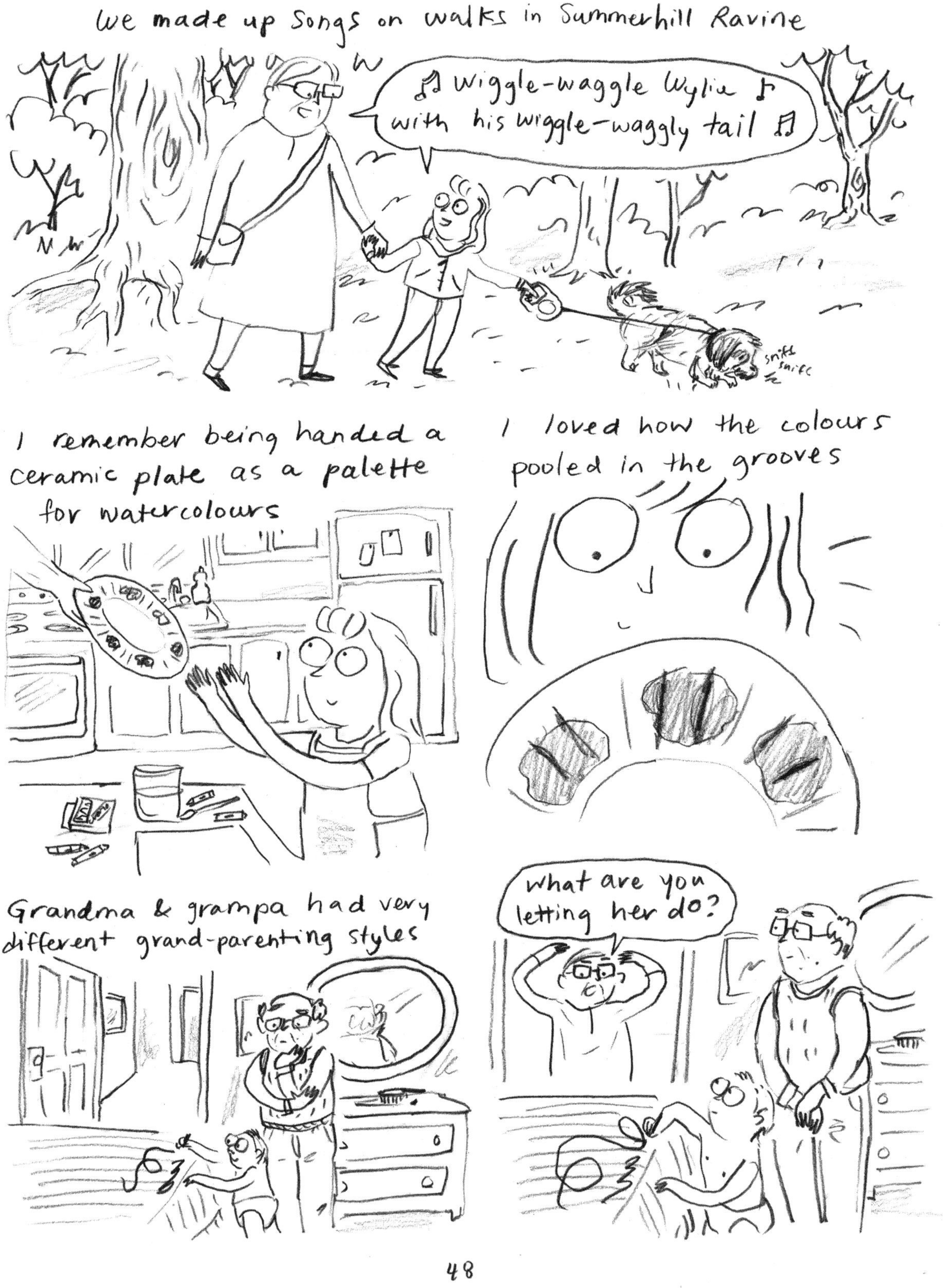
We made up songs on walks in Summerhill Ravine
♫ Wiggle-waggle Wylie ♪ with his wiggle-waggly tail ♫
sniff sniff
I remember being handed a ceramic plate as a palette for watercolours
I loved how the colours pooled in the grooves
Grandma & grampa had very different grand-parenting styles
What are you letting her do?

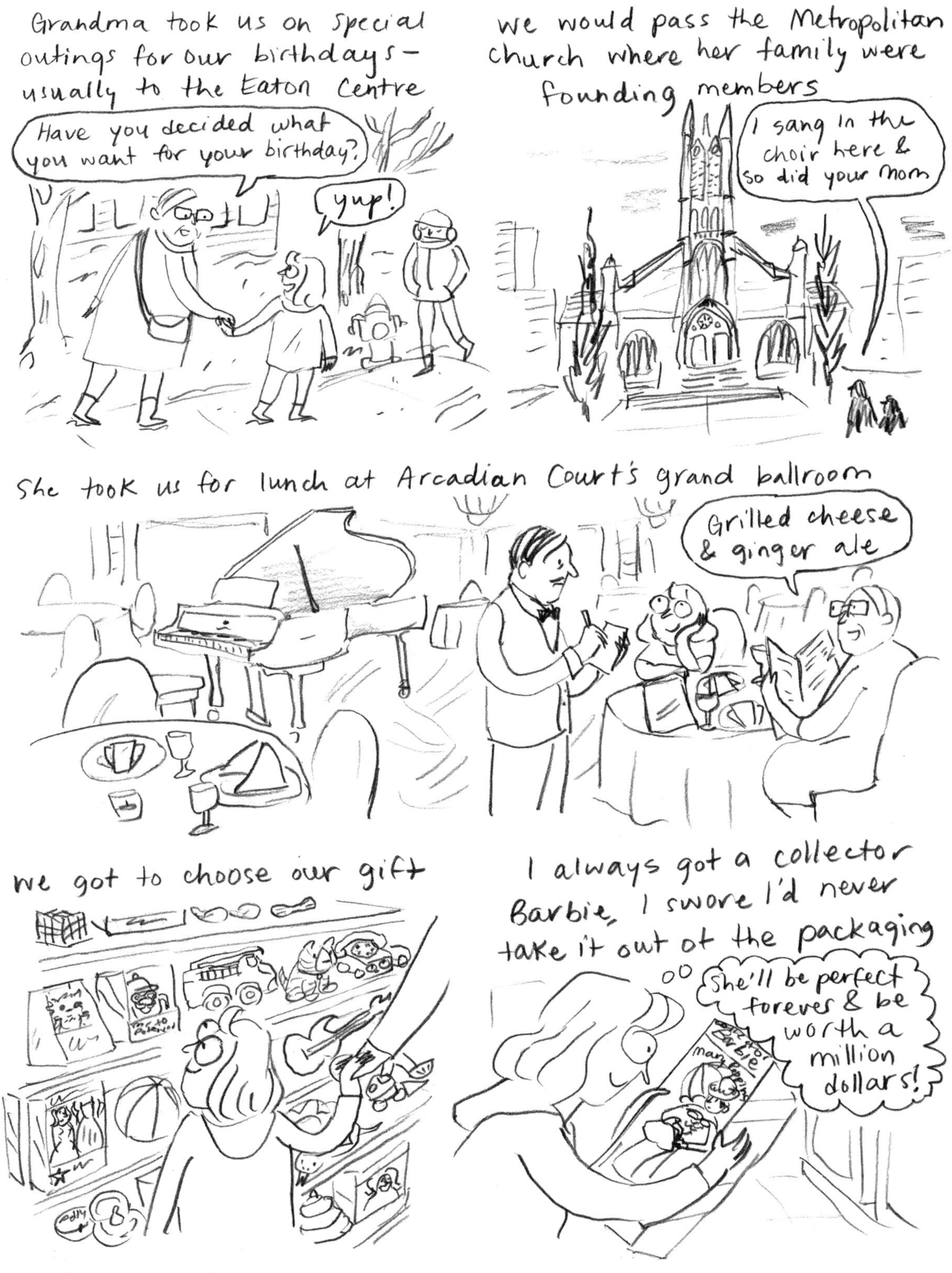
Grandma took us on special outings for our birthdays - usually to the Eaton Centre
Have you decided what you want for your birthday?
yup!
we would pass the Metropolitan church where her family were founding members
I sang in the choir here & so did your mom
She took us for lunch at Arcadian Court's grand ballroom
Grilled cheese & ginger ale
we got to choose our gift
I always got a collector Barbie, I swore I'd never take it out of the packaging
She'll be perfect forever & be worth a million dollars!

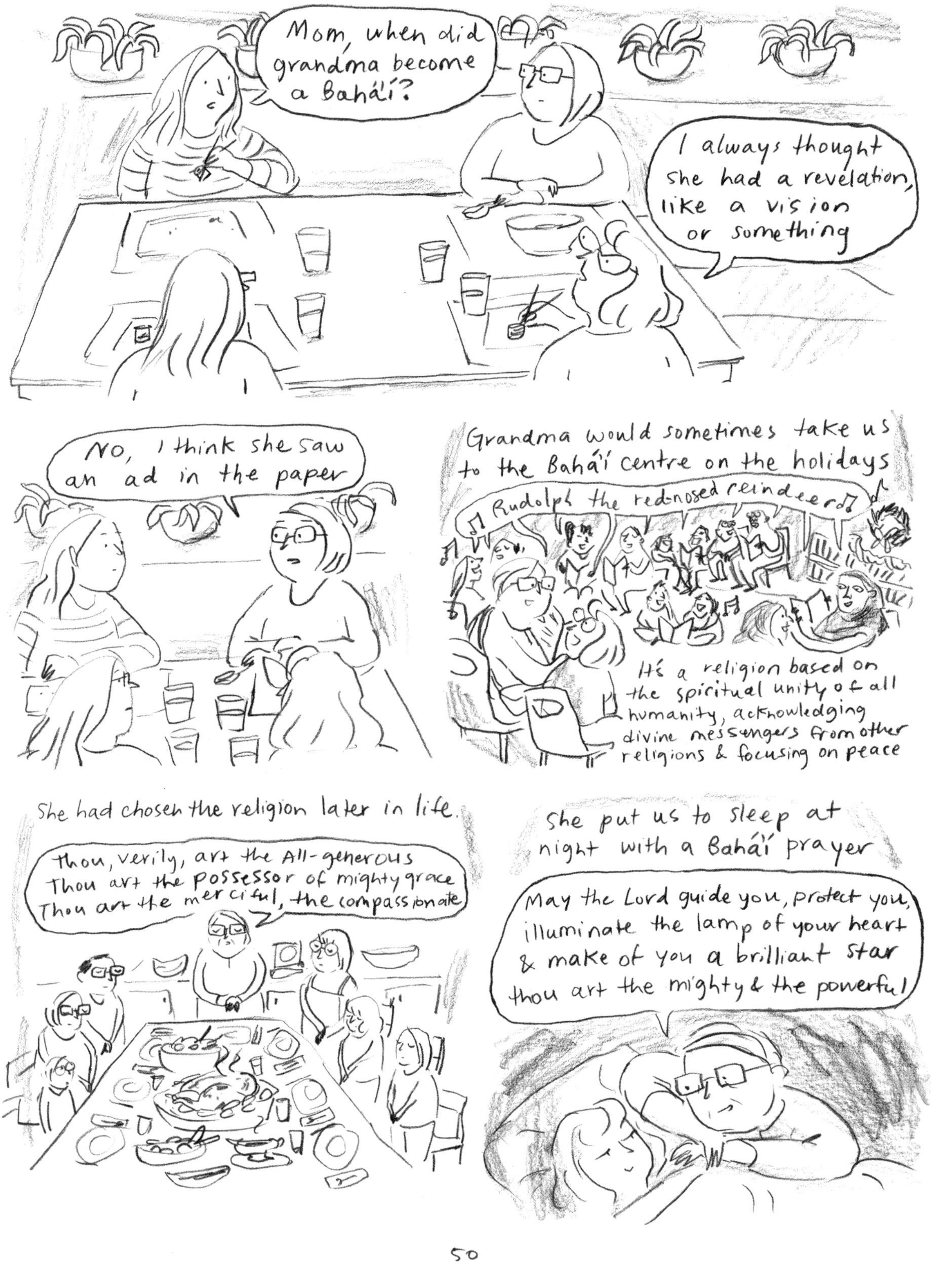

Mom, when did grandma become a Bahá'í?
I always thought she had a revelation, like a vision or something
No, I think she saw an ad in the paper
Grandma would sometimes take us to the Bahá'í centre on the holidays
♫ Rudolph the red-nosed reindeer ♫
It's a religion based on the spiritual unity of all humanity, acknowledging divine messengers from other religions & focusing on peace
She had chosen the religion later in life.
Thou, verily, art the All-generous
Thou art the possessor of mighty grace
Thou art the merciful, the compassionate
She put us to sleep at night with a Bahá'í prayer
May the Lord guide you, protect you, illuminate the lamp of your heart & make of you a brilliant star
thou art the mighty & the powerful

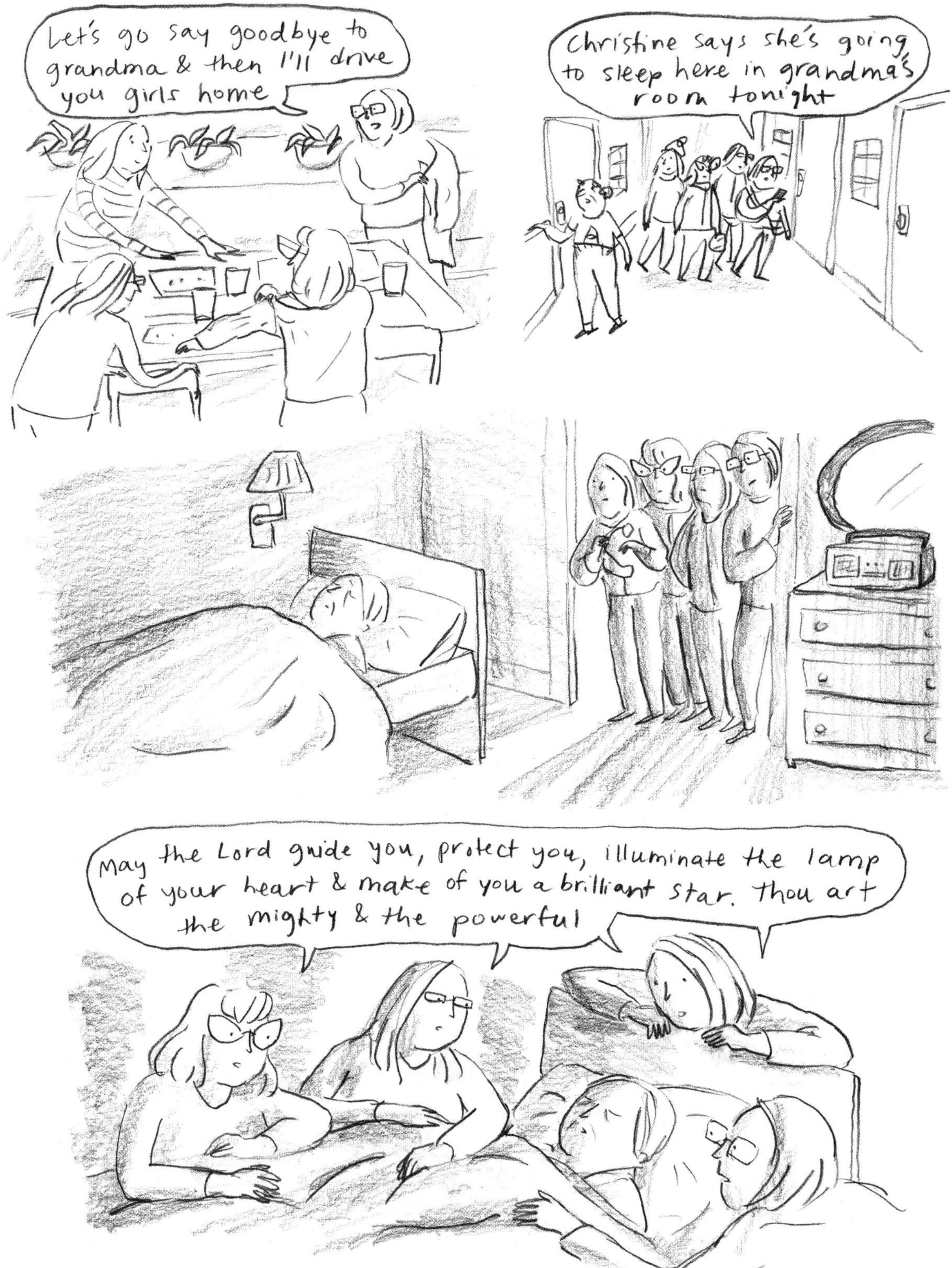
Let's go say goodbye to grandma & then I'll drive you girls home
Christine says she's going to sleep here in grandma's room tonight
May the Lord guide you, protect you, illuminate the lamp of your heart & make of you a brilliant star. Thou art the mighty & the powerful

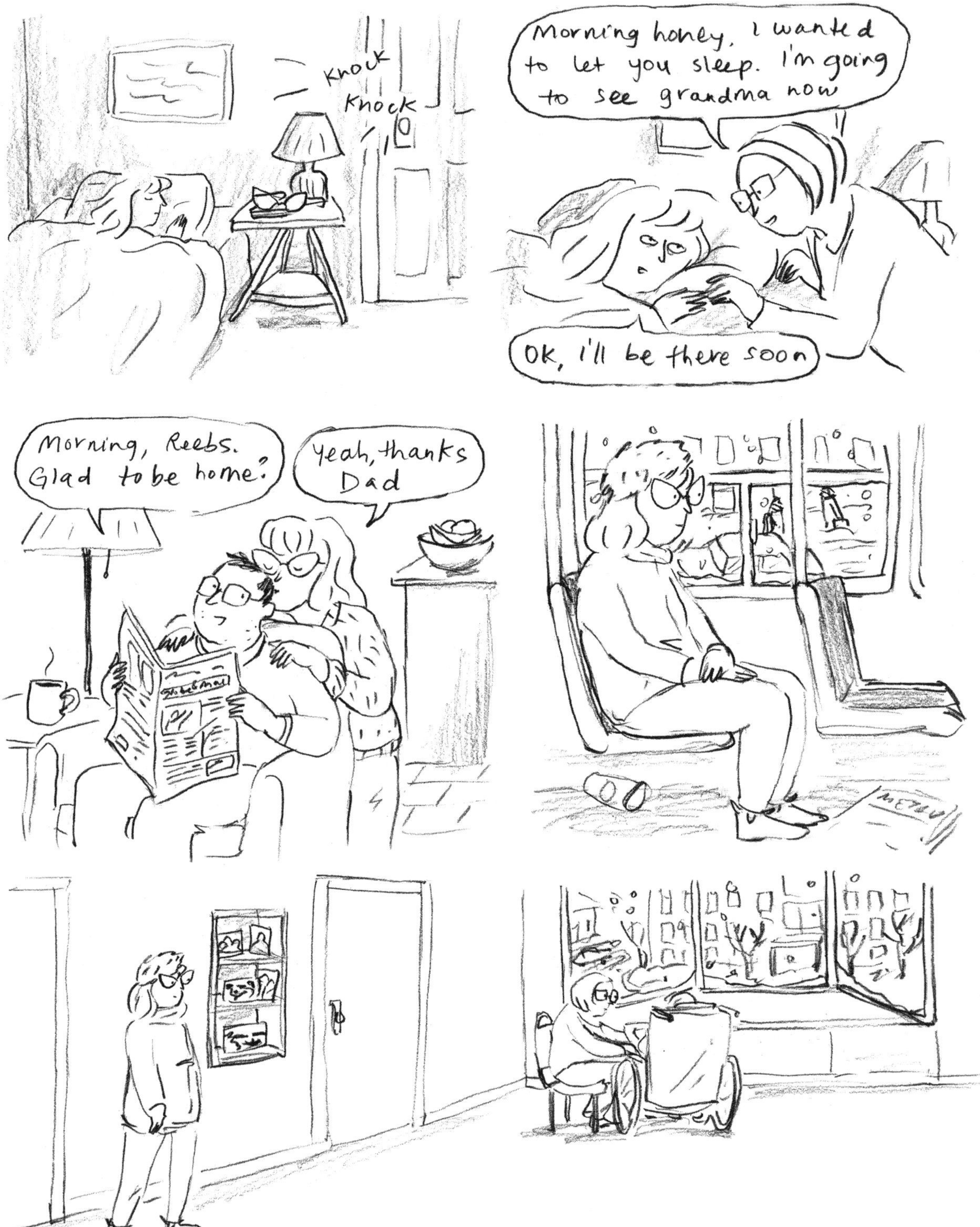
Knock
Knock
Morning honey, I wanted to let you sleep. I'm going to see grandma now
Ok, I'll be there soon
Morning, Reebs. Glad to be home?
Yeah, thanks Dad

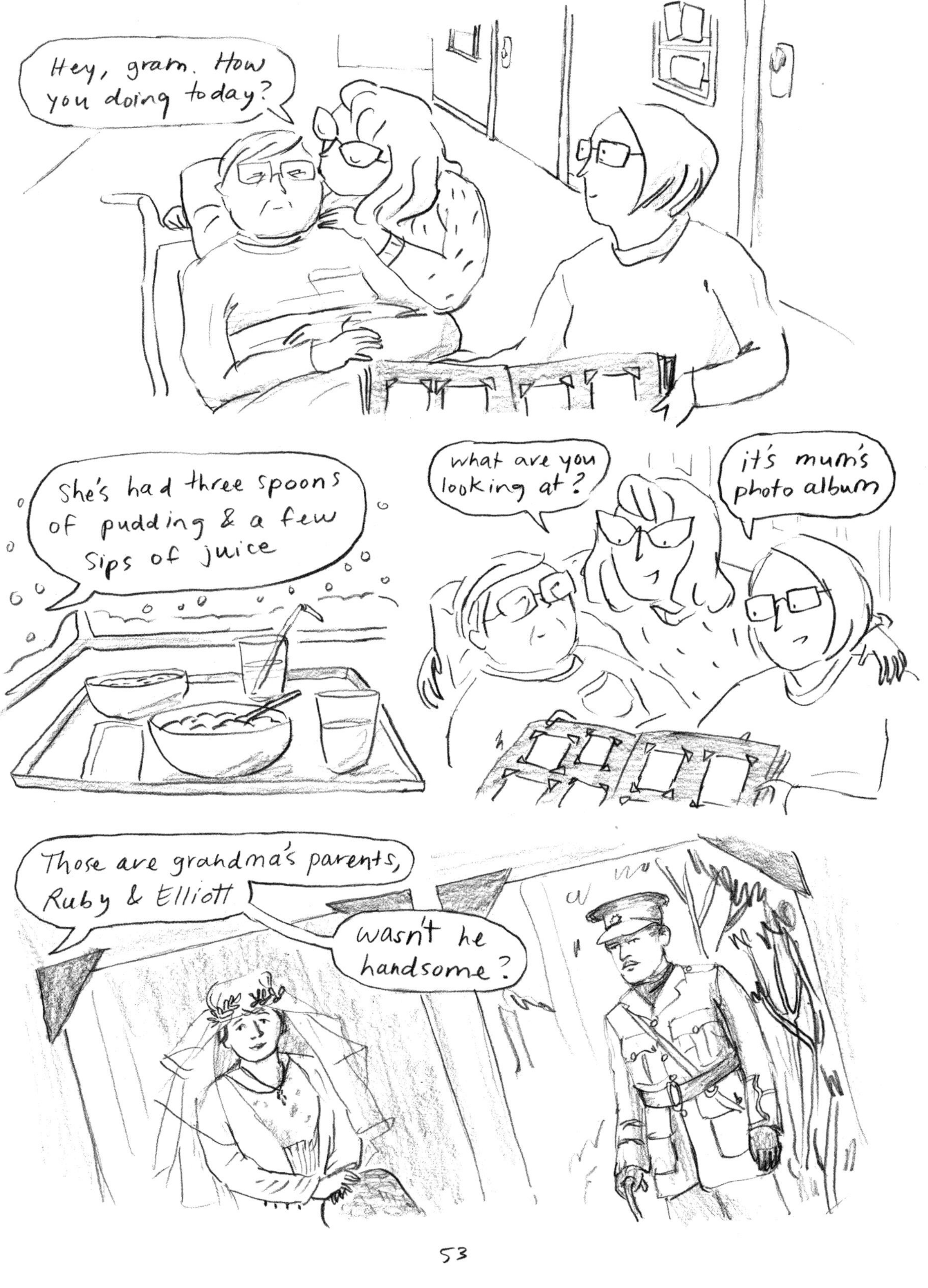
Hey, gram. How you doing today?
She's had three spoons of pudding & a few sips of juice
what are you looking at?
it's mum's photo album
Those are grandma's parents, Ruby & Elliott
wasn't he handsome?

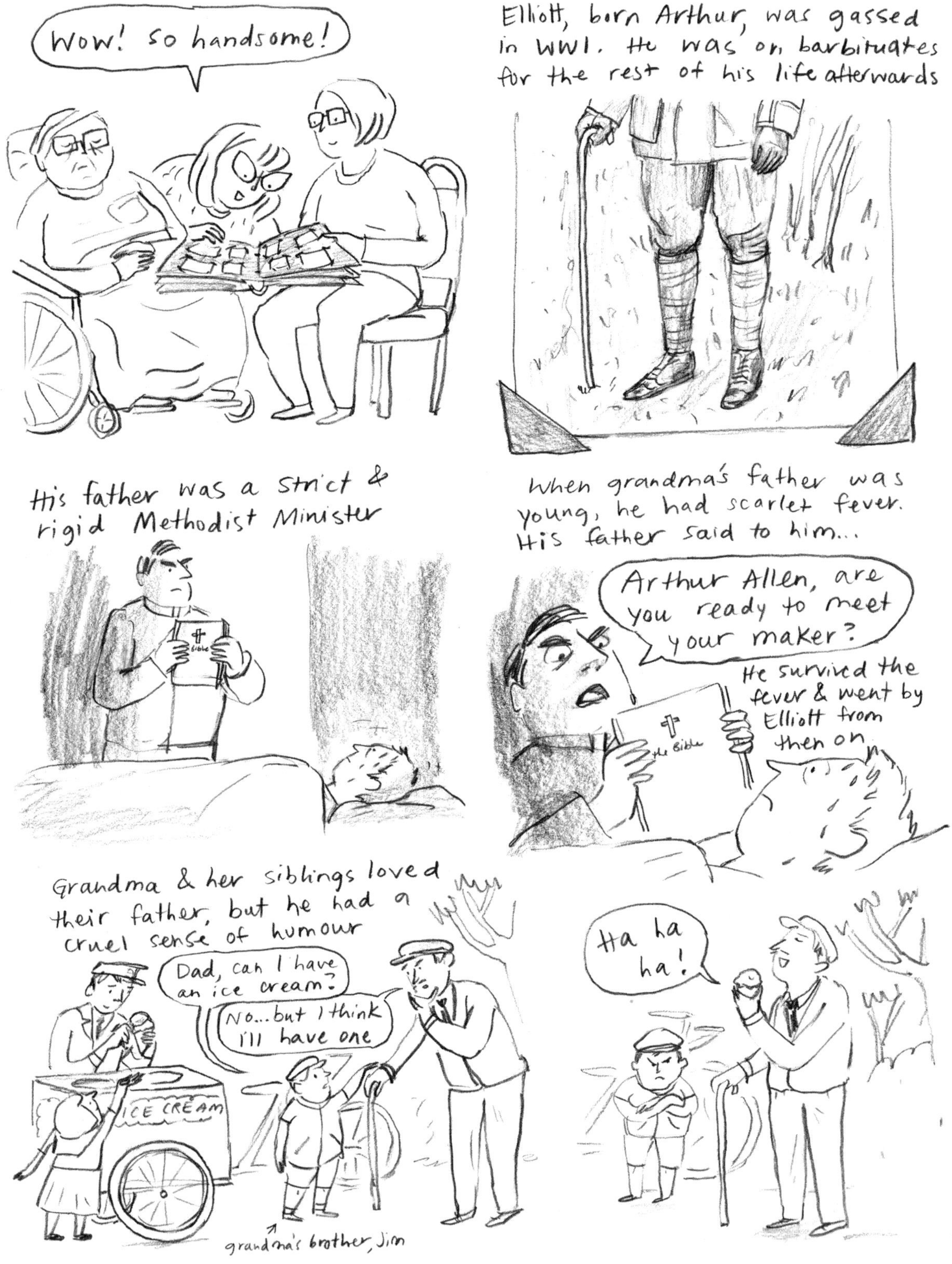
Wow! so handsome!
Elliott, born Arthur, was gassed in WWI. He was on barbituates for the rest of his life afterwards
His father was a strict & rigid Methodist Minister
Bible
When grandma's father was young, he had scarlet fever. His father said to him...
Arthur Allen, are you ready to meet your maker?
The Bible
He survived the fever & went by Elliott from then on
Grandma & her siblings loved their father, but he had a cruel sense of humour
Dad, can I have an ice cream?
No... but I think I'll have one
ICE CREAM
grandma's brother, Jim
Ha ha ha!

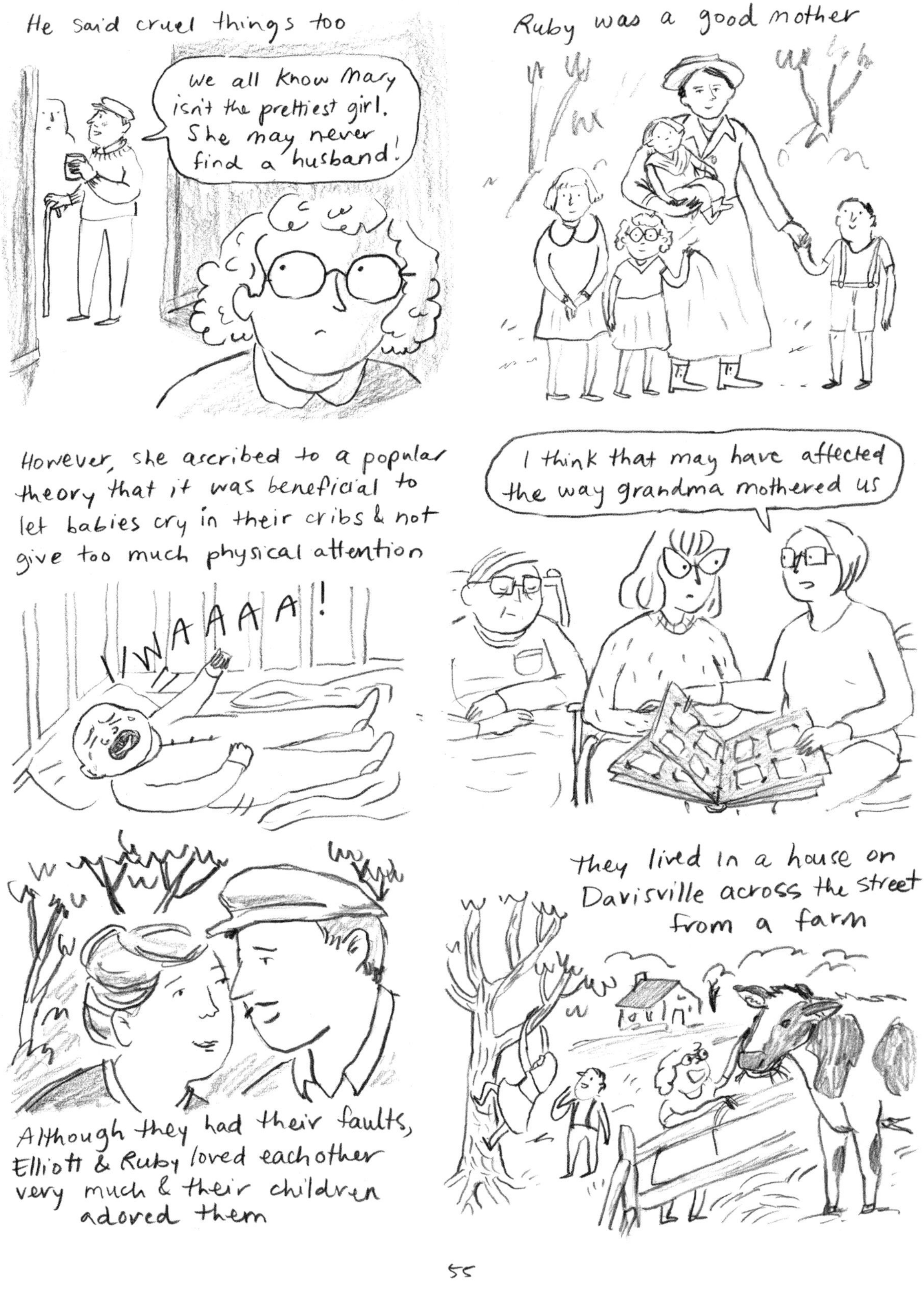
He said cruel things too
We all know Mary isn't the prettiest girl. She may never find a husband!
Ruby was a good mother
However, she ascribed to a popular theory that it was beneficial to let babies cry in their cribs & not give too much physical attention
WAAAAA!
I think that may have affected the way grandma mothered us
Although they had their faults, Elliott & Ruby loved eachother very much & their children adored them
They lived in a house on Davisville across the street from a farm

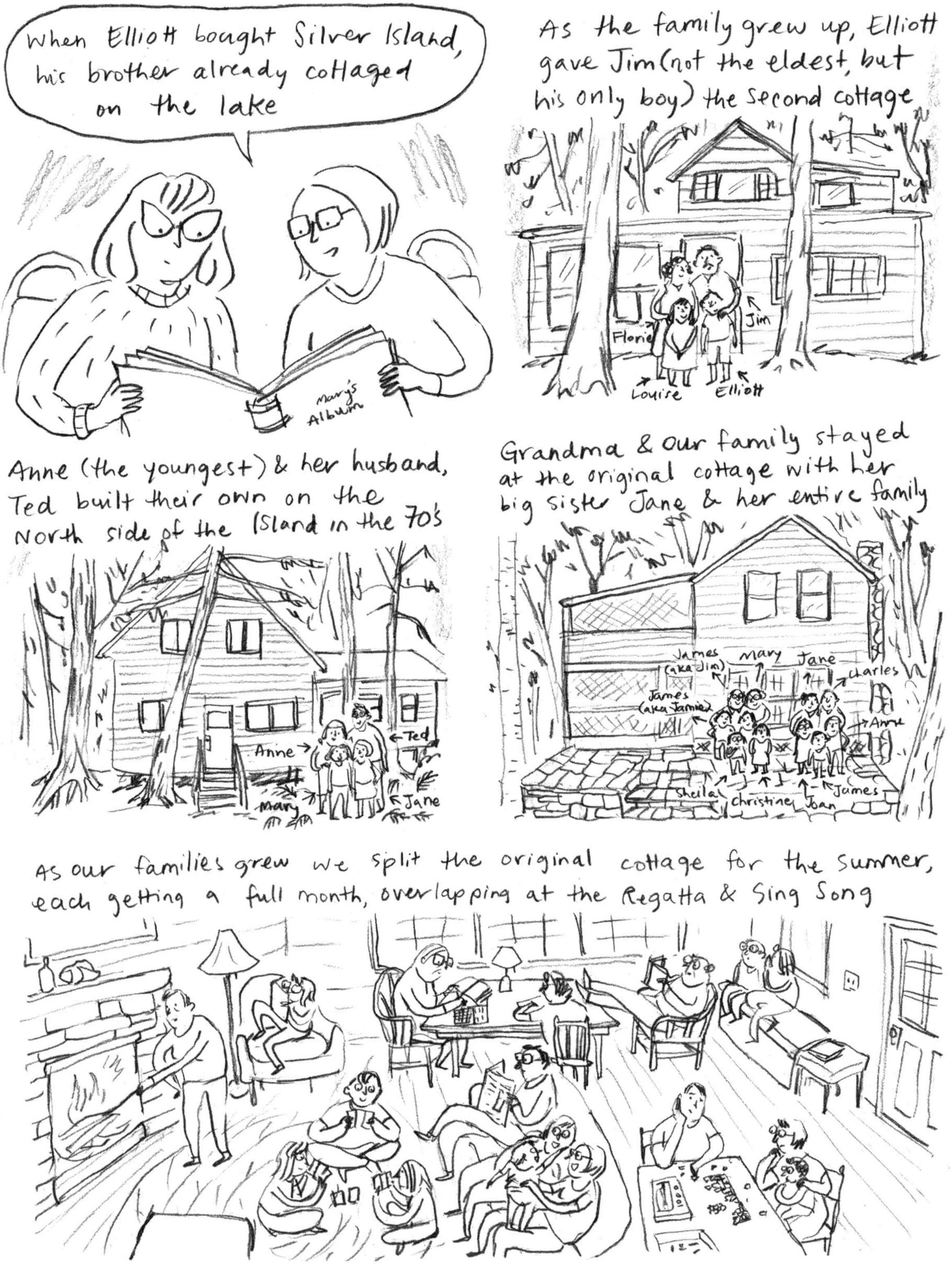

When Elliott bought Silver Island, his brother already cottaged on the lake
Mary's Album
As the family grew up, Elliott gave Jim (not the eldest, but his only boy) the second cottage
Florie
Jim
Louise
Elliott
Anne (the youngest) & her husband, Ted built their own on the North side of the Island in the 70's
Anne
Ted
Mary
Jane
Grandma & our family stayed at the original cottage with her big sister Jane & her entire family
James (aka Jim)
Mary
Jane
Charles
James (aka Jamie)
Anne
Sheila
Christine
Joan
James
As our families grew we split the original cottage for the summer, each getting a full month, overlapping at the Regatta & Sing Song

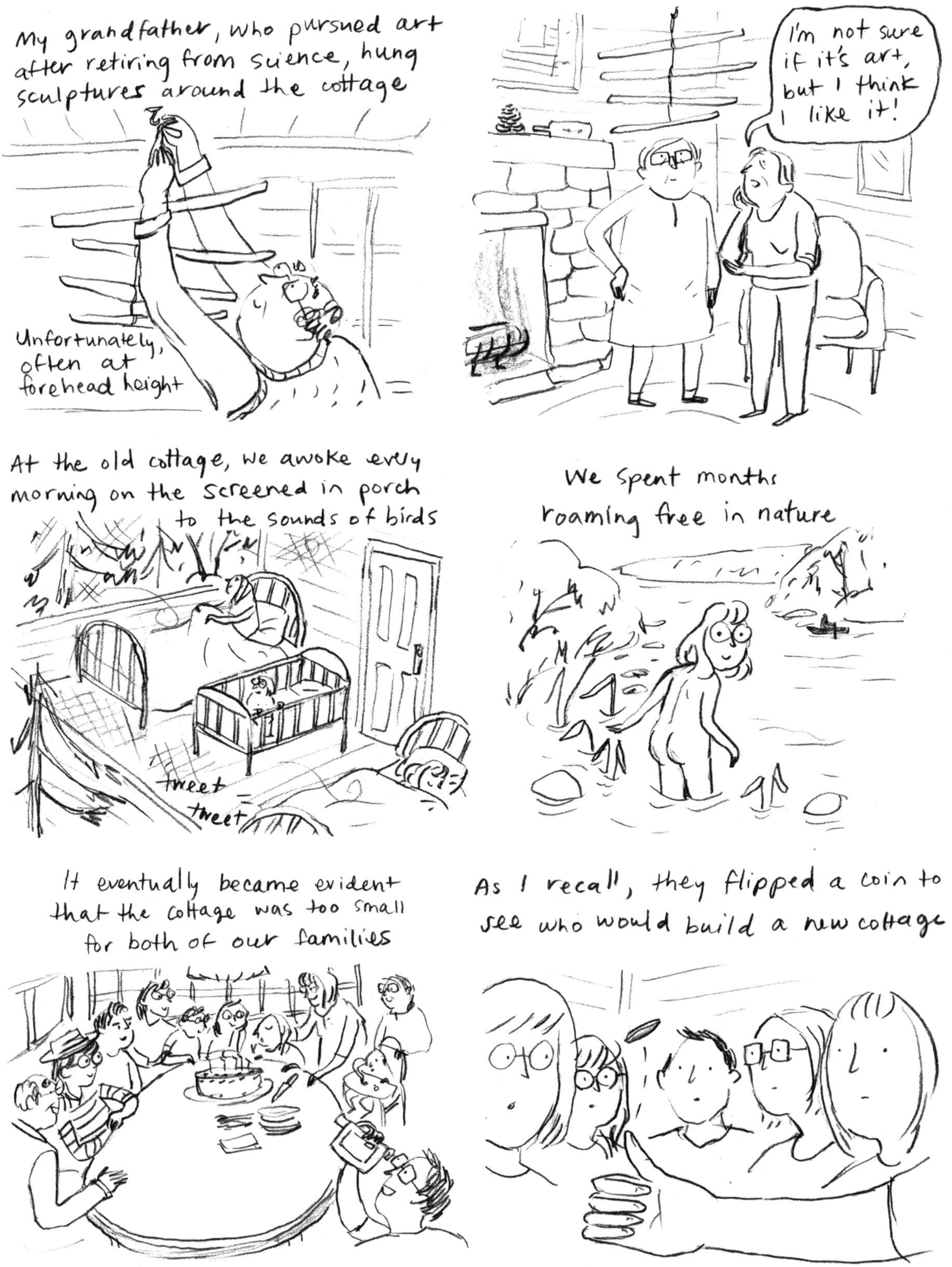
My grandfather, who pursued art after retiring from science, hung sculptures around the cottage
Unfortunately, often at forehead height
I'm not sure if it's art, but I think I like it!
At the old cottage, we awoke every morning on the screened in porch to the sounds of birds
tweet
tweet
We spent months roaming free in nature
It eventually became evident that the cottage was too small for both of our families
As I recall, they flipped a coin to see who would build a new cottage

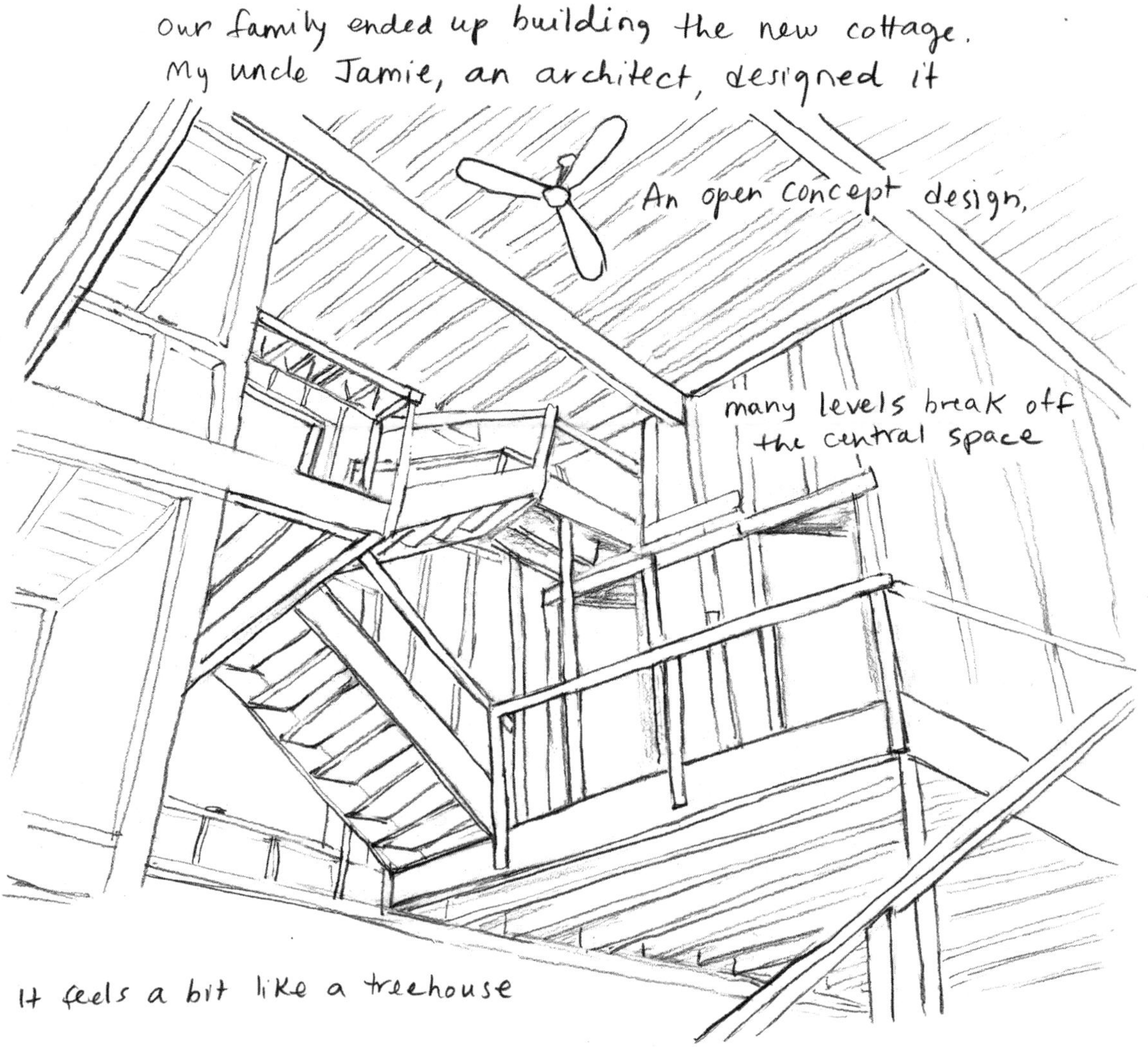
Our family ended up building the new cottage. My uncle Jamie, an architect, designed it
An open concept design,
many levels break off the central space
It feels a bit like a treehouse

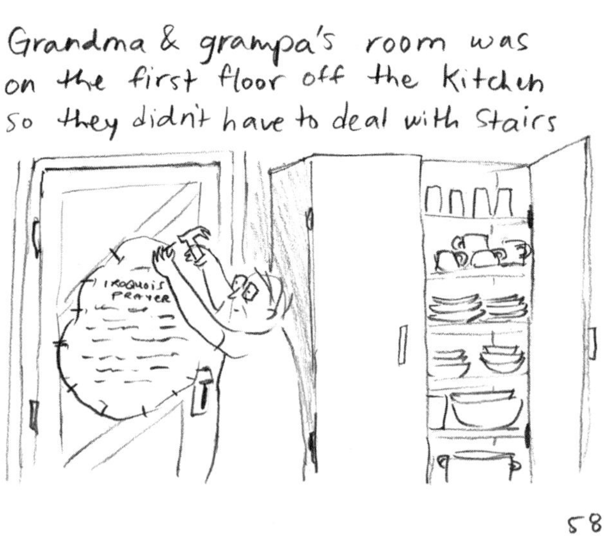
Grandma & grampa's room was on the first floor off the kitchen so they didn't have to deal with stairs
IROQUOIS PRAYER

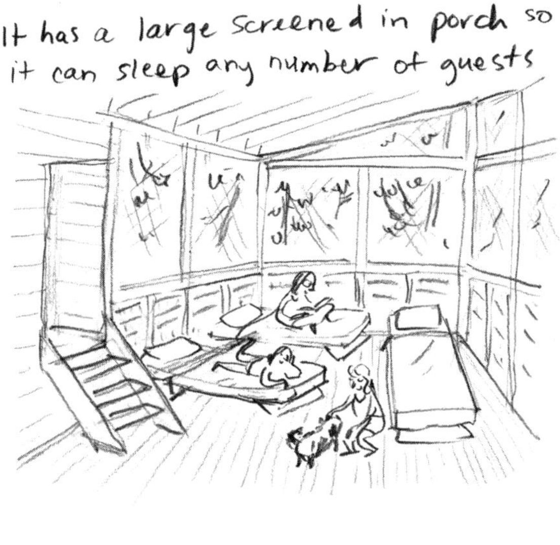
It has a large screened in porch so it can sleep any number of guests

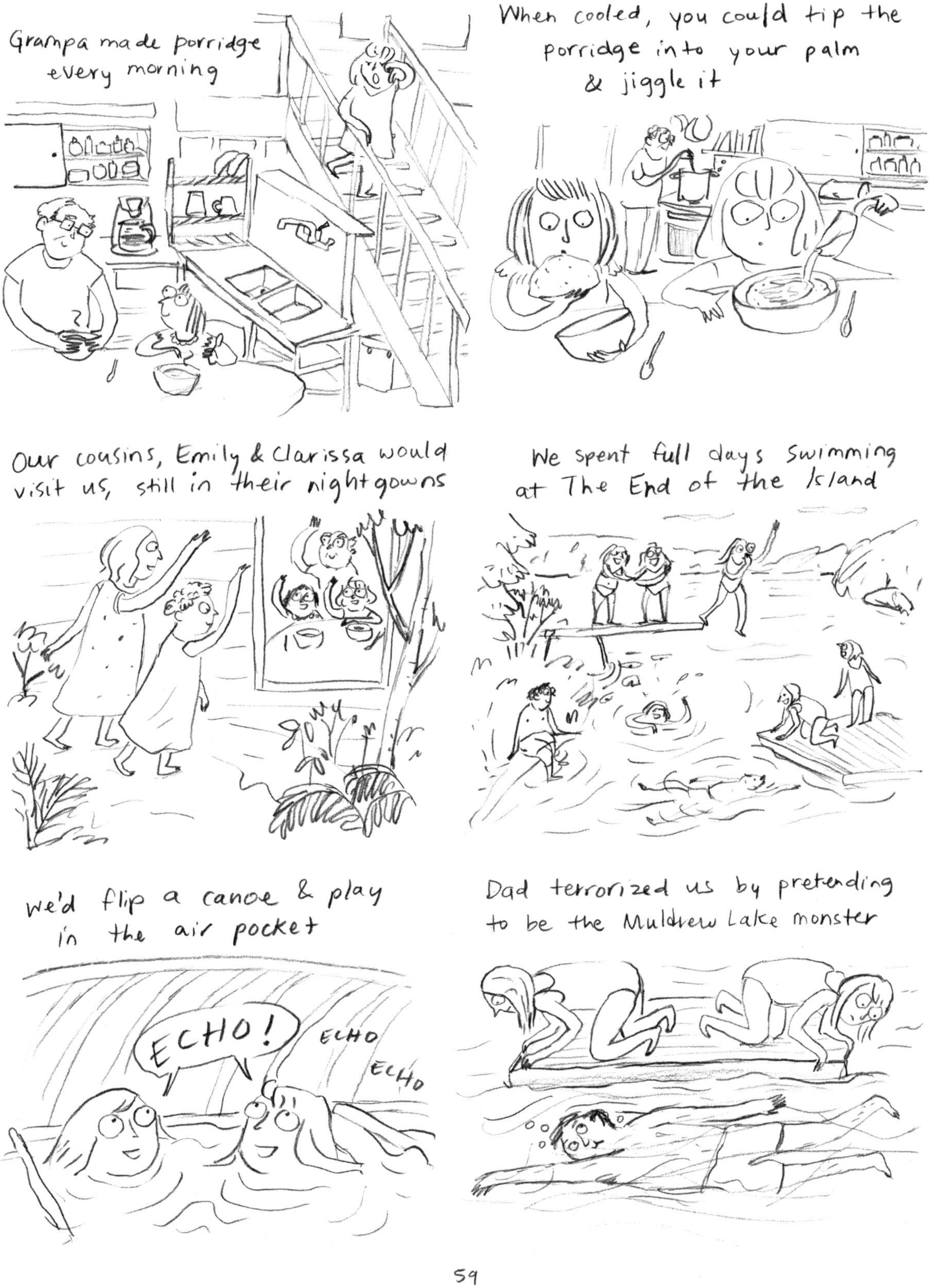
Grampa made porridge every morning
When cooled, you could tip the porridge into your palm & jiggle it
Our cousins, Emily & Clarissa would visit us, still in their nightgowns
We spent full days swimming at The End of the Island
We'd flip a canoe & play in the air pocket
ECHO!
ECHO
ECHO
Dad terrorized us by pretending to be the Muldrew Lake monster

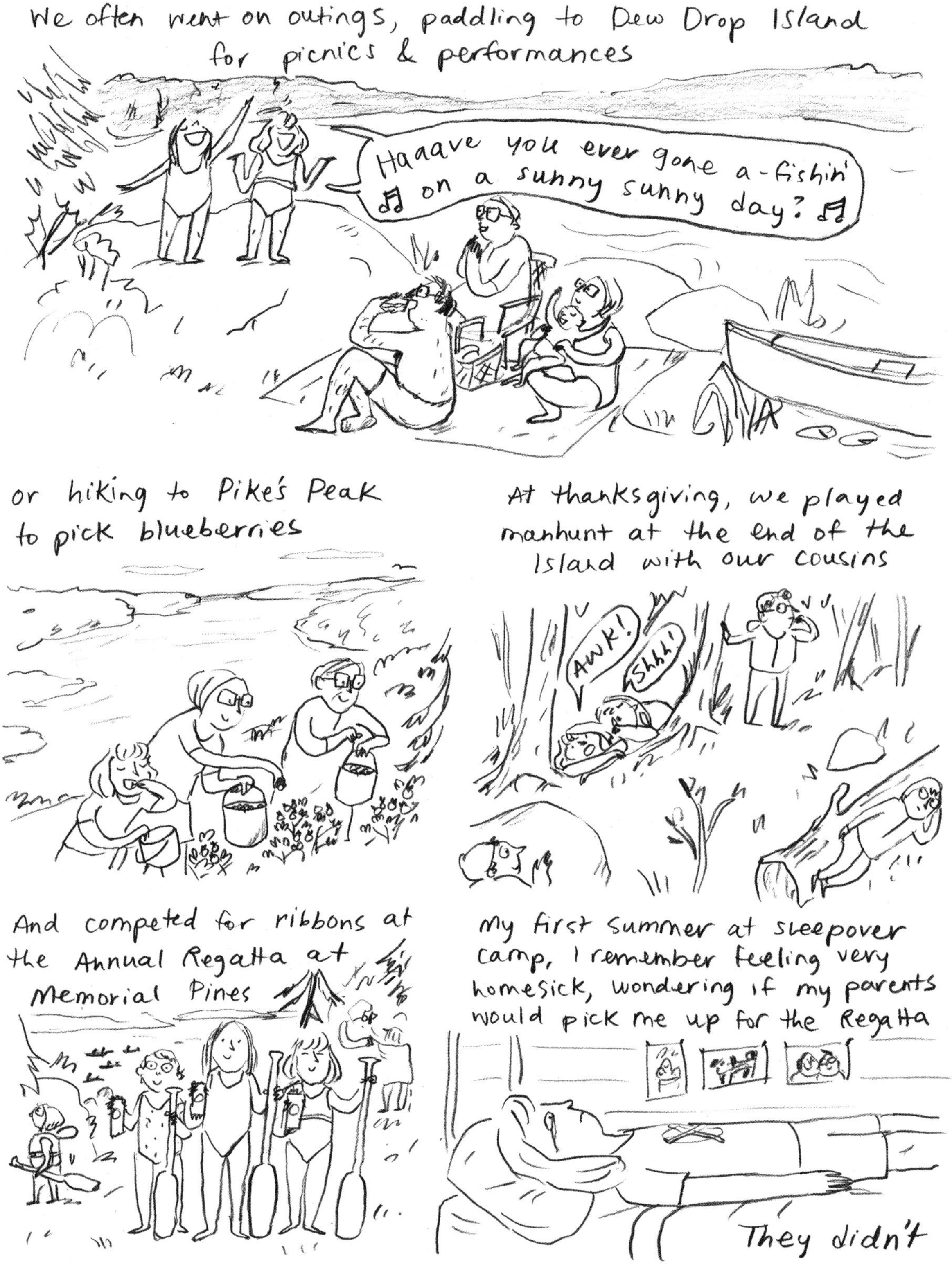
We often went on outings, paddling to Dew Drop Island for picnics & performances
Haaave you ever gone a-fishin' on a sunny sunny day?
or hiking to Pike's Peak to pick blueberries
At thanksgiving, we played manhunt at the end of the Island with our cousins
AWK!
Shhh!
And competed for ribbons at the Annual Regatta at Memorial Pines
My first summer at sleepover camp, I remember feeling very homesick, wondering if my parents would pick me up for the Regatta
They didn't

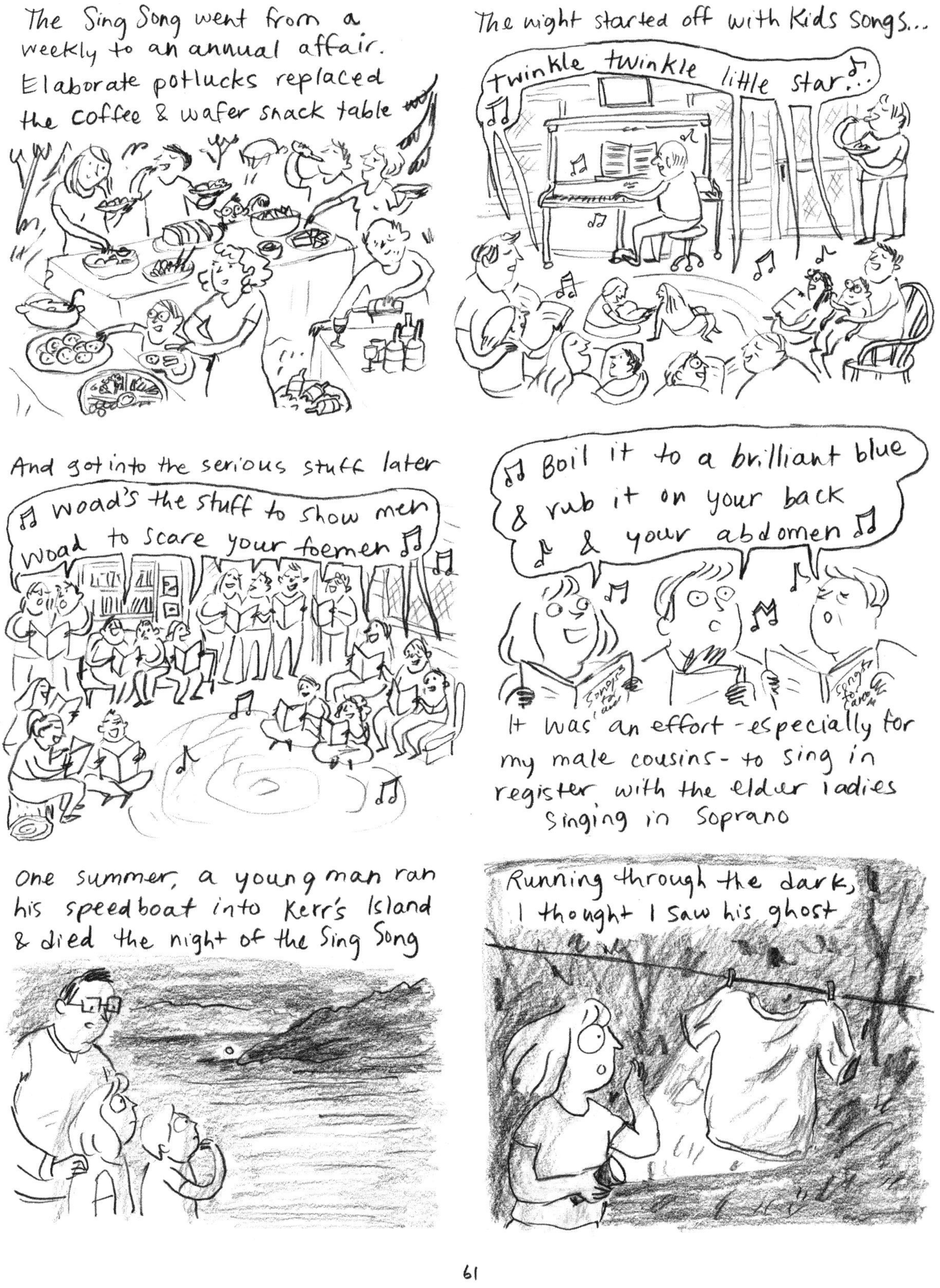
The Sing Song went from a weekly to an annual affair. Elaborate potlucks replaced the coffee & wafer snack table
The night started off with kids songs...
twinkle twinkle little star...
And got into the serious stuff later
woad's the stuff to show men woad to scare your foemen
Boil it to a brilliant blue & rub it on your back & your abdomen
It was an effort - especially for my male cousins - to sing in register with the elder ladies singing in soprano
One summer, a young man ran his speedboat into Kerr's Island & died the night of the Sing Song
Running through the dark, I thought I saw his ghost

I don't remember grandma swimming much (although I heard she did a great swan dive).
I do remember her always in boats

She had her own canoe, "Tippy", which no one else dared paddle

At the cottage, she could be found doing crossword puzzles at the kitchen table,

Rigging things up with bungee chords & duct tape,

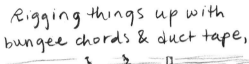

(she labeled everything in perfect cursive)

Or managing the woodpile

I would often get letters about it at camp

Dear Rebecca,   July 15 1998
    How is camp? The weather is fine here on Muldrew. The woodpile is really shaping up! A few pines came down last winter, so I've asked Elliott to chainsaw them for me will have plenty of wood in the fall.
    Sheila & the cats are fine. We went

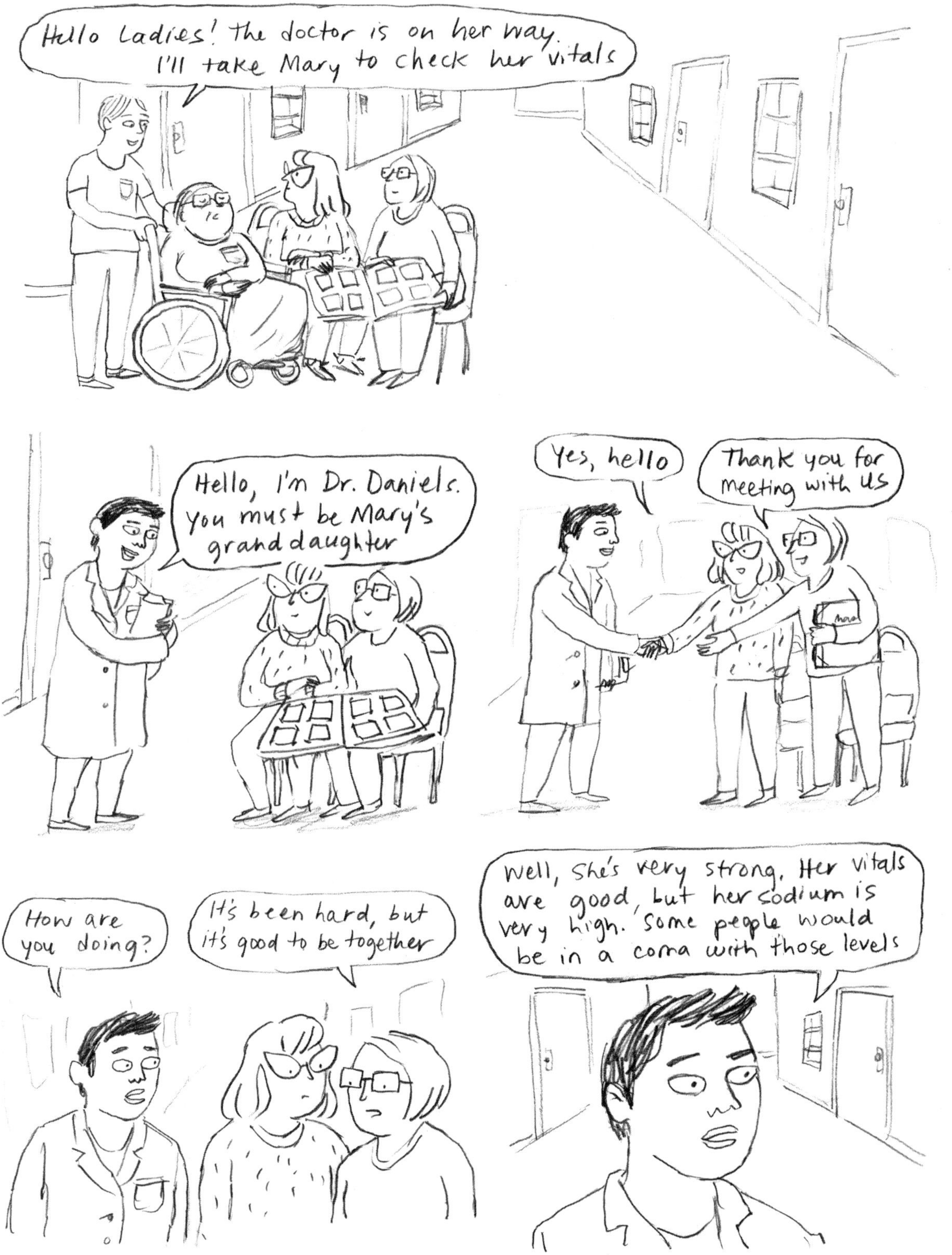

Hello Ladies! the doctor is on her way. I'll take Mary to check her vitals
Hello, I'm Dr. Daniels. You must be Mary's granddaughter
Yes, hello
Thank you for meeting with us
How are you doing?
It's been hard, but it's good to be together
Well, she's very strong. Her vitals are good, but her sodium is very high. Some people would be in a coma with those levels

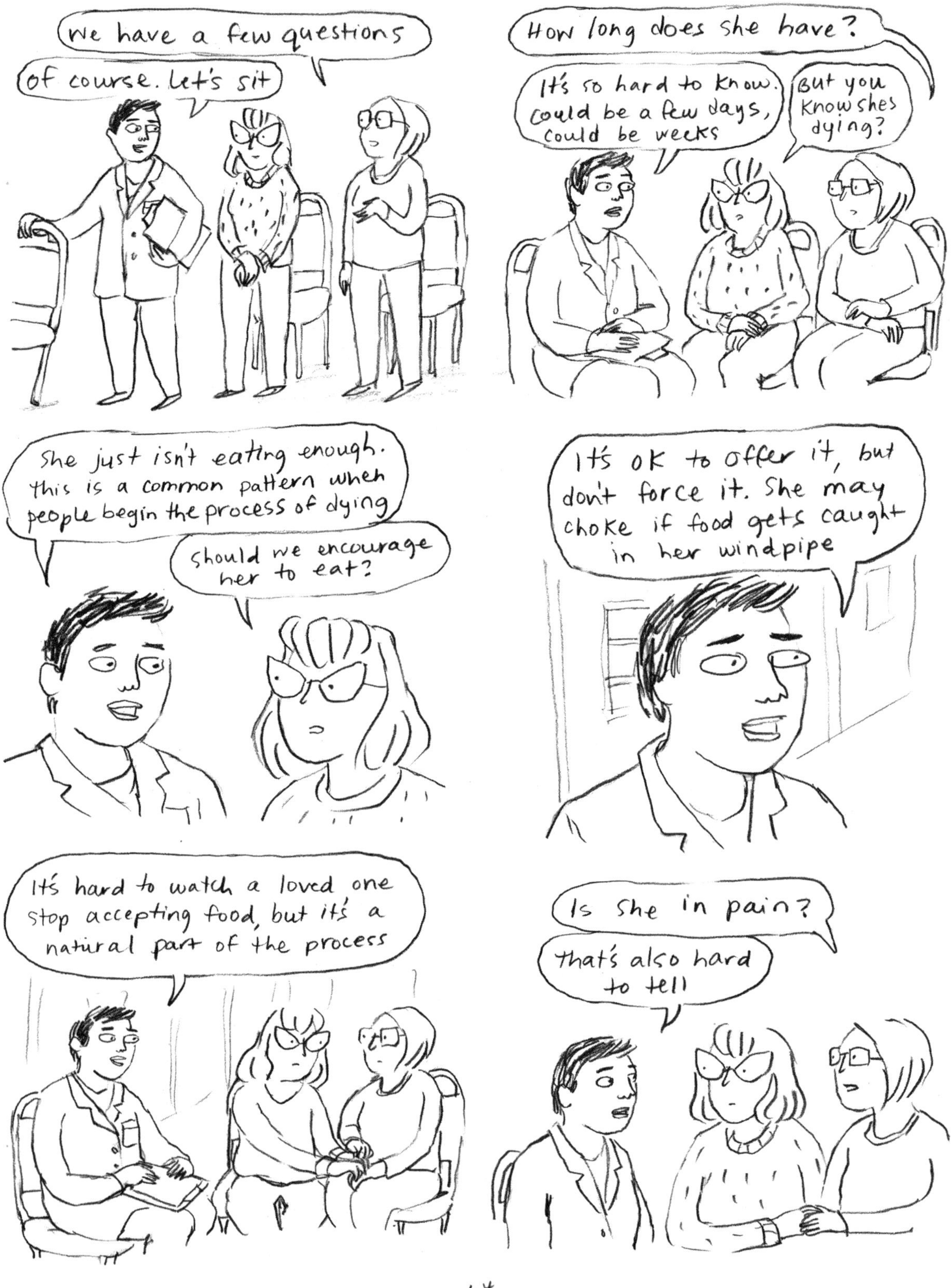
We have a few questions
of course. Let's sit
How long does she have?
It's so hard to know. could be a few days, could be weeks
But you know shes dying?
She just isn't eating enough. this is a common pattern when people begin the process of dying
should we encourage her to eat?
It's OK to offer it, but don't force it. She may choke if food gets caught in her windpipe
It's hard to watch a loved one stop accepting food, but it's a natural part of the process
Is she in pain?
that's also hard to tell

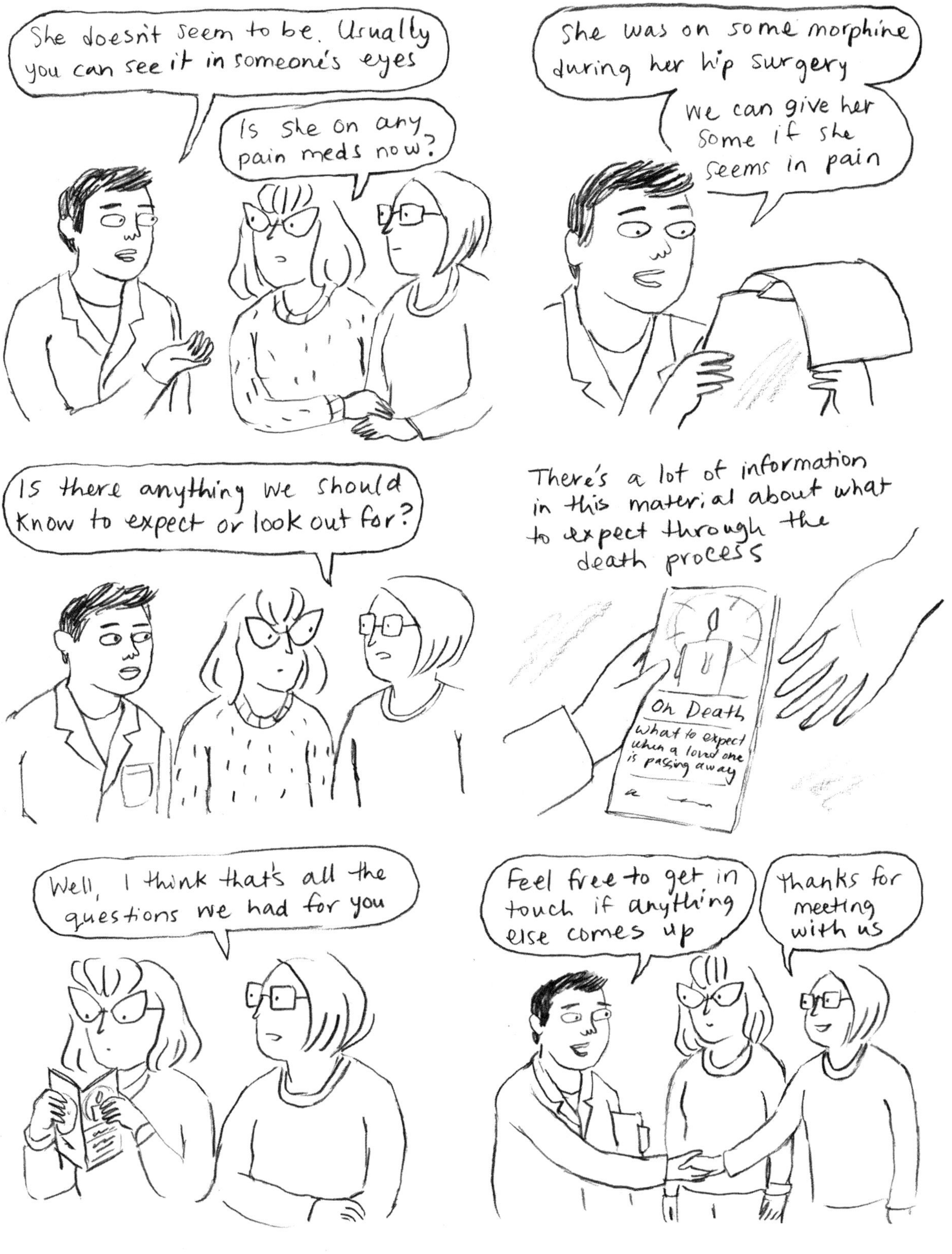
She doesn't seem to be. Usually you can see it in someone's eyes
Is she on any pain meds now?
She was on some morphine during her hip surgery
We can give her some if she seems in pain
Is there anything we should know to expect or look out for?
There's a lot of information in this material about what to expect through the death process
On Death
what to expect when a loved one is passing away
Well, I think that's all the questions we had for you
Feel free to get in touch if anything else comes up
Thanks for meeting with us

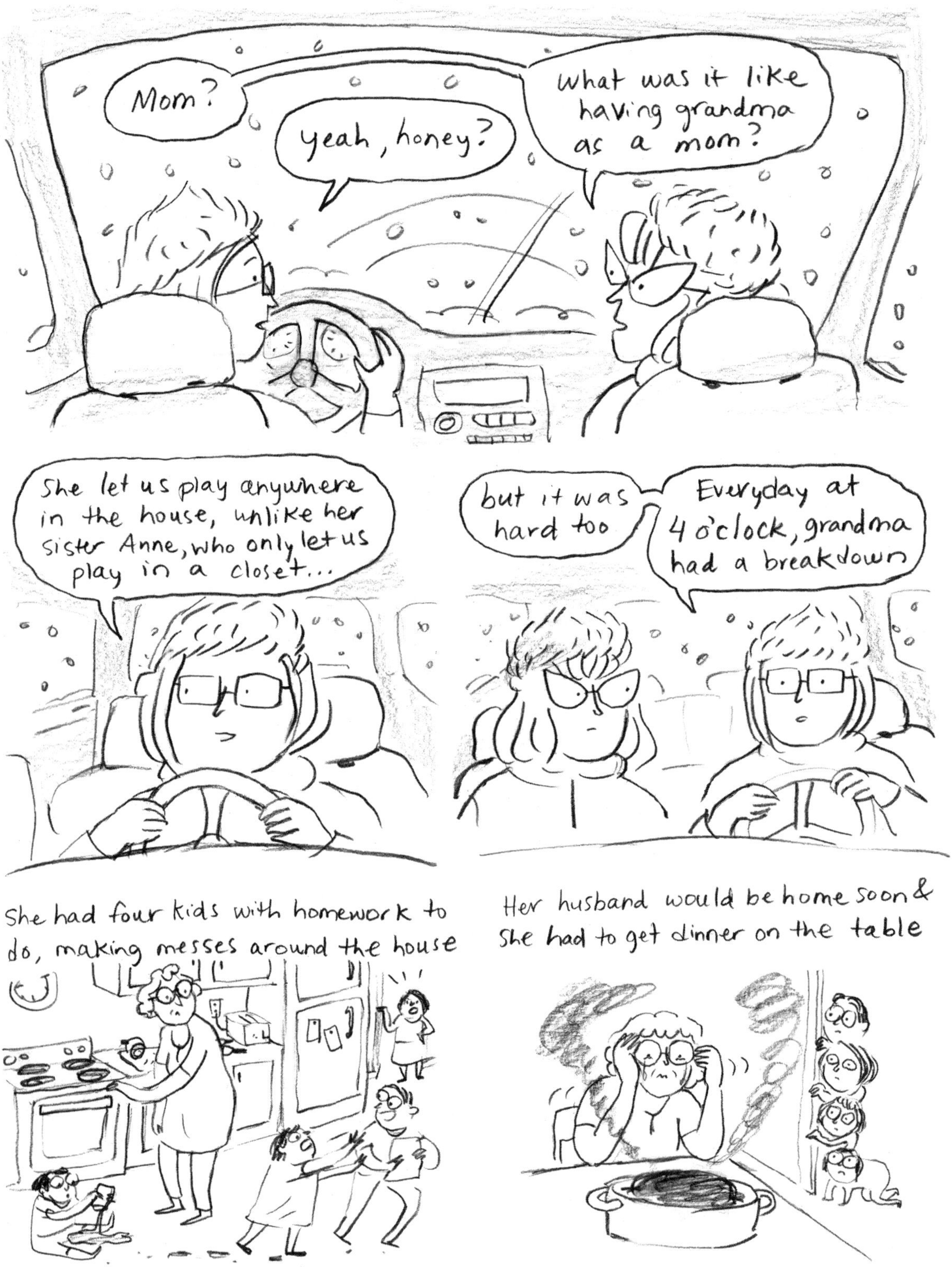

Mom?
yeah, honey?
What was it like having grandma as a mom?
She let us play anywhere in the house, unlike her sister Anne, who only let us play in a closet...
but it was hard too
Everyday at 4 o'clock, grandma had a breakdown
She had four kids with homework to do, making messes around the house
Her husband would be home soon & she had to get dinner on the table

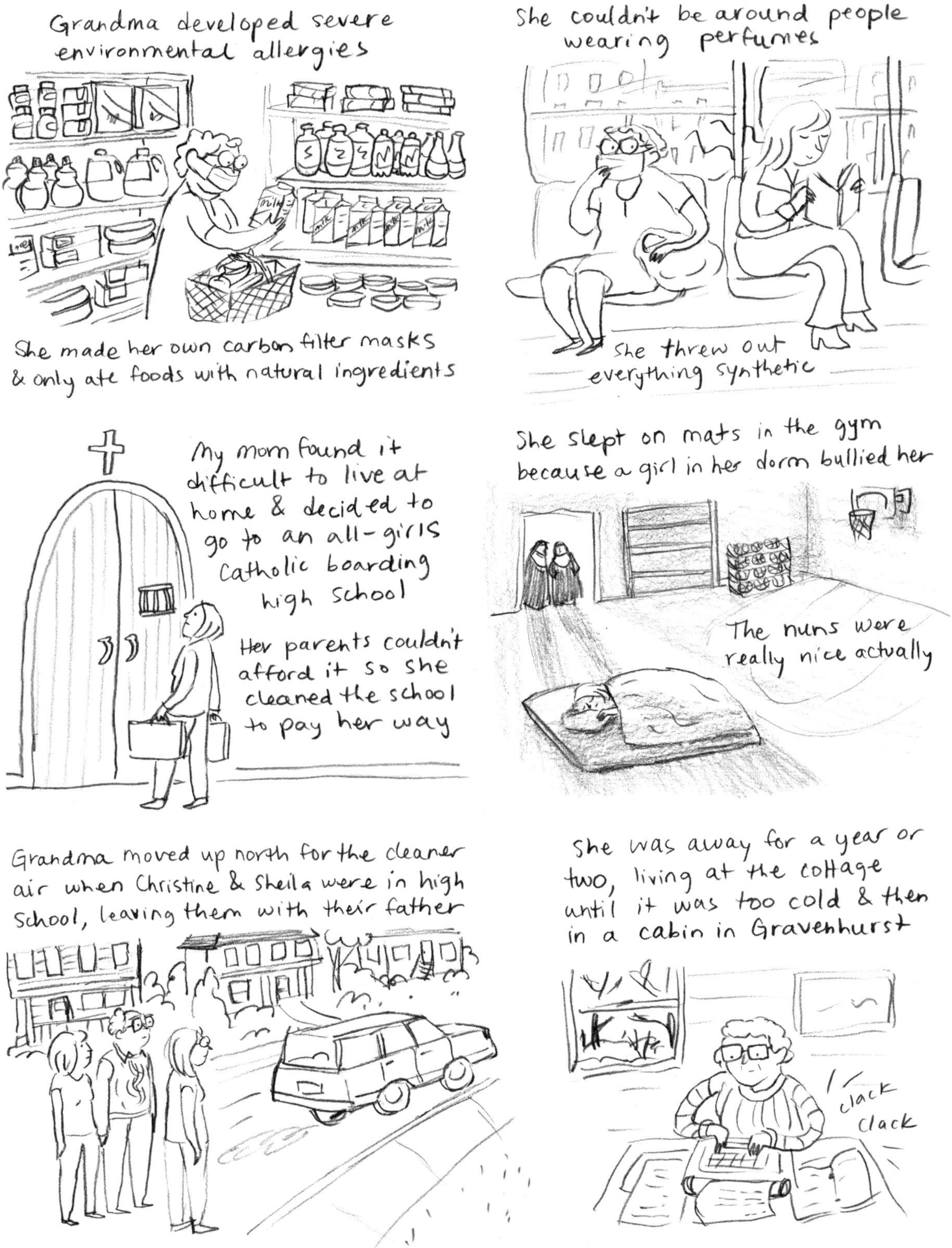
Grandma developed severe environmental allergies
She made her own carbon filter masks & only ate foods with natural ingredients
Milk
She couldn't be around people wearing perfumes
She threw out everything synthetic
My mom found it difficult to live at home & decided to go to an all-girls Catholic boarding high school
Her parents couldn't afford it so she cleaned the school to pay her way
She slept on mats in the gym because a girl in her dorm bullied her
The nuns were really nice actually
Grandma moved up north for the cleaner air when Christine & Sheila were in high school, leaving them with their father
She was away for a year or two, living at the cottage until it was too cold & then in a cabin in Gravenhurst
clack clack

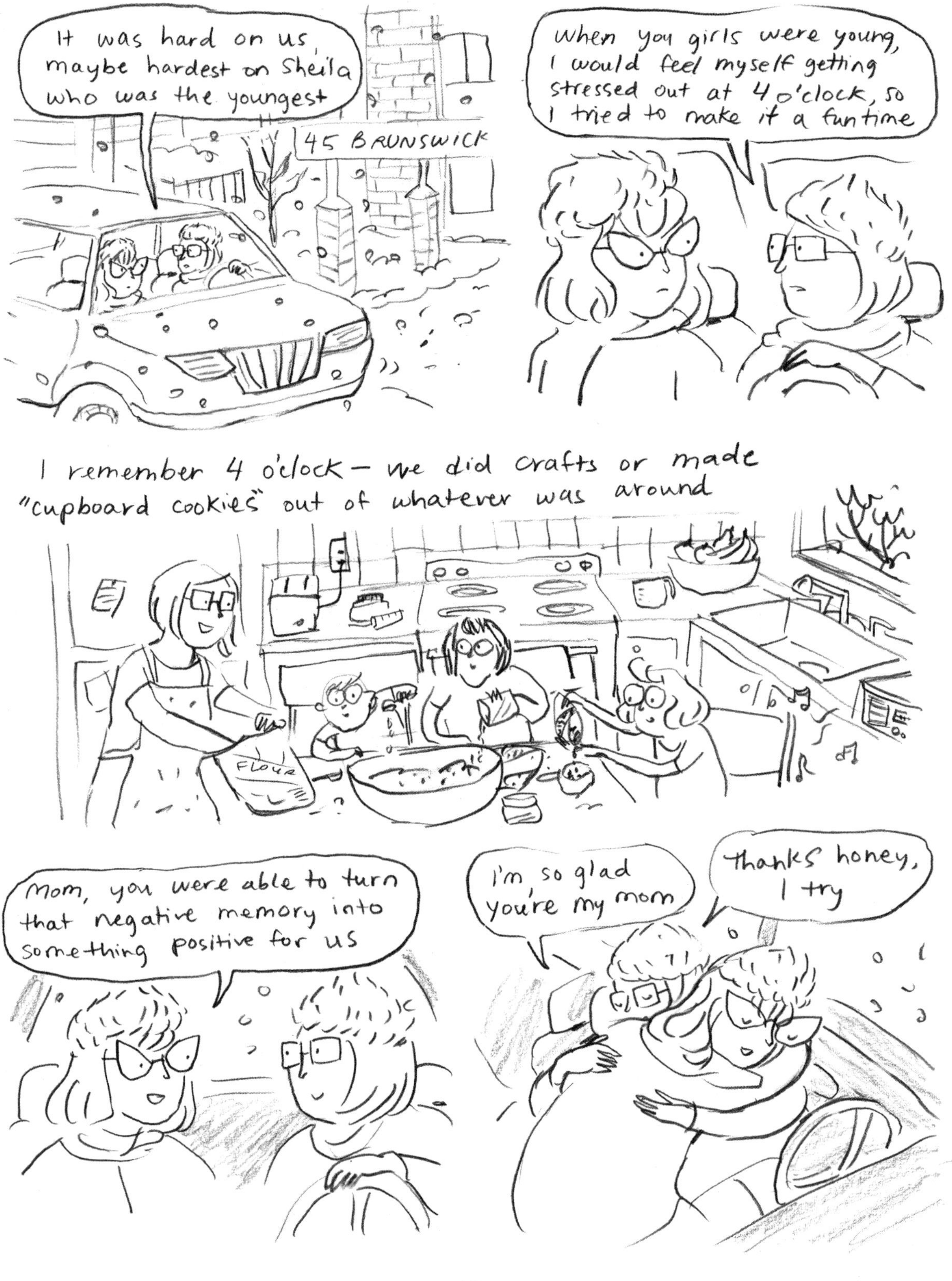

It was hard on us, maybe hardest on Sheila who was the youngest
45 BRUNSWICK
When you girls were young, I would feel myself getting stressed out at 4 o'clock, so I tried to make it a funtime
I remember 4 o'clock — we did crafts or made "cupboard cookies" out of whatever was around
FLOUR
Mom, you were able to turn that negative memory into something positive for us
I'm so glad you're my mom
thanks honey, I try

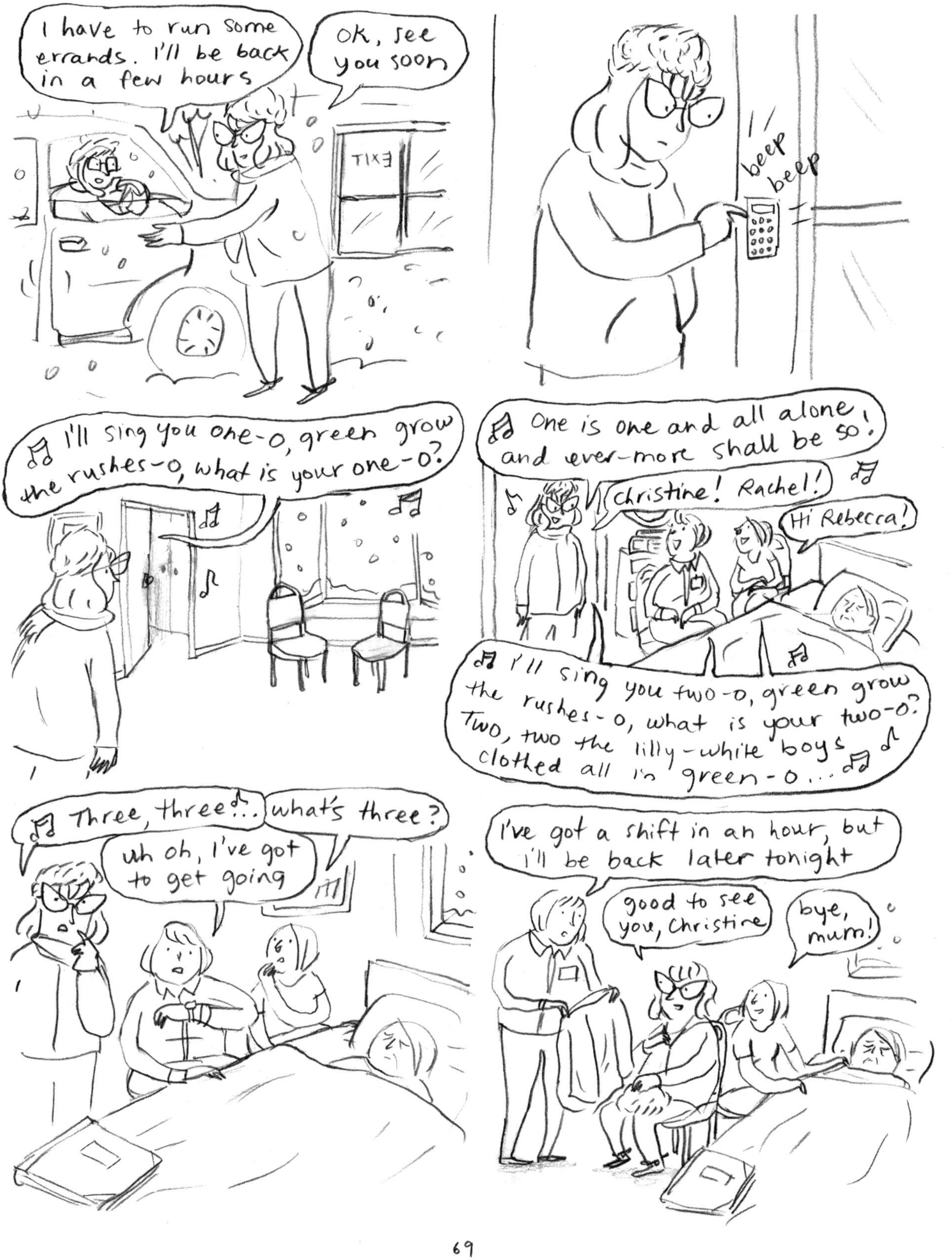
I have to run some errands. I'll be back in a few hours
Ok, see you soon
EXIT
beep beep
I'll sing you one-o, green grow the rushes-o, what is your one-o?
One is one and all alone, and ever-more shall be so!
Christine! Rachel!
Hi Rebecca!
I'll sing you two-o, green grow the rushes-o, what is your two-o? Two, two the lilly-white boys clothed all in green-o...
Three, three...
what's three?
uh oh, I've got to get going
I've got a shift in an hour, but I'll be back later tonight
good to see you, Christine
bye, mum!

"Have you guys been looking at photo albums?"

Grandma made an album for each of her children

"This one's Sheila's"

Our aunt Sheila was gentle, loving & kind

She named her cats Tessa & Diana after mother Teresa & Princess Diana

She volunteered for Riders with Disabilities

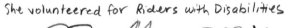

She loved
Lord of
the Dance

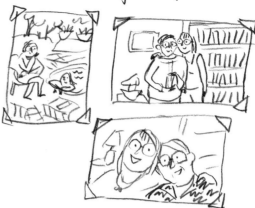

She & grandma were
basically inseparable

Sheila swam around the island every day at the cottage
Grandma paddled beside her

It's time for
Mary's bath

You can step out
for a few minutes

Thank you, we'll
be in the hall

hello, Mary!

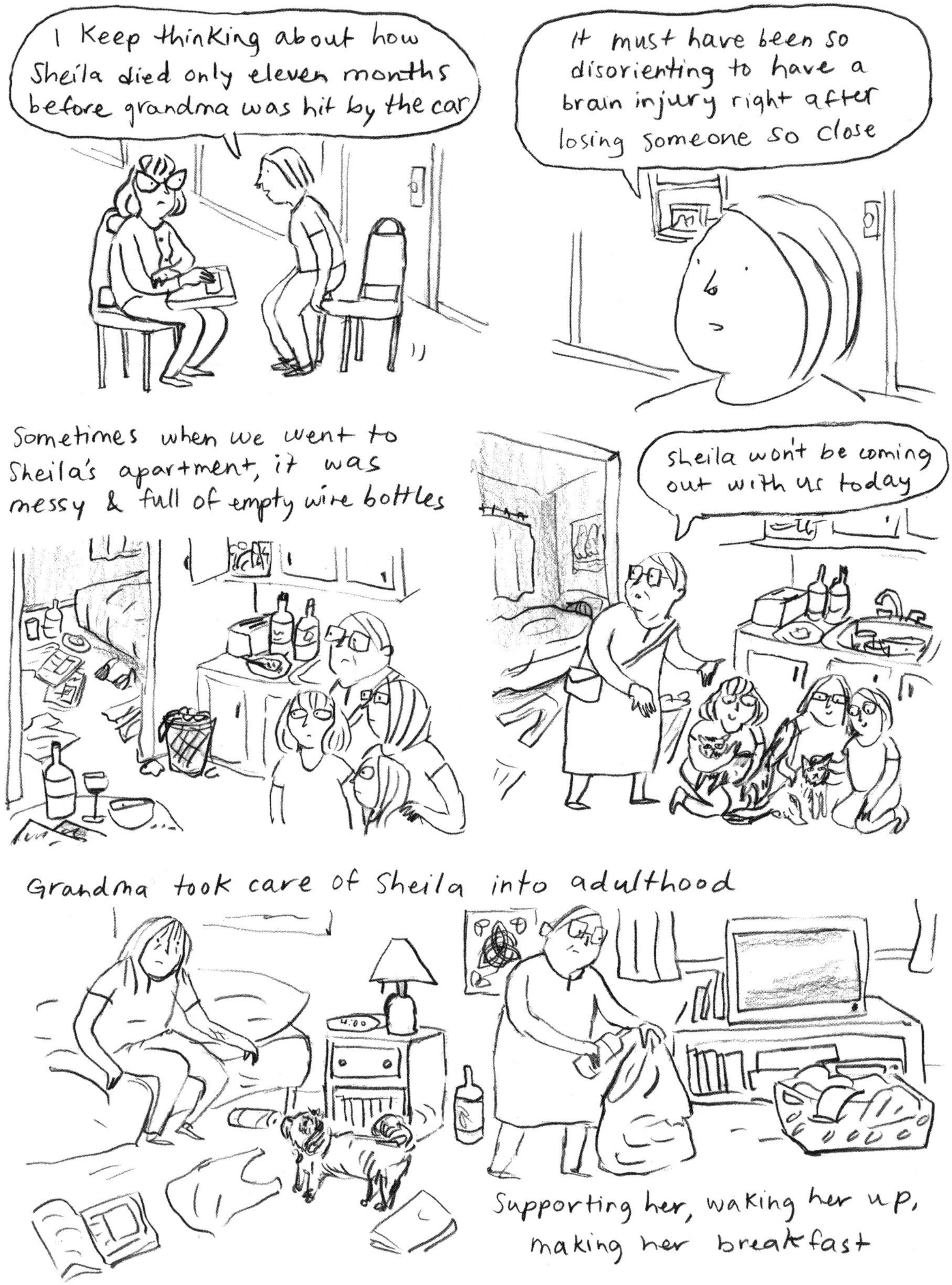
I Keep thinking about how Sheila died only eleven months before grandma was hit by the car
It must have been so disorienting to have a brain injury right after losing someone so close
Sometimes when we went to Sheila's apartment, it was messy & full of empty wire bottles
Sheila won't be coming out with us today
Grandma took care of Sheila into adulthood
Supporting her, waking her up, making her breakfast

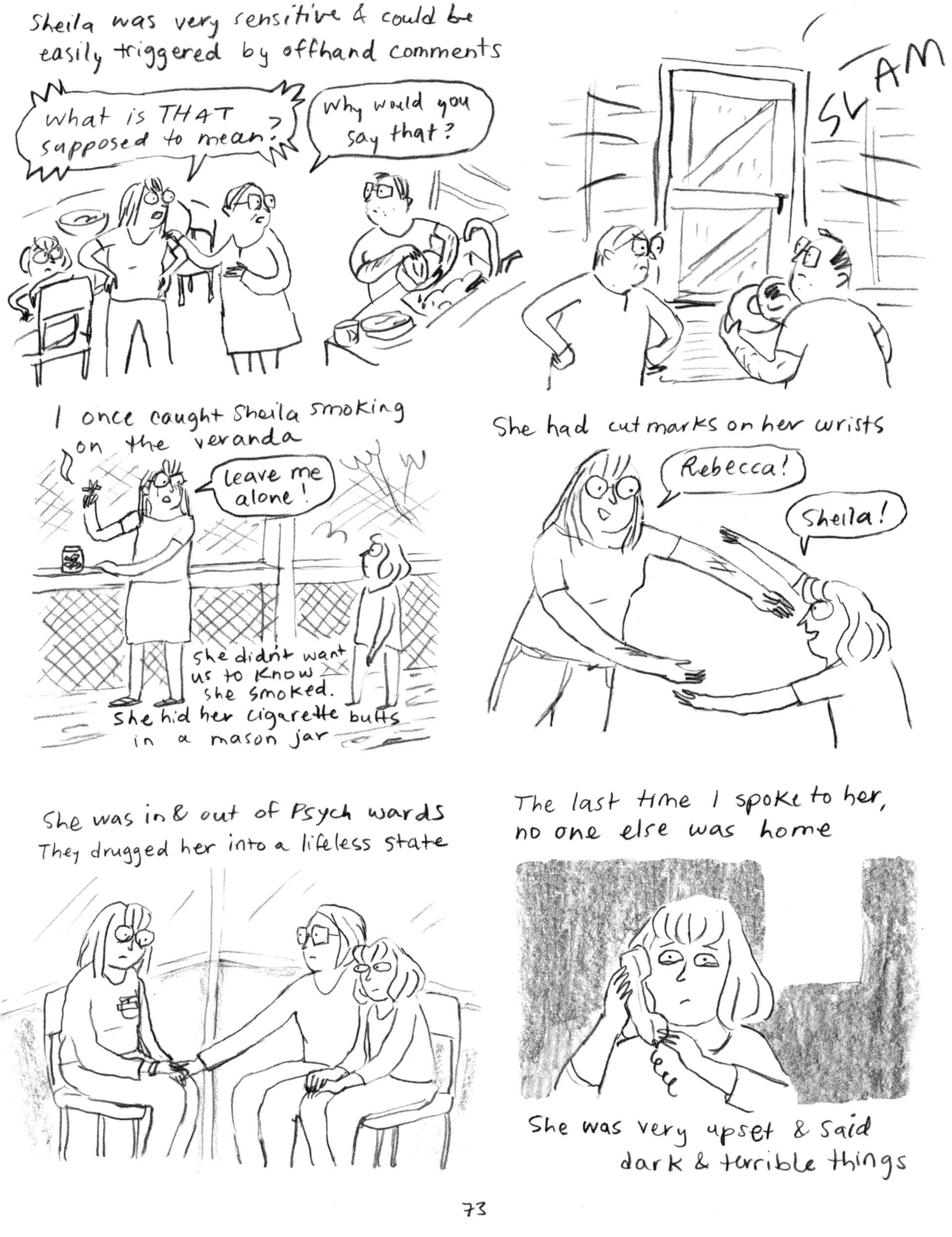
Sheila was very sensitive & could be easily triggered by offhand comments
what is THAT supposed to mean?
Why would you say that?
SLAM
I once caught Sheila smoking on the veranda
leave me alone!
she didn't want us to know she smoked. She hid her cigarette butts in a mason jar
She had cut marks on her wrists
Rebecca!
Sheila!
She was in & out of Psych wards They drugged her into a lifeless state
The last time I spoke to her, no one else was home
She was very upset & said dark & terrible things

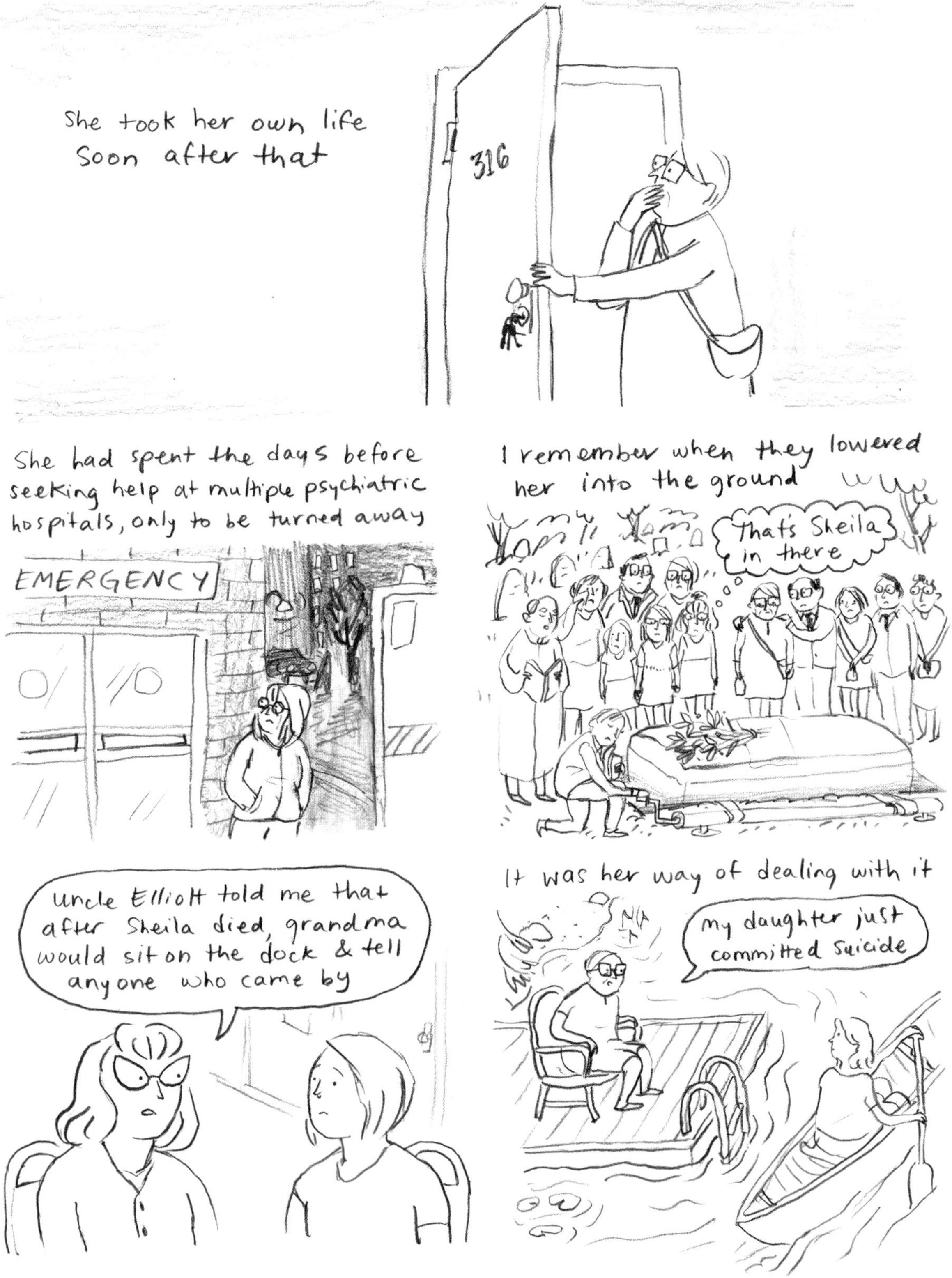
She took her own life soon after that
316
She had spent the days before seeking help at multiple psychiatric hospitals, only to be turned away
EMERGENCY
I remember when they lowered her into the ground
That's Sheila in there
Uncle Elliott told me that after Sheila died, grandma would sit on the dock & tell anyone who came by
It was her way of dealing with it
My daughter just committed suicide

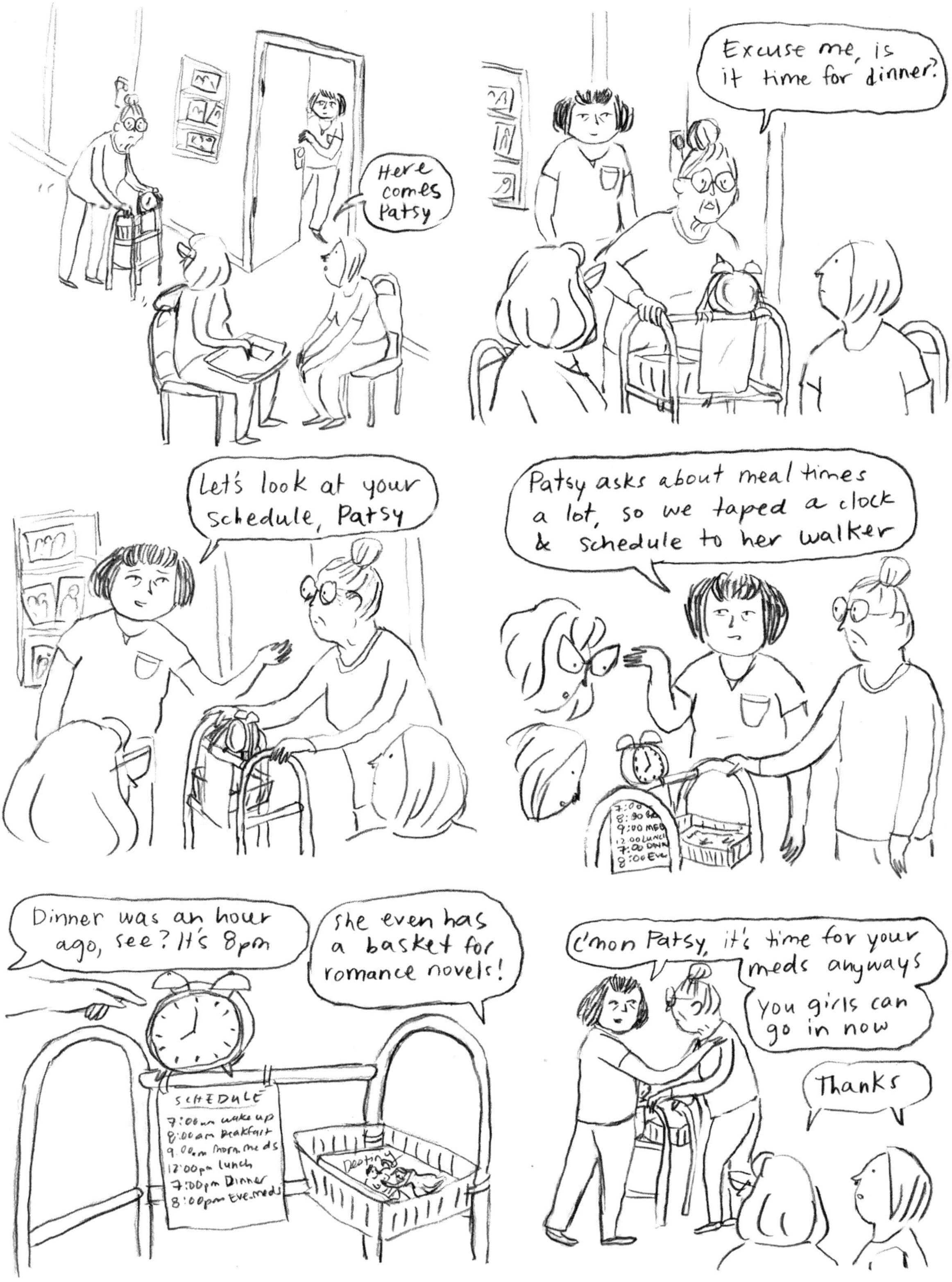
Here comes Patsy
Excuse me, is it time for dinner?
Let's look at your schedule, Patsy
Patsy asks about meal times a lot, so we taped a clock & schedule to her walker
Dinner was an hour ago, see? It's 8pm
She even has a basket for romance novels!
SCHEDULE
7:00am wake up
8:00am Breakfast
9:00am Morn. meds
12:00pm Lunch
7:00pm Dinner
8:00pm Eve. meds
C'mon Patsy, it's time for your meds anyways
You girls can go in now
Thanks

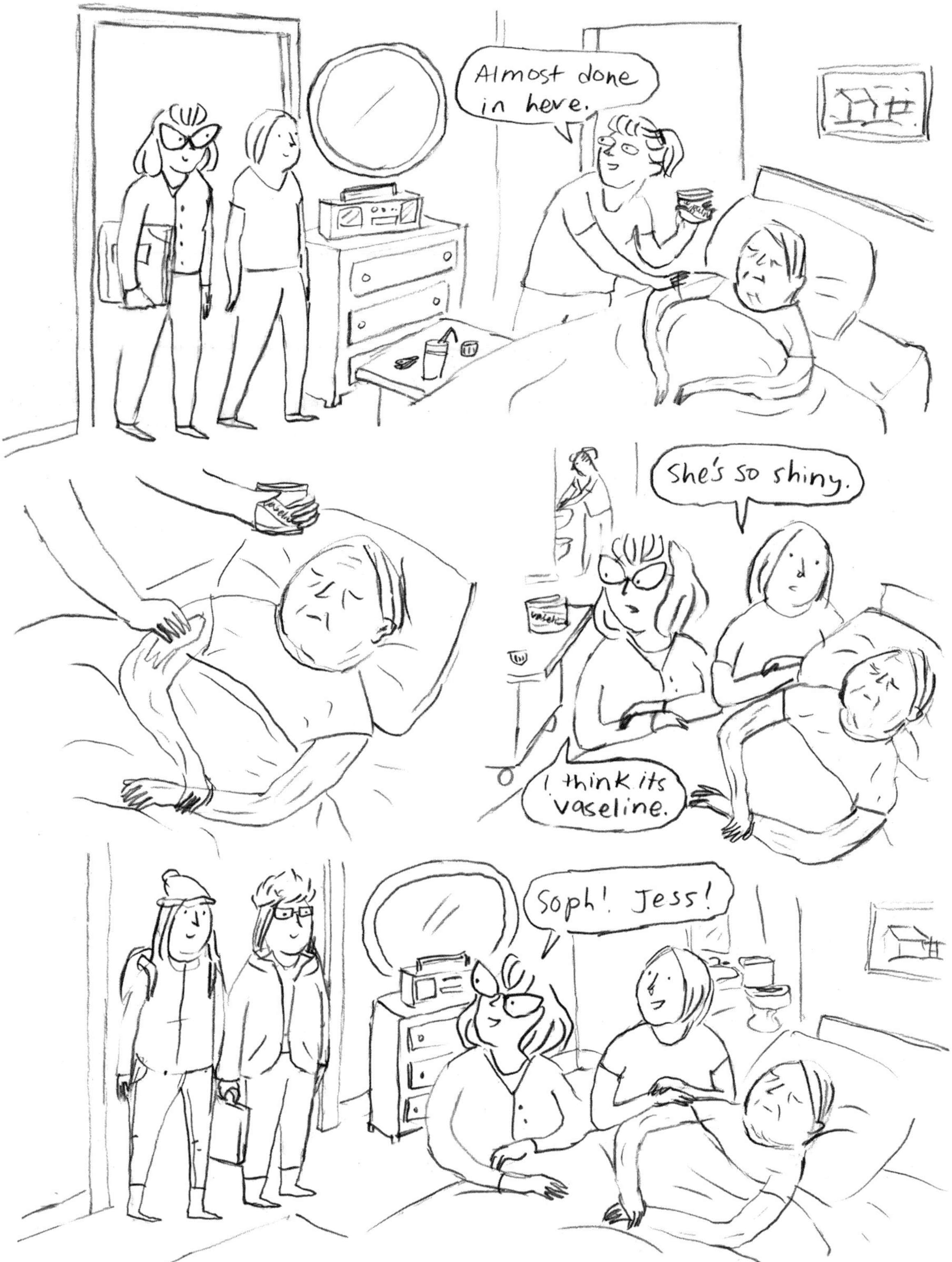
Almost done in here.
She's so shiny.
I think its vaseline.
Soph! Jess!

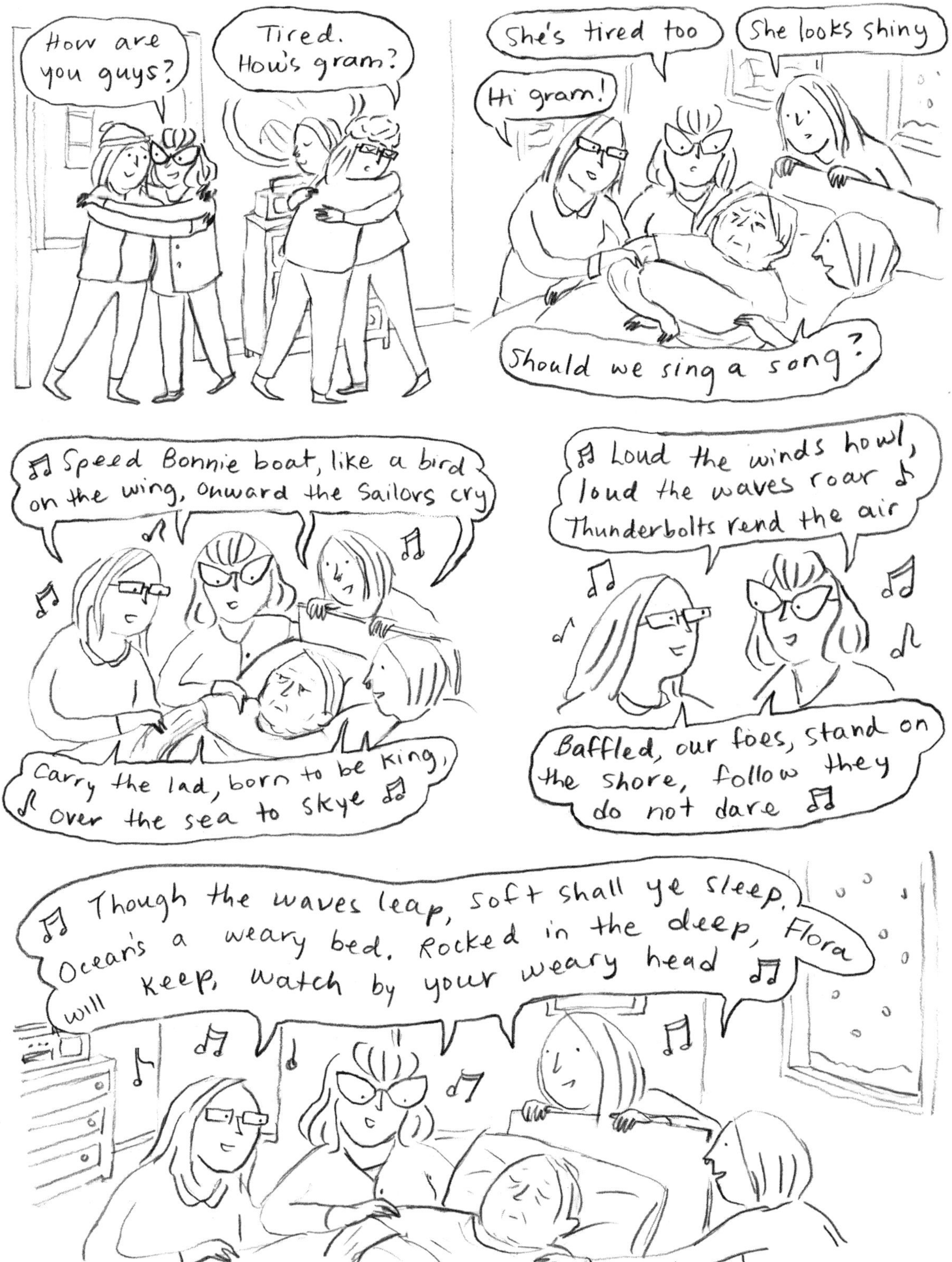
How are you guys?
Tired. How's gram?
She's tired too
She looks shiny
Hi gram!
Should we sing a song?
Speed Bonnie boat, like a bird on the wing, onward the Sailors cry
Carry the lad, born to be king, over the sea to skye
Loud the winds howl, loud the waves roar
Thunderbolts rend the air
Baffled, our foes, stand on the shore, follow they do not dare
Though the waves leap, soft shall ye sleep, Ocean's a weary bed. Rocked in the deep, Flora will keep, watch by your weary head

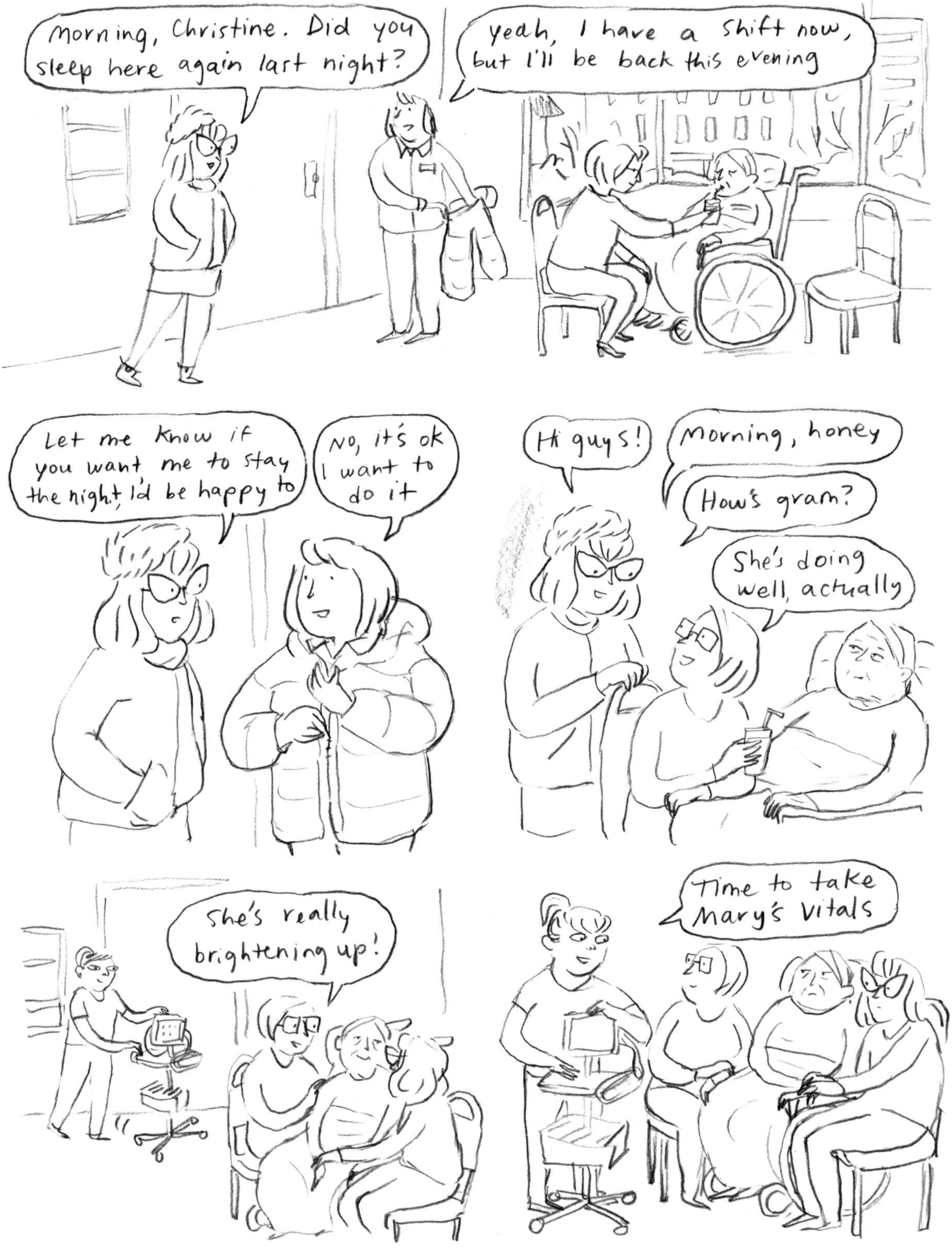
Morning, Christine. Did you sleep here again last night?
yeah, I have a shift now, but I'll be back this evening
Let me know if you want me to stay the night, I'd be happy to
No, it's ok I want to do it
Hi guys!
Morning, honey
How's gram?
She's doing well, actually
She's really brightening up!
Time to take Mary's vitals

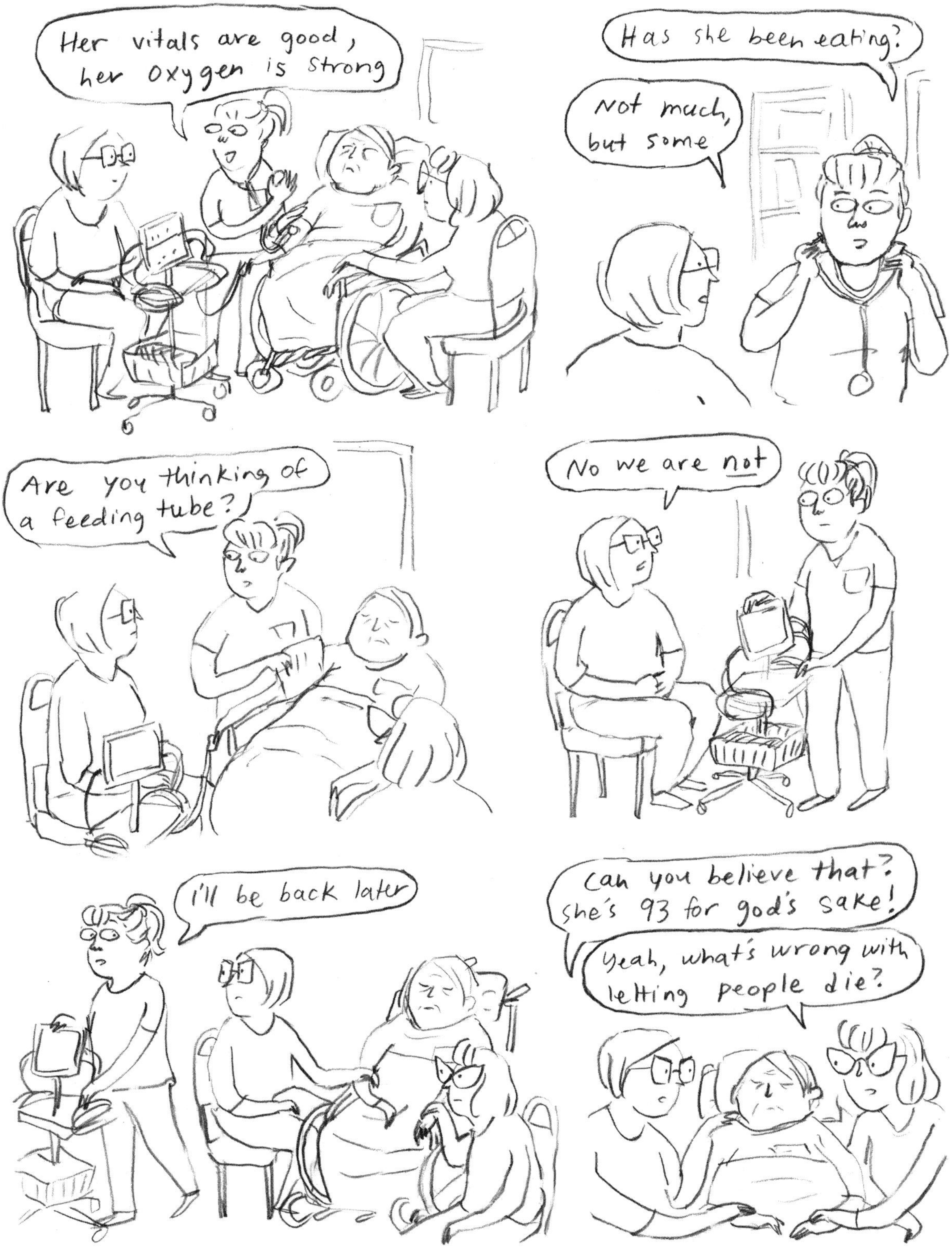
Her vitals are good, her oxygen is strong
Has she been eating?
Not much, but some
Are you thinking of a feeding tube?
No we are not
I'll be back later
Can you believe that? She's 93 for god's sake!
Yeah, what's wrong with letting people die?

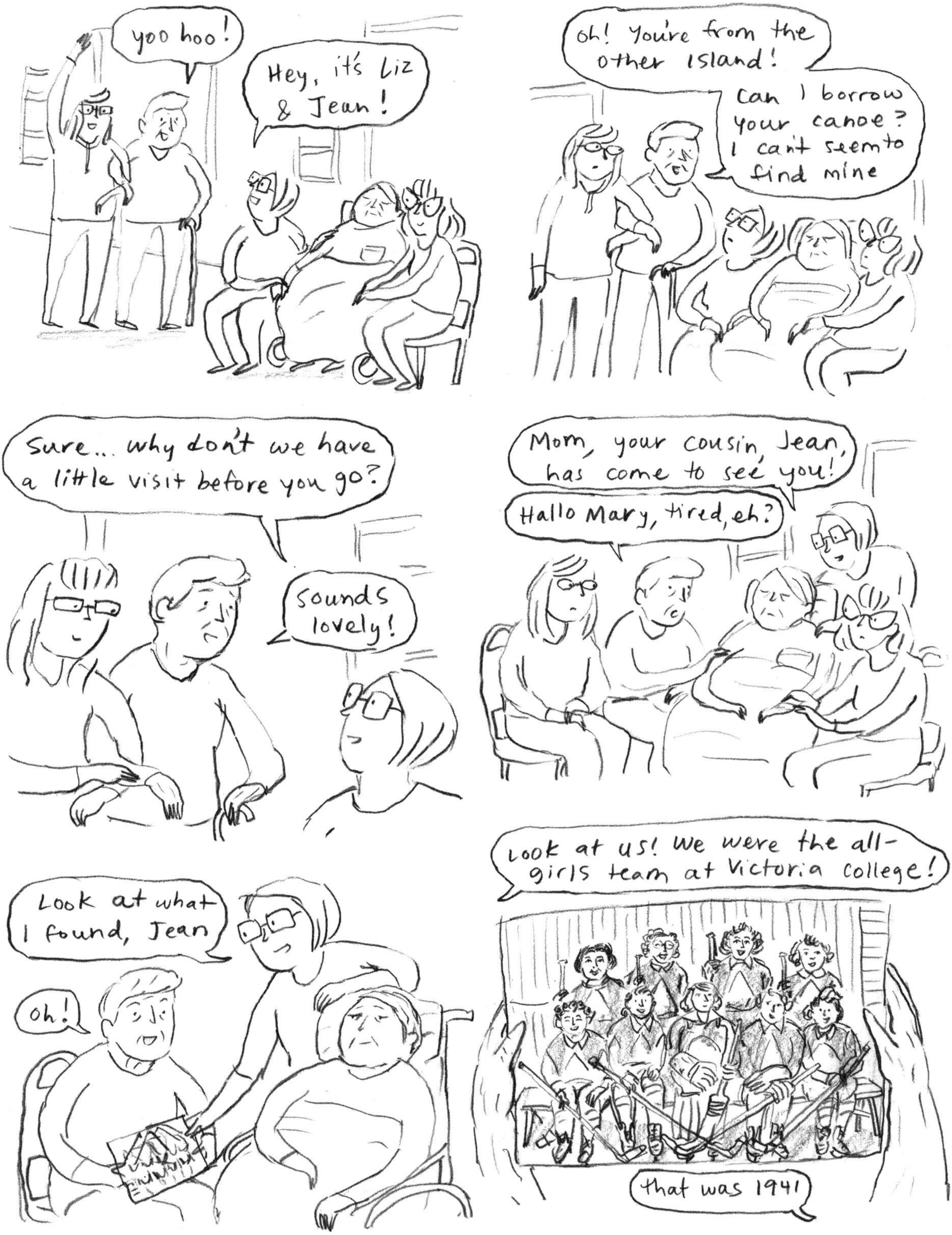
yoo hoo!
Hey, it's Liz & Jean!
oh! You're from the other Island!
Can I borrow your canoe? I can't seem to find mine
Sure... why don't we have a little visit before you go?
sounds lovely!
Mom, your cousin, Jean, has come to see you!
Hallo Mary, tired, eh?
Look at what I found, Jean
oh!
Look at us! We were the all-girls team at Victoria College!
that was 1941

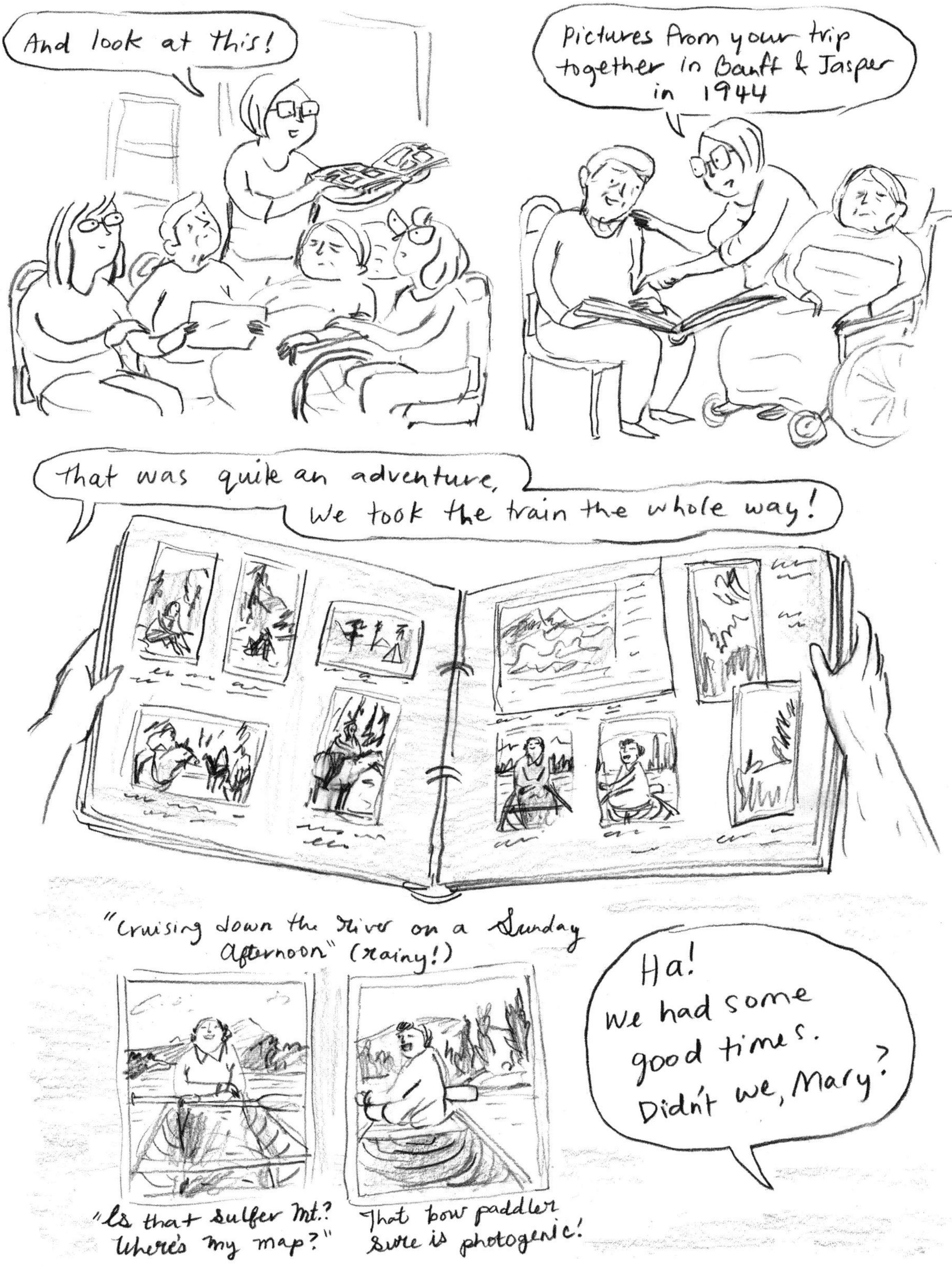
And look at this!
Pictures from your trip together in Banff & Jasper in 1944
That was quite an adventure,
We took the train the whole way!
"Cruising down the river on a Sunday afternoon" (rainy!)
Ha! We had some good times. Didn't we, Mary?
"Is that Sulfer Mt.? Where's my map?"
That bow paddler sure is photogenic!

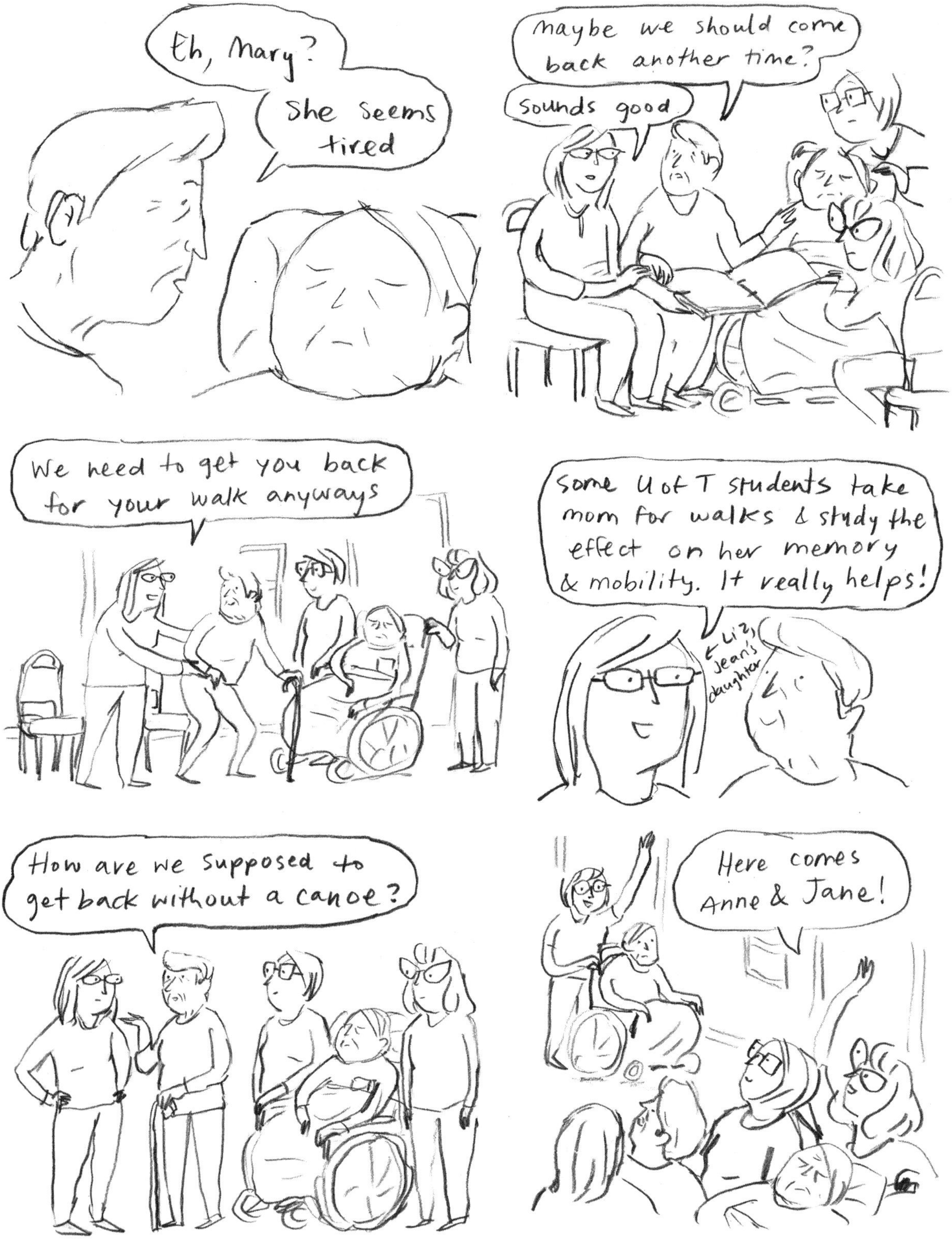
Eh, Mary?
She seems tired
maybe we should come back another time?
Sounds good
We need to get you back for your walk anyways
Some U of T students take mom for walks & study the effect on her memory & mobility. It really helps!
← Liz, Jean's daughter
How are we supposed to get back without a canoe?
Here comes Anne & Jane!

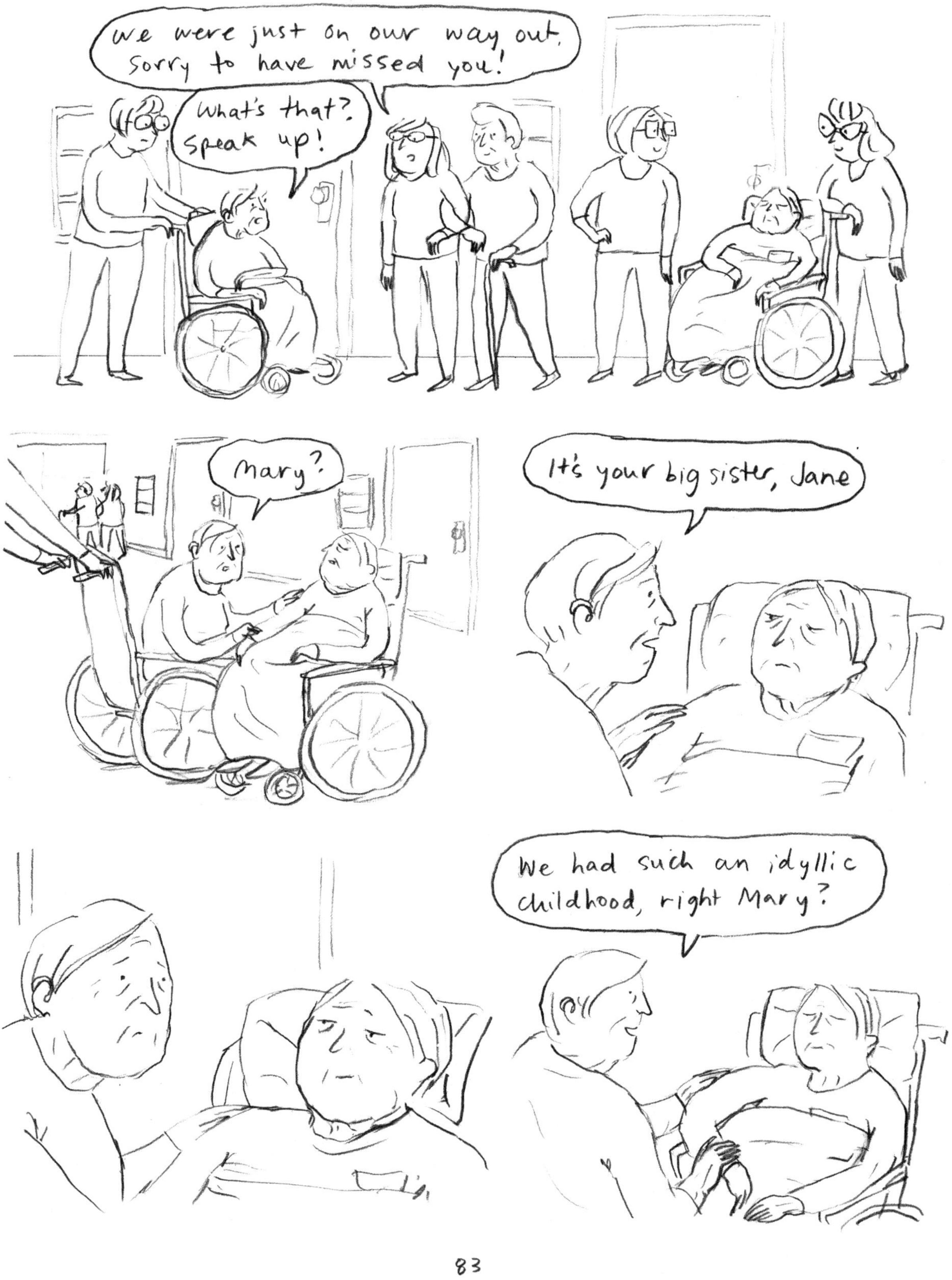
we were just on our way out, sorry to have missed you!
What's that? Speak up!
Mary?
It's your big sister, Jane
We had such an idyllic childhood, right Mary?

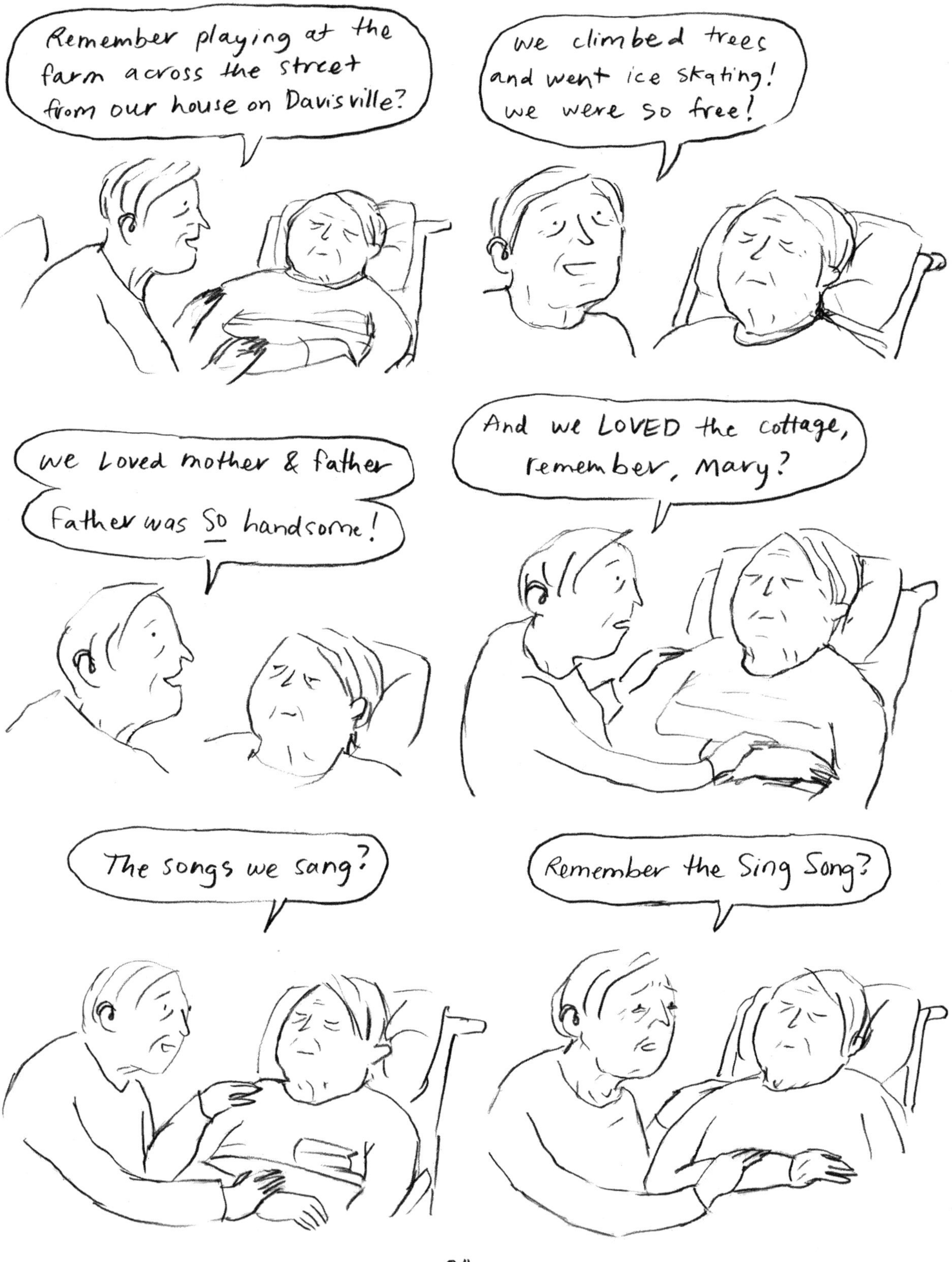

Remember playing at the farm across the street from our house on Davisville?
We climbed trees and went ice skating! We were so free!
We loved mother & father
Father was SO handsome!
And we LOVED the cottage, remember, Mary?
The songs we sang?
Remember the Sing Song?

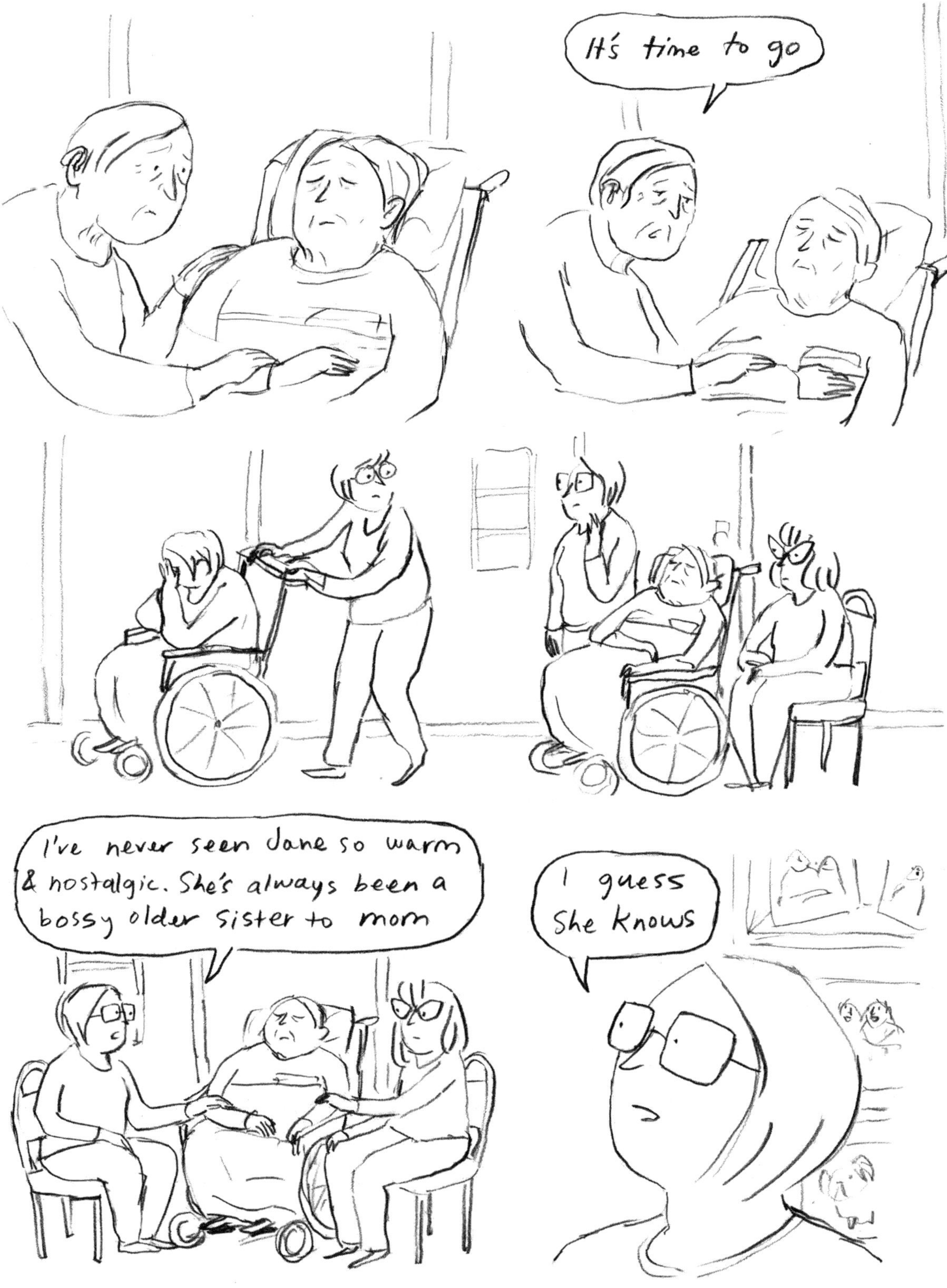
It's time to go
I've never seen Jane so warm & nostalgic. She's always been a bossy older sister to mom
I guess She knows

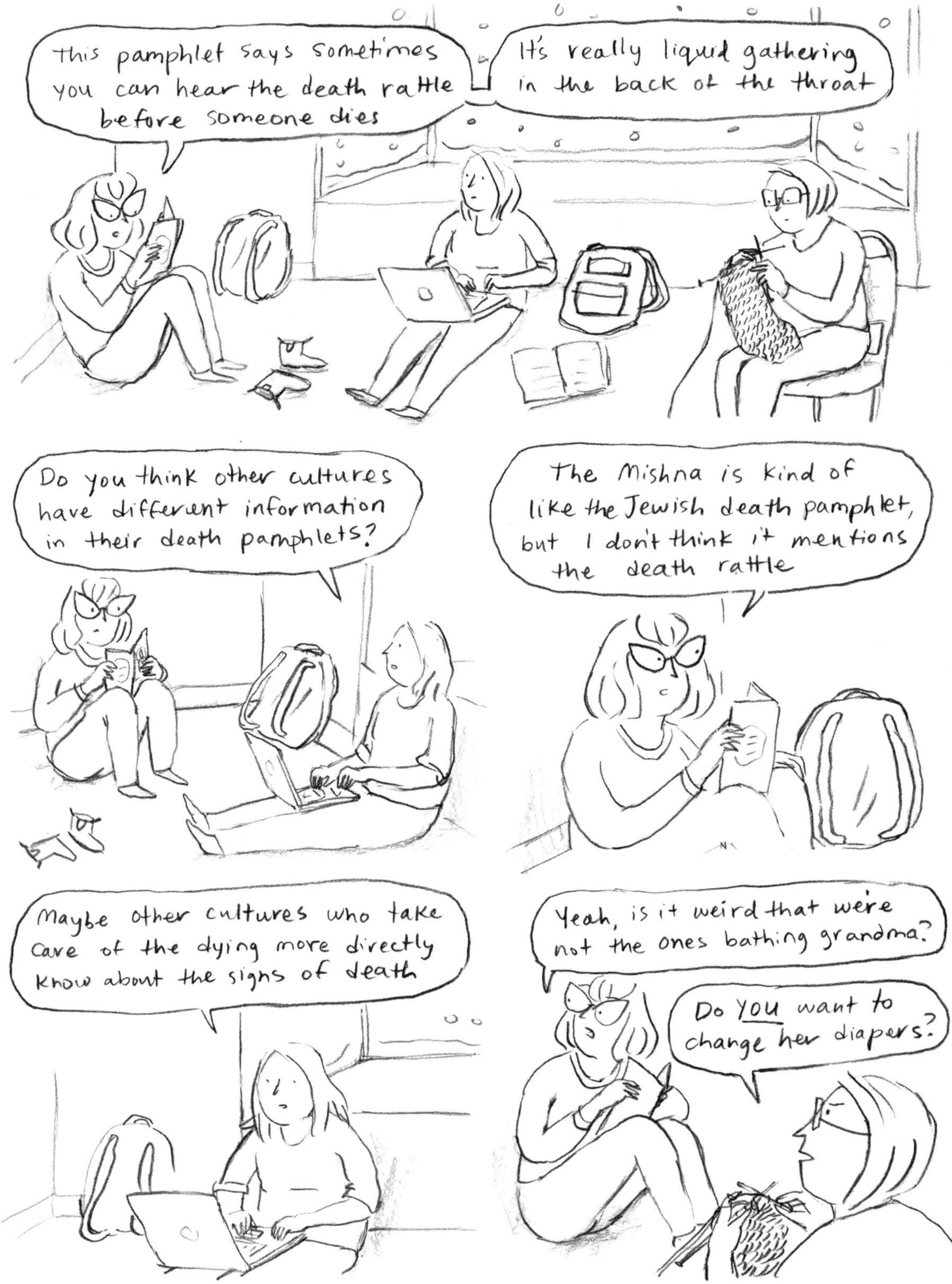
This pamphlet says sometimes you can hear the death rattle before someone dies
It's really liquid gathering in the back of the throat
Do you think other cultures have different information in their death pamphlets?
The Mishna is kind of like the Jewish death pamphlet, but I don't think it mentions the death rattle
Maybe other cultures who take care of the dying more directly know about the signs of death
Yeah, is it weird that we're not the ones bathing grandma?
Do YOU want to change her diapers?

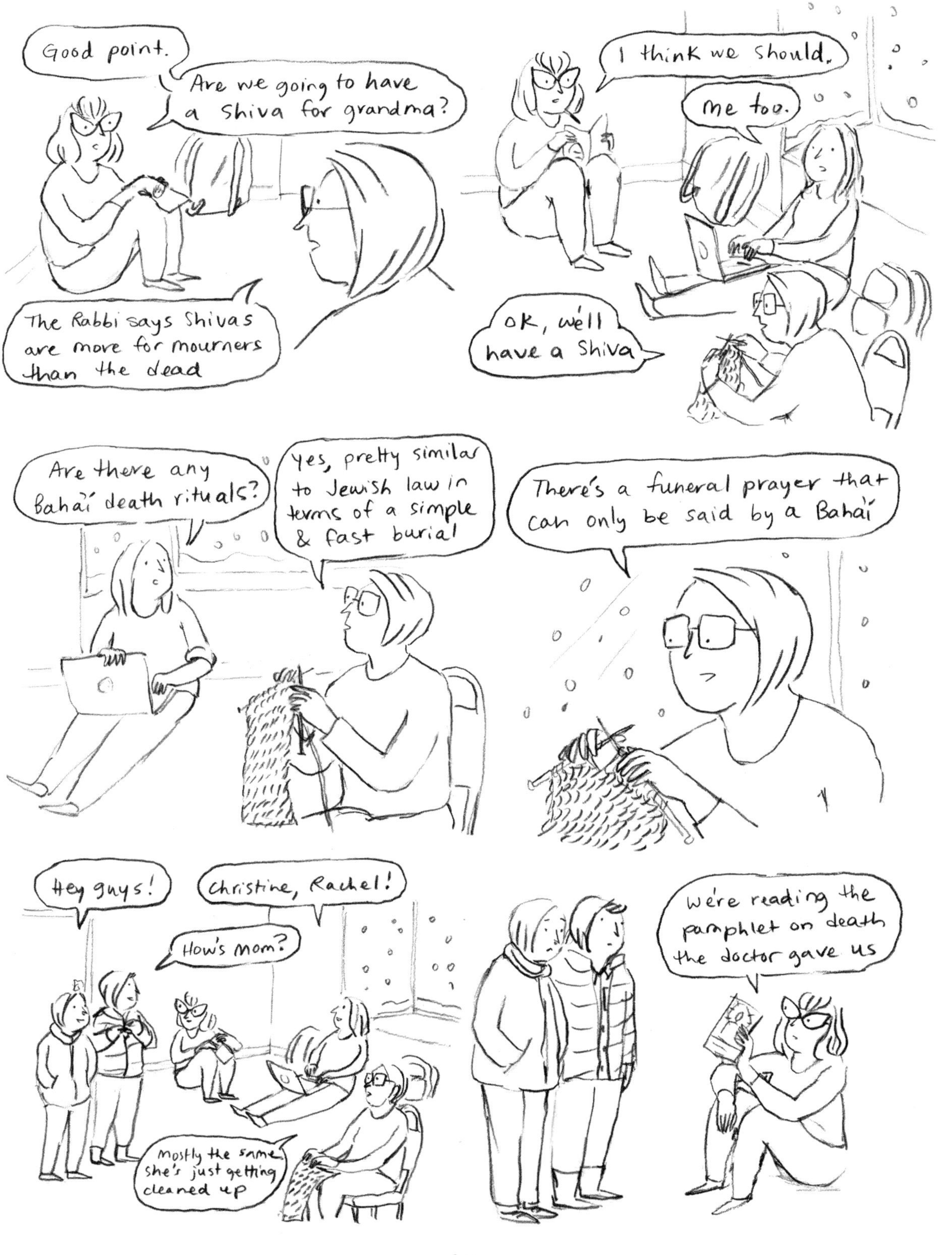
Good point.
Are we going to have a Shiva for grandma?
The Rabbi says Shivas are more for mourners than the dead
I think we should.
Me too.
OK, we'll have a Shiva
Are there any Bahai death rituals?
Yes, pretty similar to Jewish law in terms of a simple & fast burial
There's a funeral prayer that can only be said by a Bahai
Hey guys!
Christine, Rachel!
How's Mom?
Mostly the same she's just getting cleaned up
We're reading the pamphlet on death the doctor gave us

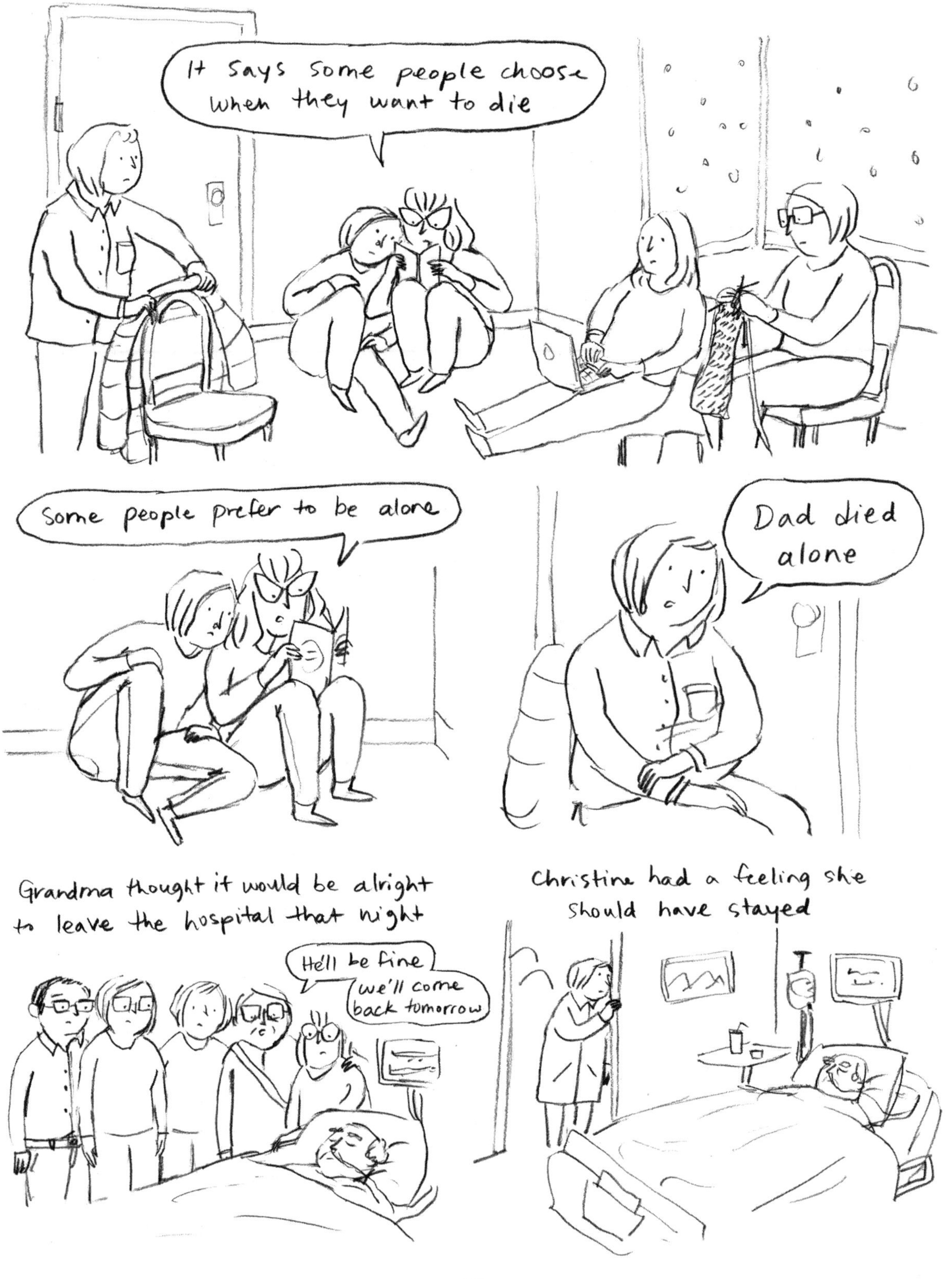
It says some people choose when they want to die
Some people prefer to be alone
Dad died alone
Grandma thought it would be alright to leave the hospital that night
He'll be fine
we'll come back tomorrow
Christine had a feeling she should have stayed

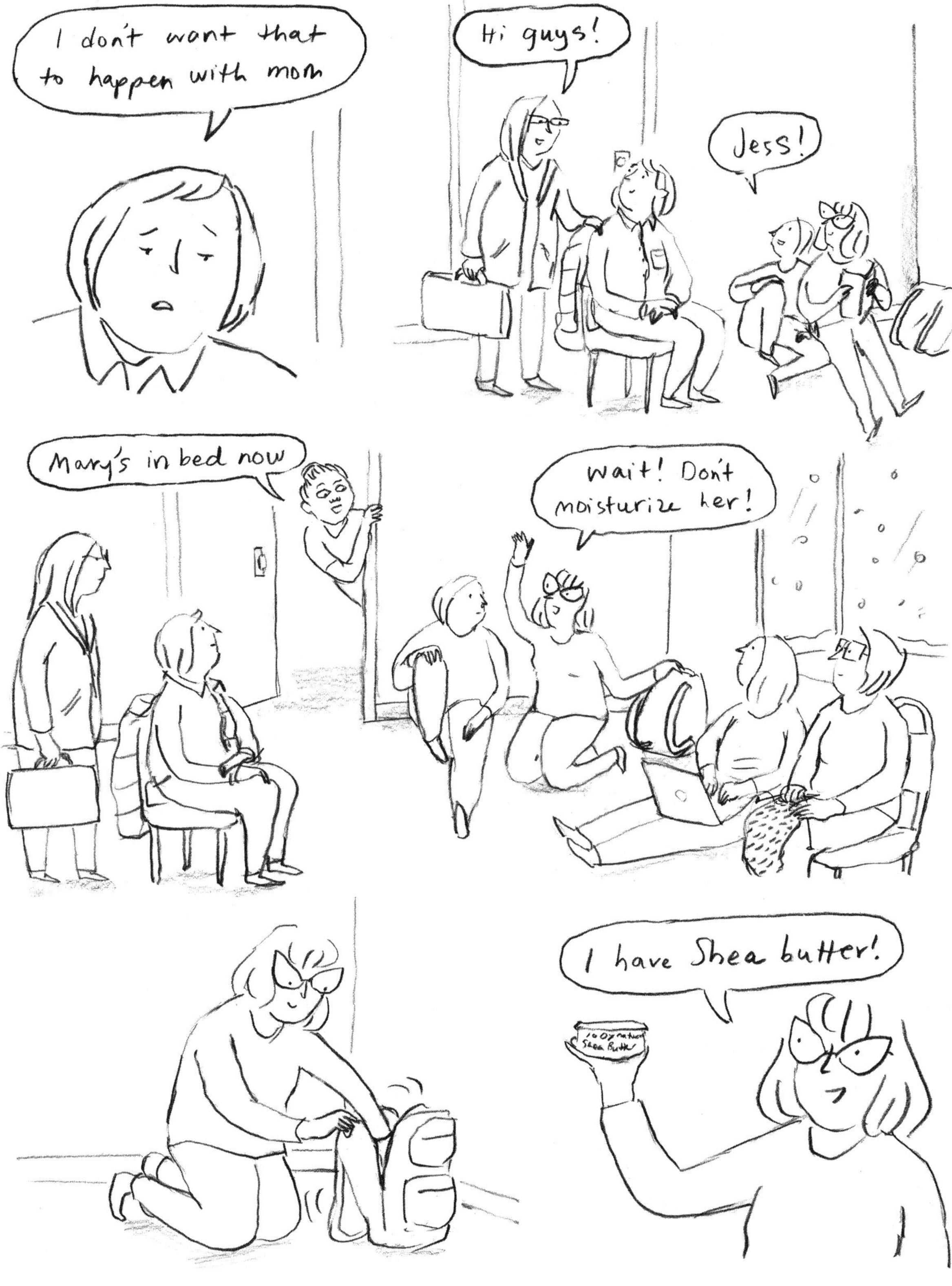
I don't want that to happen with mom
Hi guys!
Jess!
Mary's in bed now
Wait! Don't moisturize her!
I have Shea butter!
100% natural Shea Butter

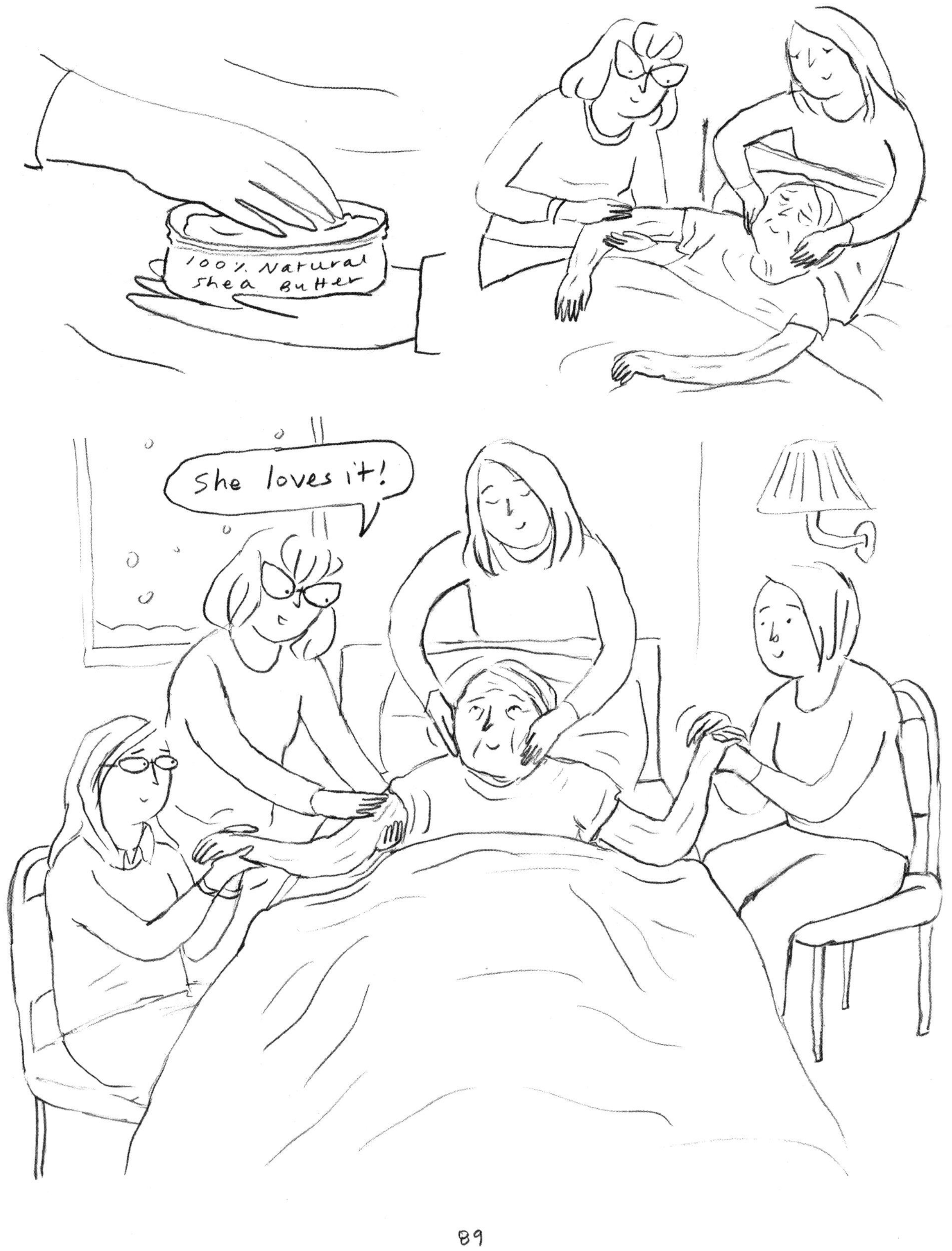
100% Natural Shea Butter
She loves it!

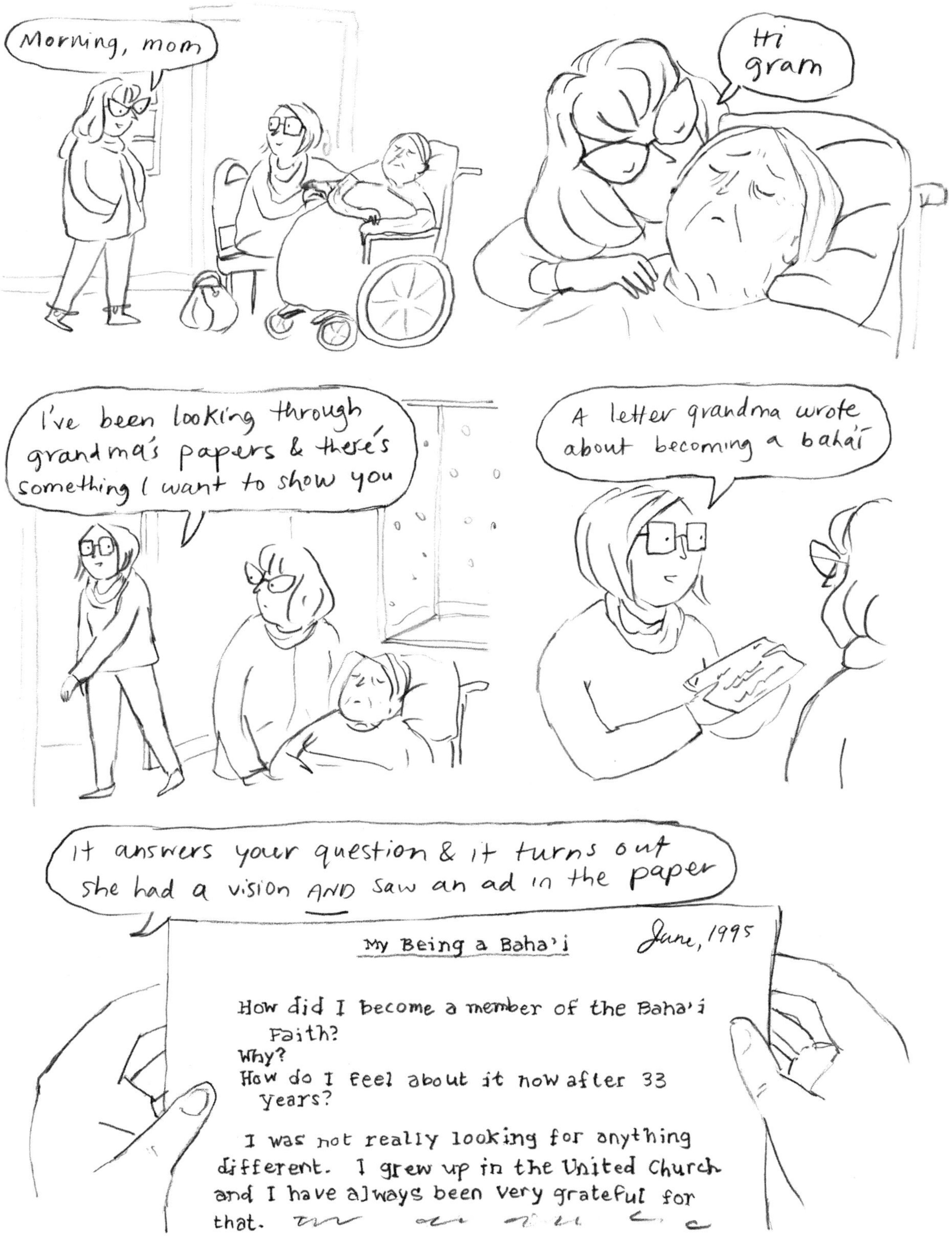
Morning, mom
Hi gram
I've been looking through grandma's papers & there's something I want to show you
A letter grandma wrote about becoming a bahá'í
It answers your question & it turns out she had a vision AND saw an ad in the paper
My Being a Baha'i
June, 1995
How did I become a member of the Baha'i Faith?
Why?
How do I feel about it now after 33 years?
I was not really looking for anything different. I grew up in the United Church and I have always been very grateful for that.

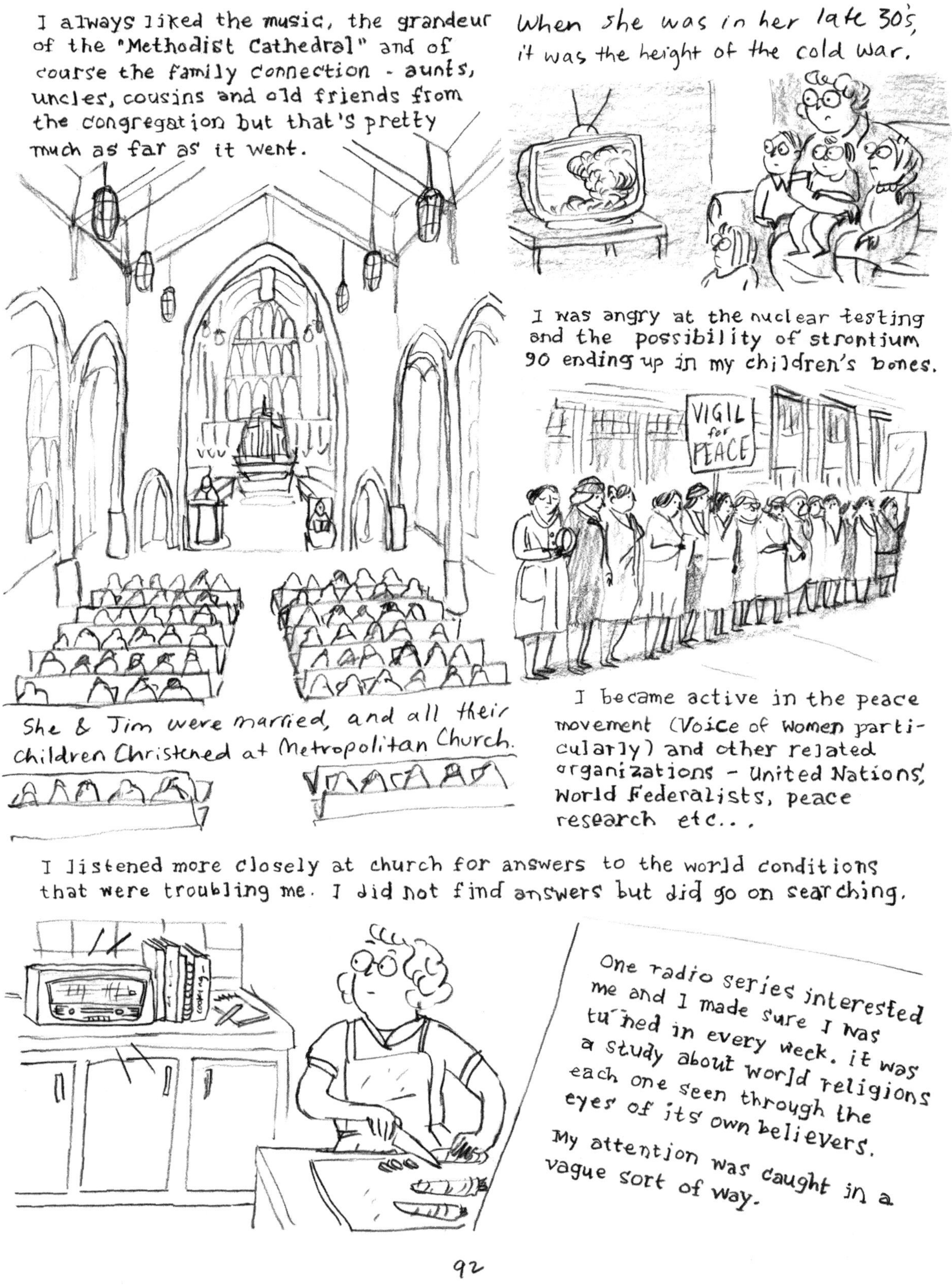
I always liked the music, the grandeur of the "Methodist Cathedral" and of course the family connection - aunts, uncles, cousins and old friends from the congregation but that's pretty much as far as it went.
When she was in her late 30's, it was the height of the cold war.
I was angry at the nuclear testing and the possibility of strontium 90 ending up in my children's bones.
VIGIL for PEACE
She & Jim were married, and all their children Christened at Metropolitan Church.
I became active in the peace movement (Voice of Women particularly) and other related organizations - United Nations, World Federalists, peace research etc...
I listened more closely at church for answers to the world conditions that were troubling me. I did not find answers but did go on searching.
cooking
One radio series interested me and I made sure I was tuned in every week. it was a study about world religions each one seen through the eyes of its own believers.
My attention was caught in a vague sort of way.

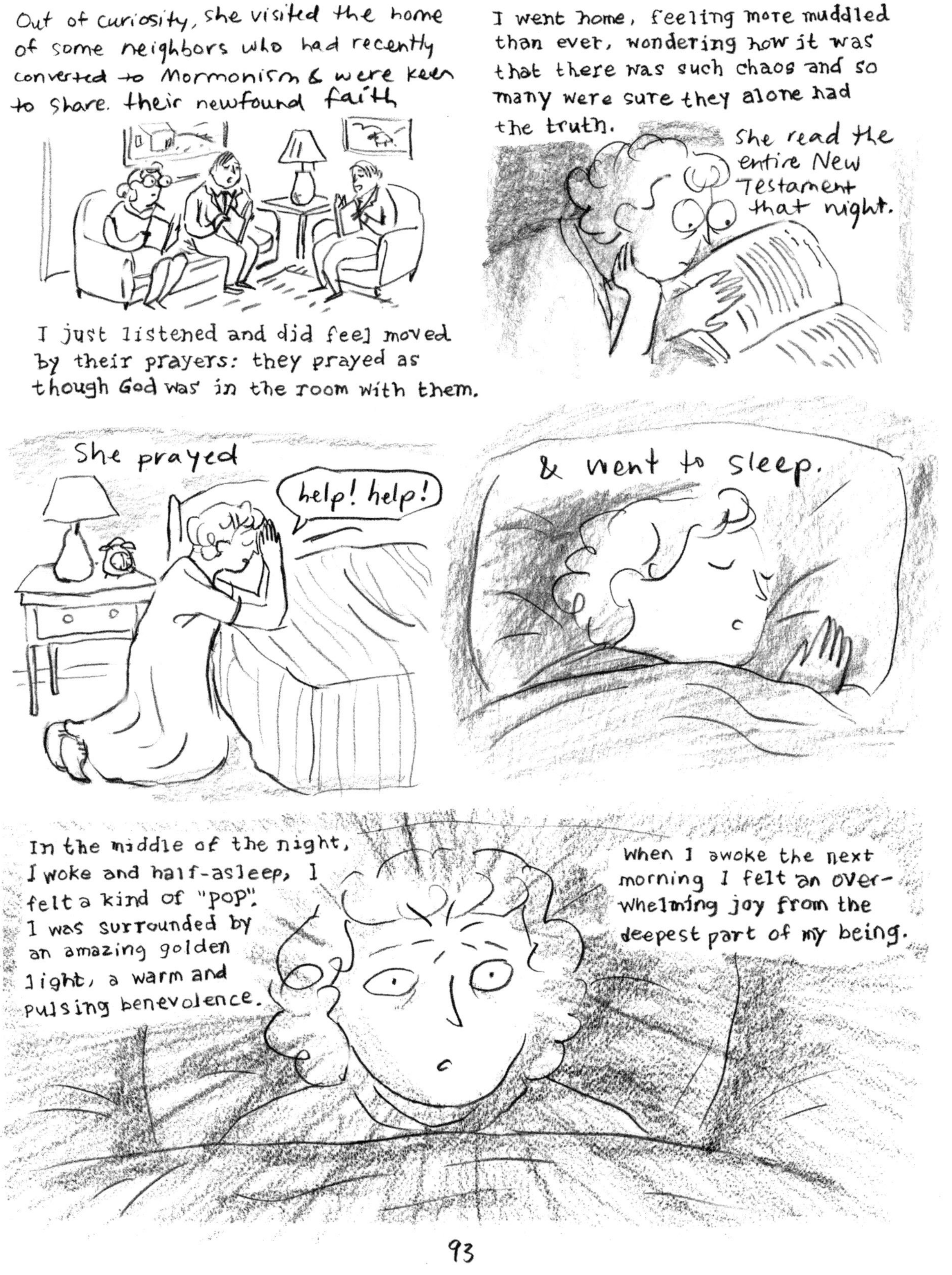
Out of curiosity, she visited the home of some neighbors who had recently converted to Mormonism & were keen to share their newfound faith
I just listened and did feel moved by their prayers: they prayed as though God was in the room with them.
I went home, feeling more muddled than ever, wondering how it was that there was such chaos and so many were sure they alone had the truth.
She read the entire New Testament that night.
She prayed
help! help!
& went to sleep.
In the middle of the night, I woke and half-asleep, I felt a kind of "POP". I was surrounded by an amazing golden light, a warm and pulsing benevolence.
When I awoke the next morning I felt an over-whelming joy from the deepest part of my being.

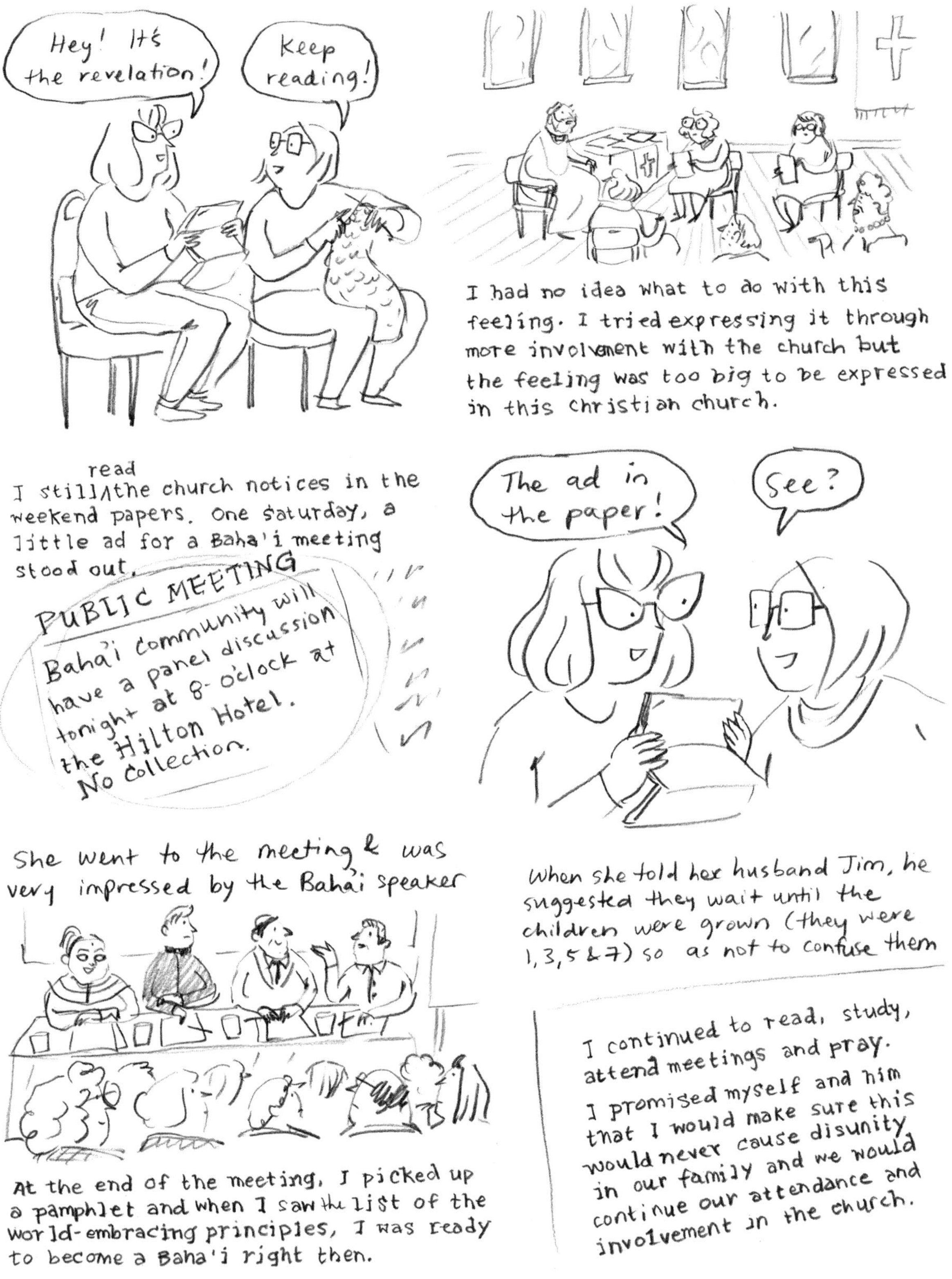
Hey! It's the revelation!
Keep reading!
I had no idea what to do with this feeling. I tried expressing it through more involvement with the church but the feeling was too big to be expressed in this christian church.
I still read the church notices in the weekend papers. One saturday, a little ad for a Baha'i meeting stood out.
PUBLIC MEETING
Baha'i community will have a panel discussion tonight at 8 o'clock at the Hilton Hotel. No collection.
The ad in the paper!
See?
She went to the meeting & was very impressed by the Bahai speaker
At the end of the meeting, I picked up a pamphlet and when I saw the list of the world-embracing principles, I was ready to become a Baha'i right then.
When she told her husband Jim, he suggested they wait until the children were grown (they were 1, 3, 5 & 7) so as not to confuse them
I continued to read, study, attend meetings and pray. I promised myself and him that I would make sure this would never cause disunity in our family and we would continue our attendance and involvement in the church.

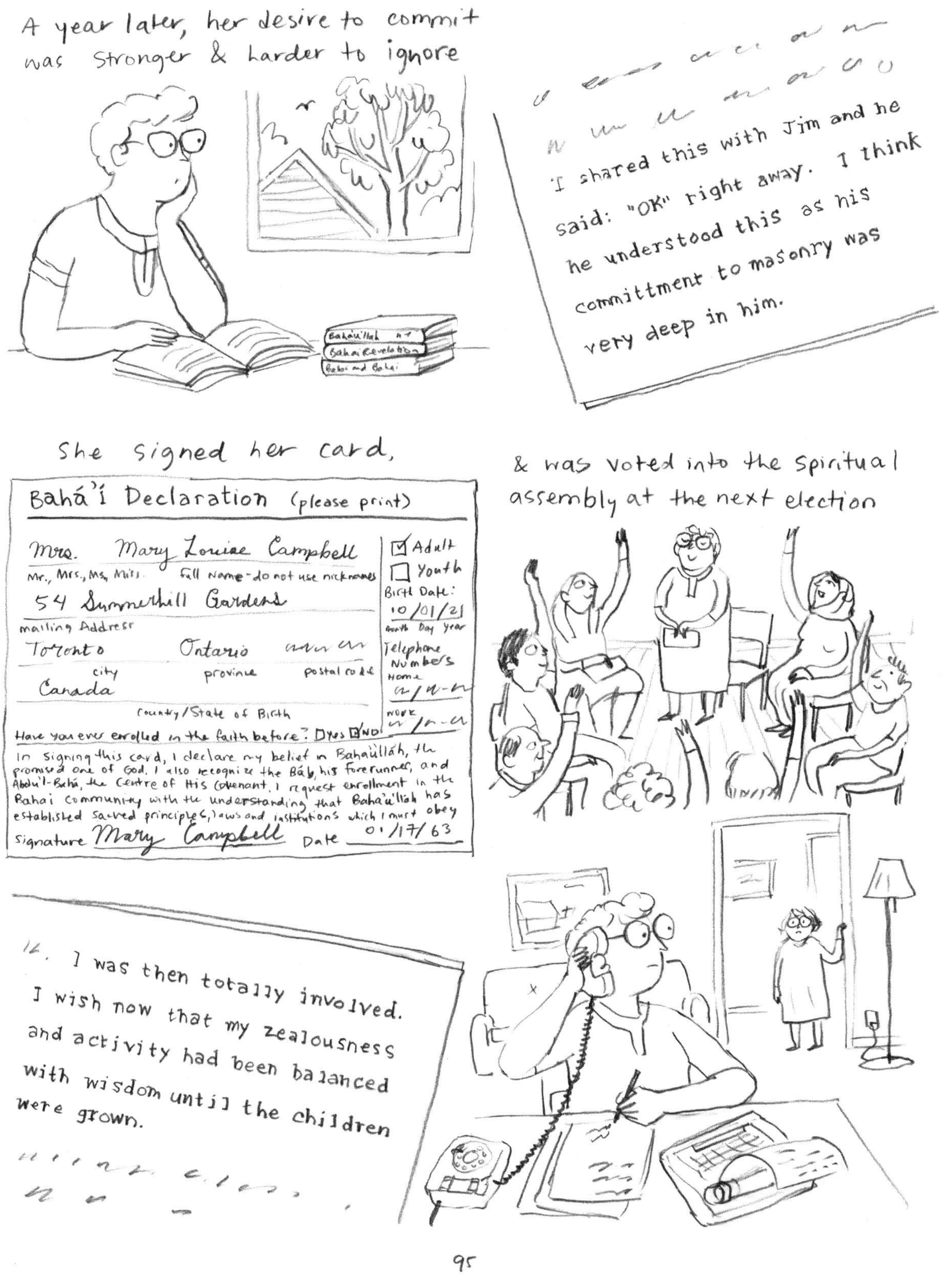
A year later, her desire to commit was stronger & harder to ignore
Bahá'u'lláh
Bahá'í Revelation
Bábí and Bahá'í
I shared this with Jim and he said: "OK" right away. I think he understood this as his committment to masonry was very deep in him.
She signed her card,
Bahá'í Declaration (please print)
Mrs. Mary Louise Campbell
Mr., Mrs., Ms, Miss. full Name - do not use nicknames
54 Summerhill Gardens
mailing Address
Toronto Ontario
city province postal code
Canada
country/State of Birth
Adult
Youth
Birth Date: 10/01/21
Month Day Year
Telephone Numbers
Home
Work
Have you ever enrolled in the faith before? Yes NO
In signing this card, I declare my belief in Bahá'u'lláh, the promised one of God. I also recognize the Báb, his forerunner, and Abdu'l-Bahá, the Centre of His Covenant. I request enrollment in the Bahai community with the understanding that Bahá'u'lláh has established sacred principles, laws and institutions which I must obey
Signature Mary Campbell Date 01/17/63
& was voted into the spiritual assembly at the next election
I was then totally involved. I wish now that my zealousness and activity had been balanced with wisdom until the children were grown.

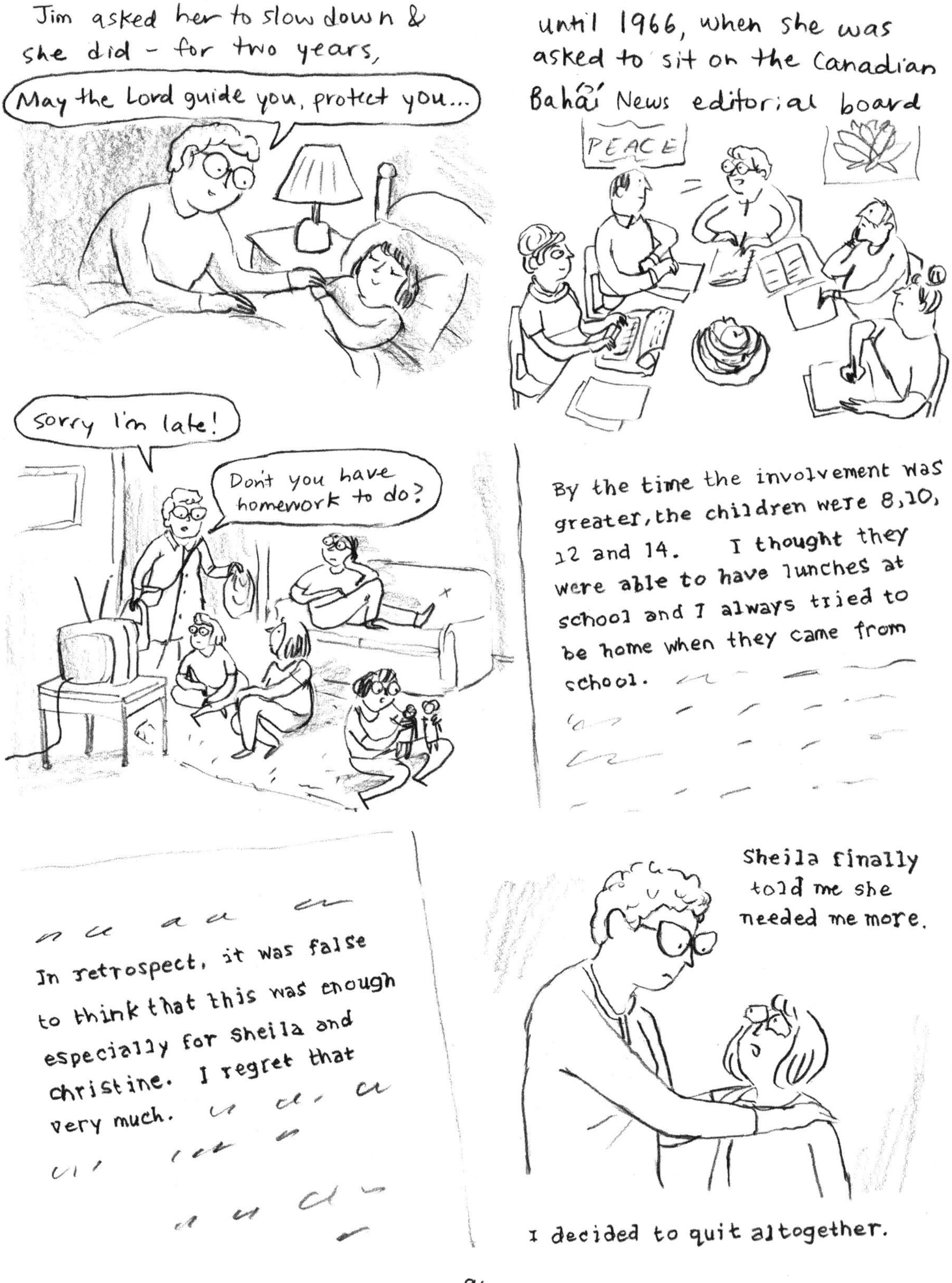
Jim asked her to slow down & she did - for two years,
May the Lord guide you, protect you...
until 1966, when she was asked to sit on the Canadian Bahá'í News editorial board
PEACE
Sorry I'm late!
Don't you have homework to do?
By the time the involvement was greater, the children were 8, 10, 12 and 14. I thought they were able to have lunches at school and I always tried to be home when they came from school.
In retrospect, it was false to think that this was enough for Sheila and especially for Christine. I regret that very much.
Sheila finally told me she needed me more.
I decided to quit altogether.

It was now 1973 and I was beginning to suffer from the effect of the chemical sensitivities.

My activity in the Baha'i community stopped altogether when my energy and wellness decreased and I finally had to move to Gravenhurst.

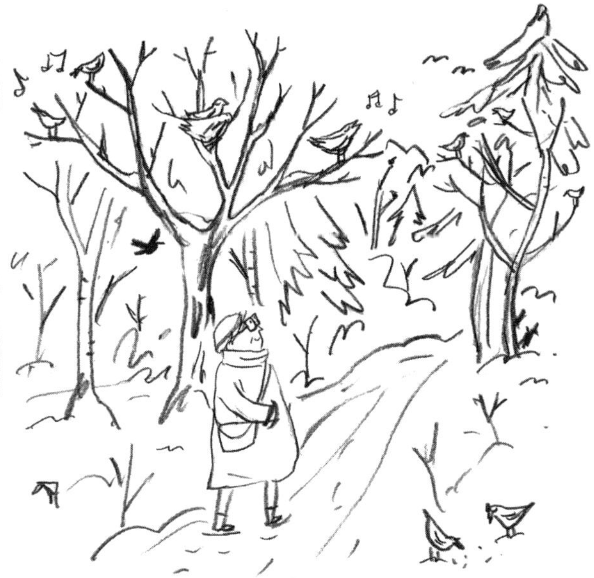

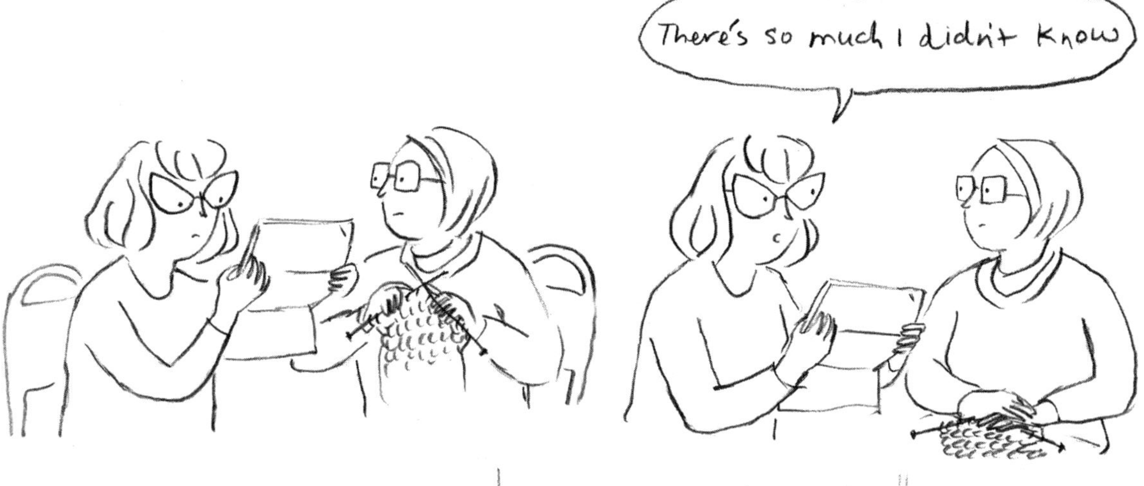
There's so much I didn't know

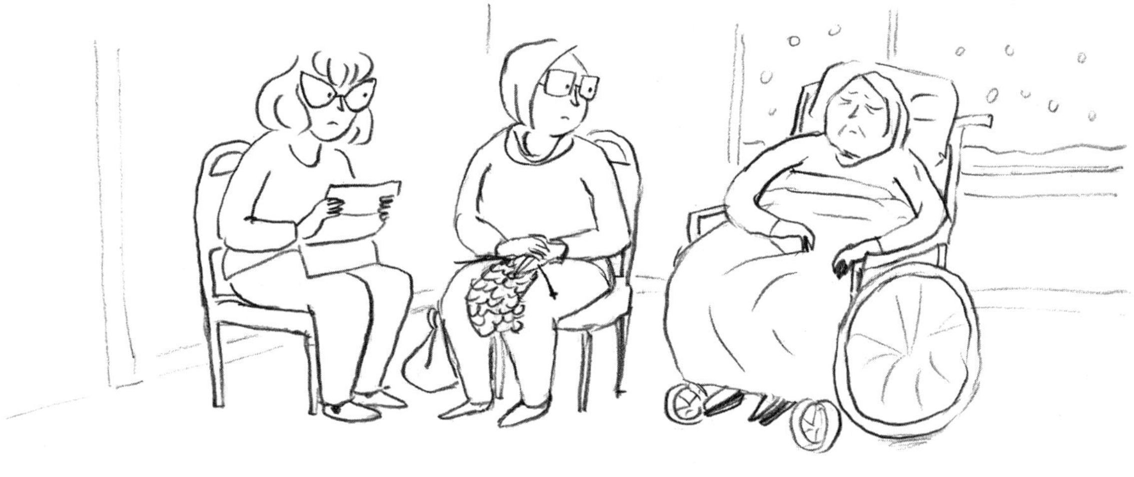

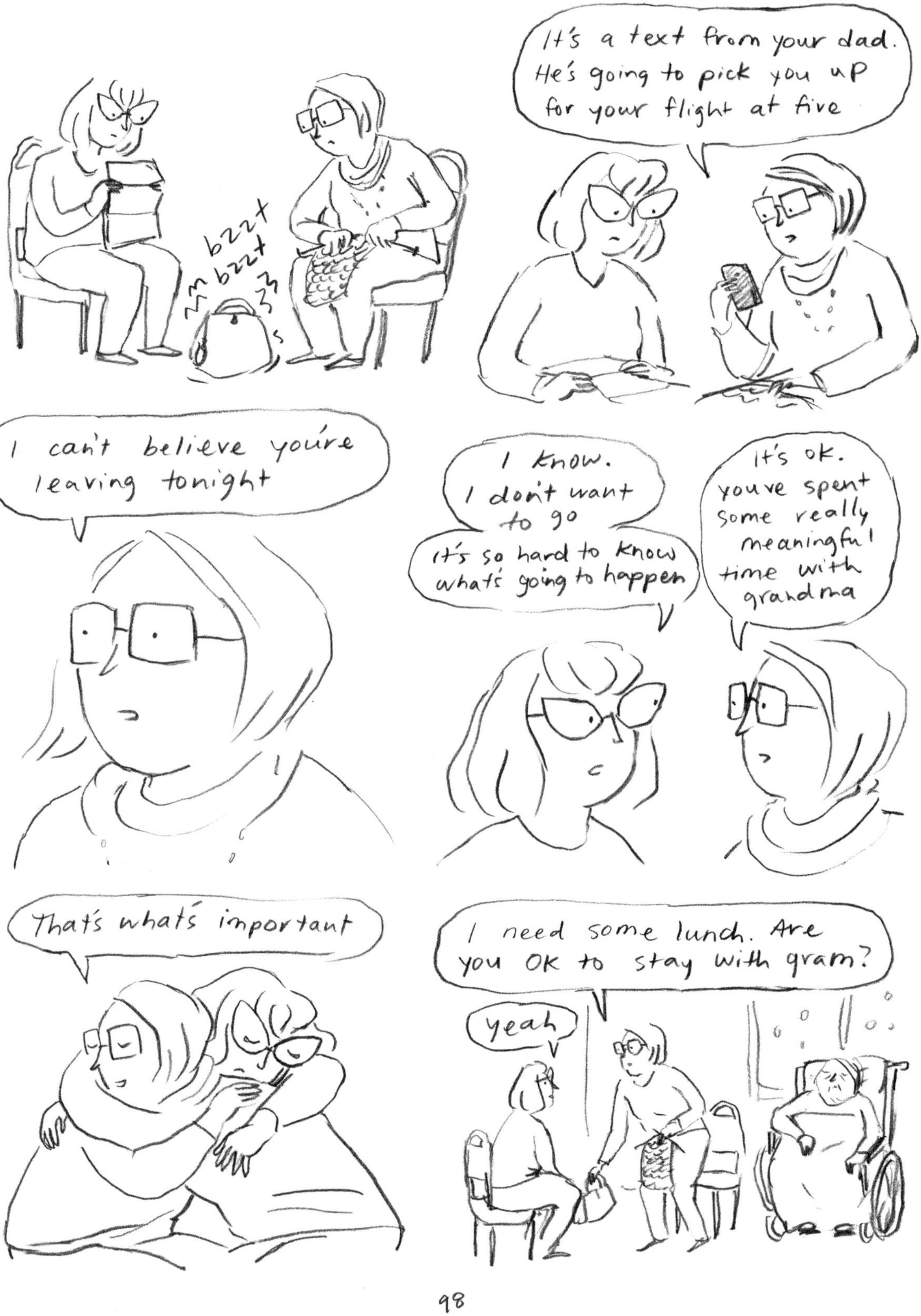
bzzzt bzzzt
It's a text from your dad. He's going to pick you up for your flight at five
I can't believe you're leaving tonight
I know. I don't want to go
It's so hard to know what's going to happen
It's ok. You've spent some really meaningful time with grandma
That's what's important
I need some lunch. Are you OK to stay with gram?
yeah

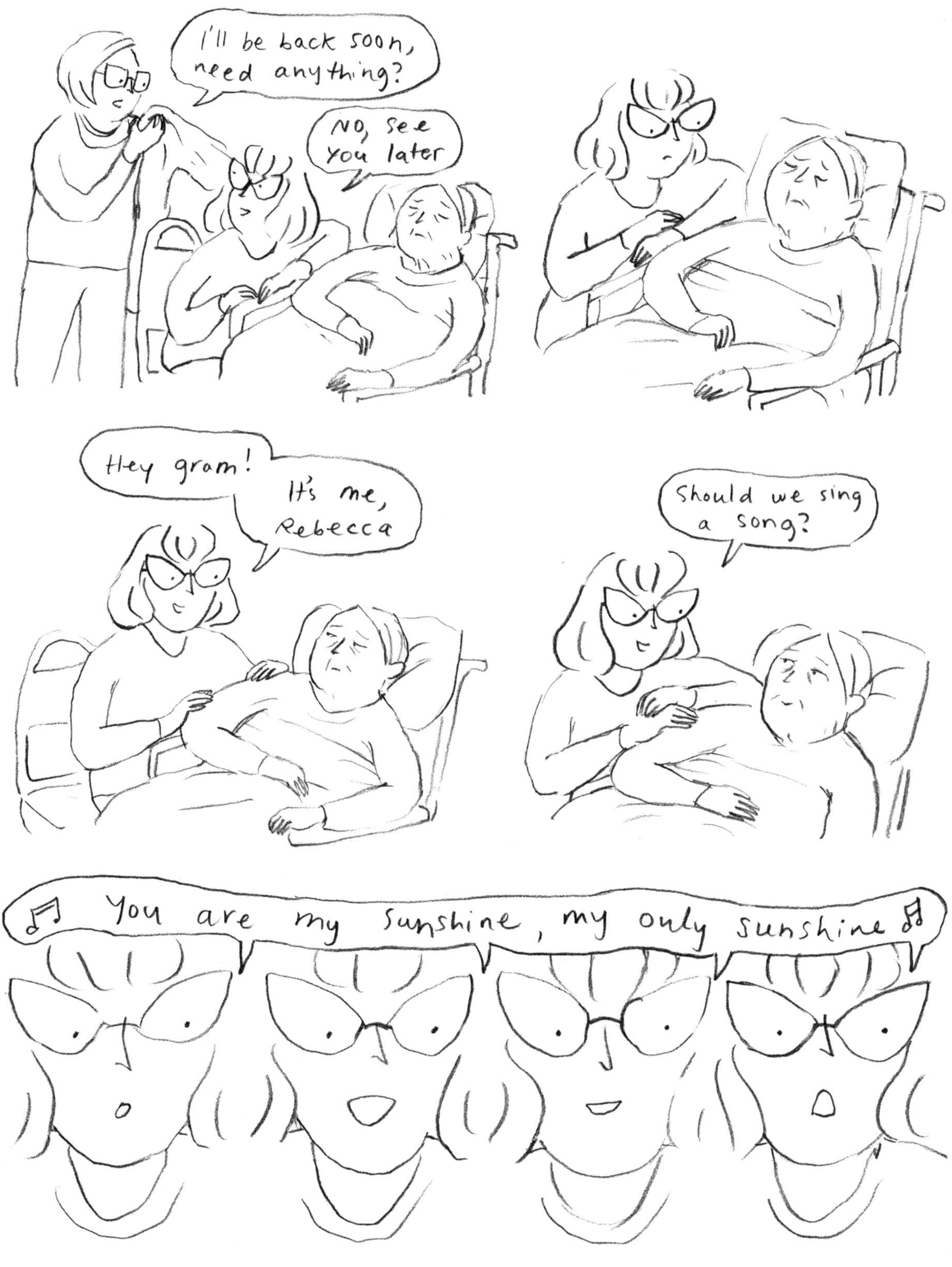
I'll be back soon, need anything?
No, see you later
Hey gram!
It's me, Rebecca
Should we sing a song?
You are my sunshine, my only sunshine

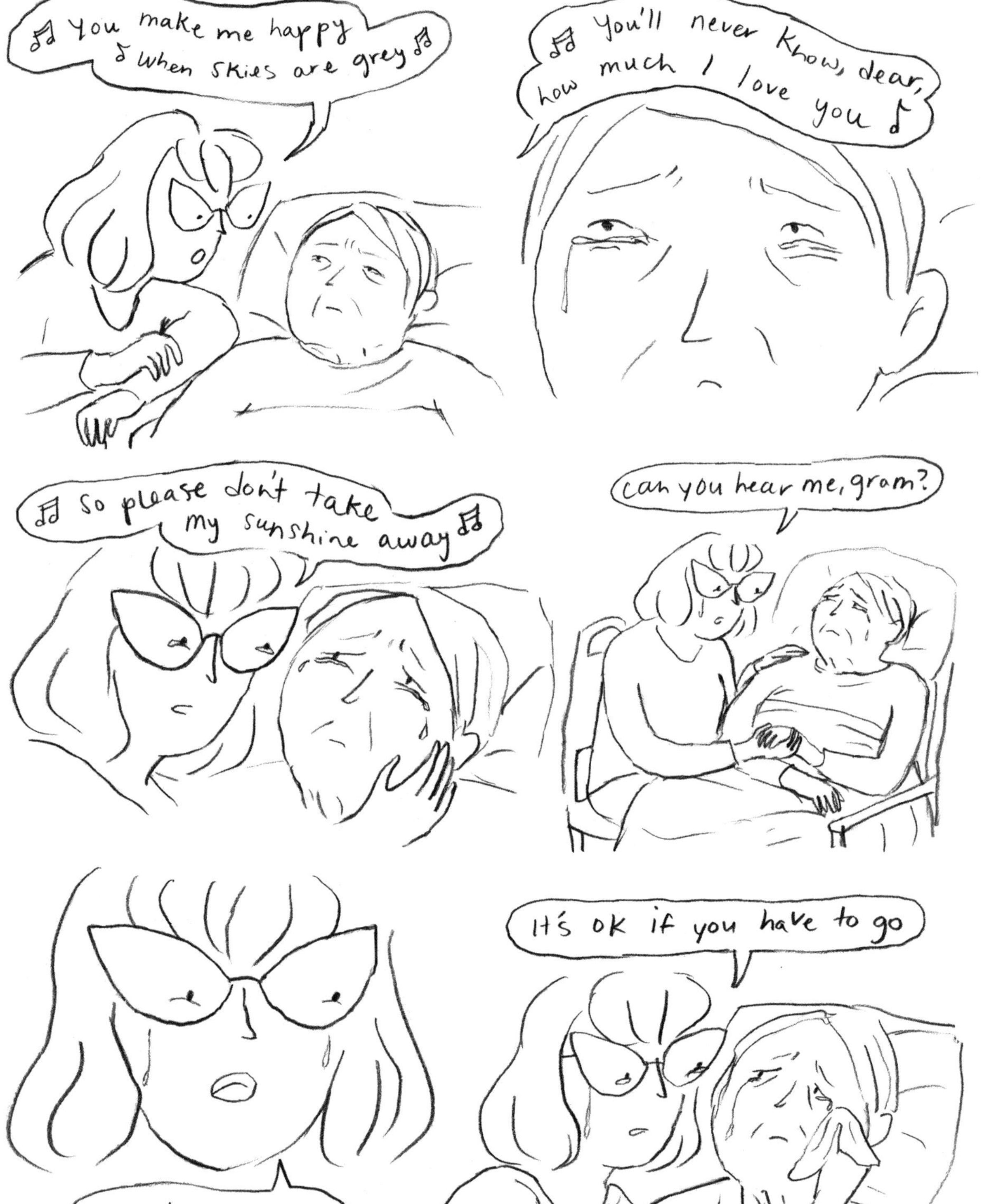
You make me happy when skies are grey
You'll never know, dear, how much I love you
So please don't take my sunshine away
Can you hear me, gram?
I love you
It's ok if you have to go

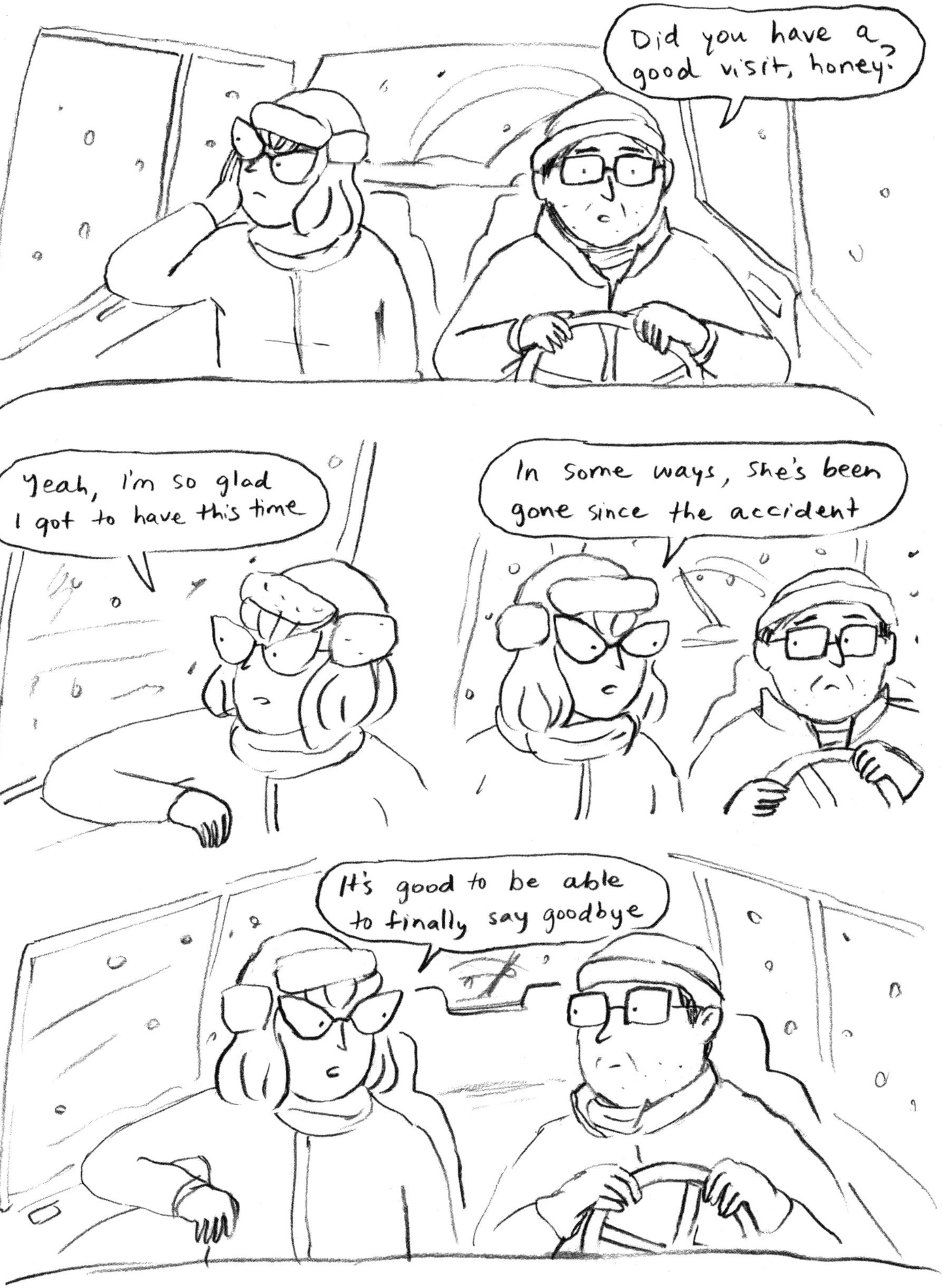
Did you have a good visit, honey?
Yeah, I'm so glad I got to have this time
In some ways, she's been gone since the accident
It's good to be able to finally say goodbye

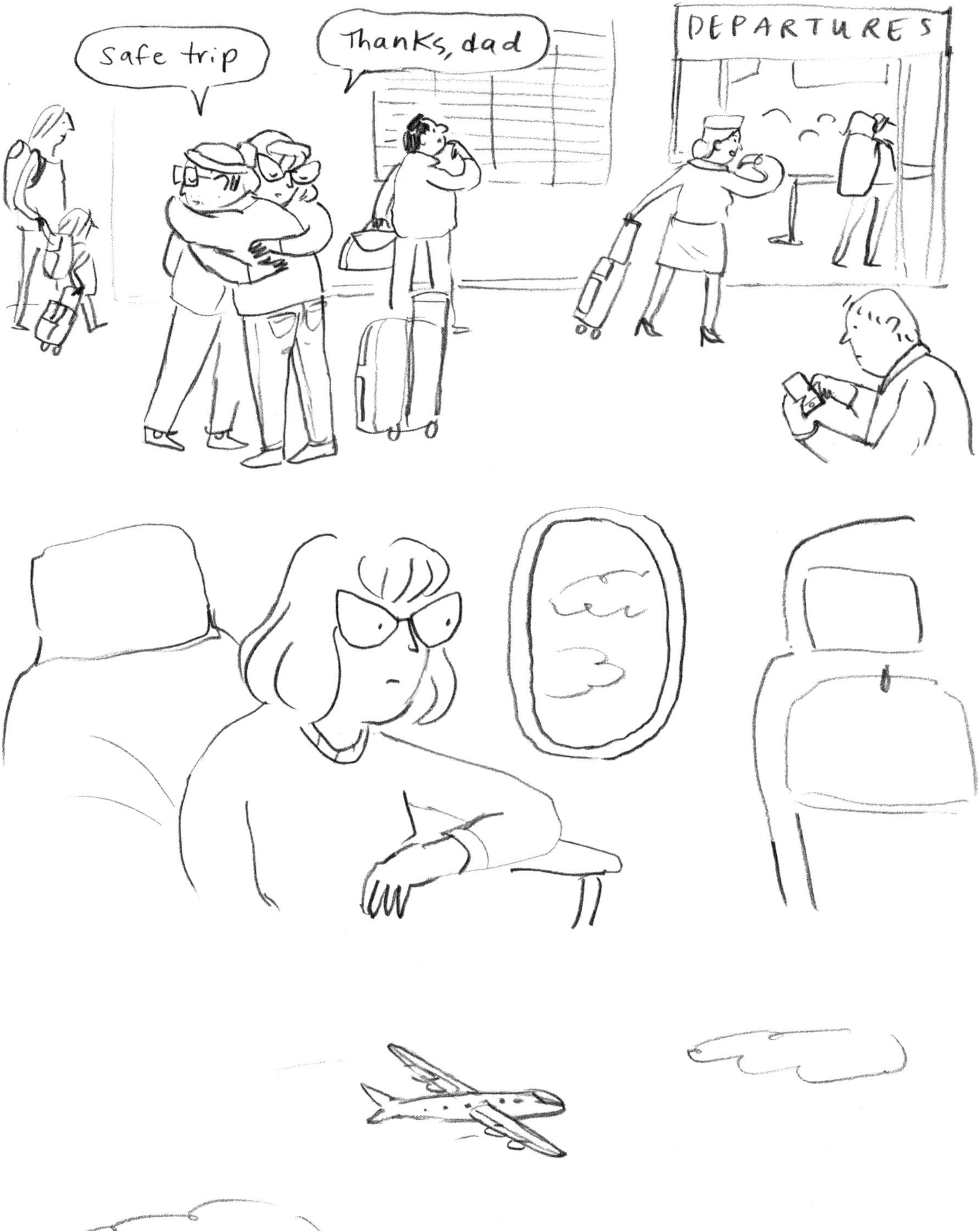
Safe trip
Thanks, dad
DEPARTURES

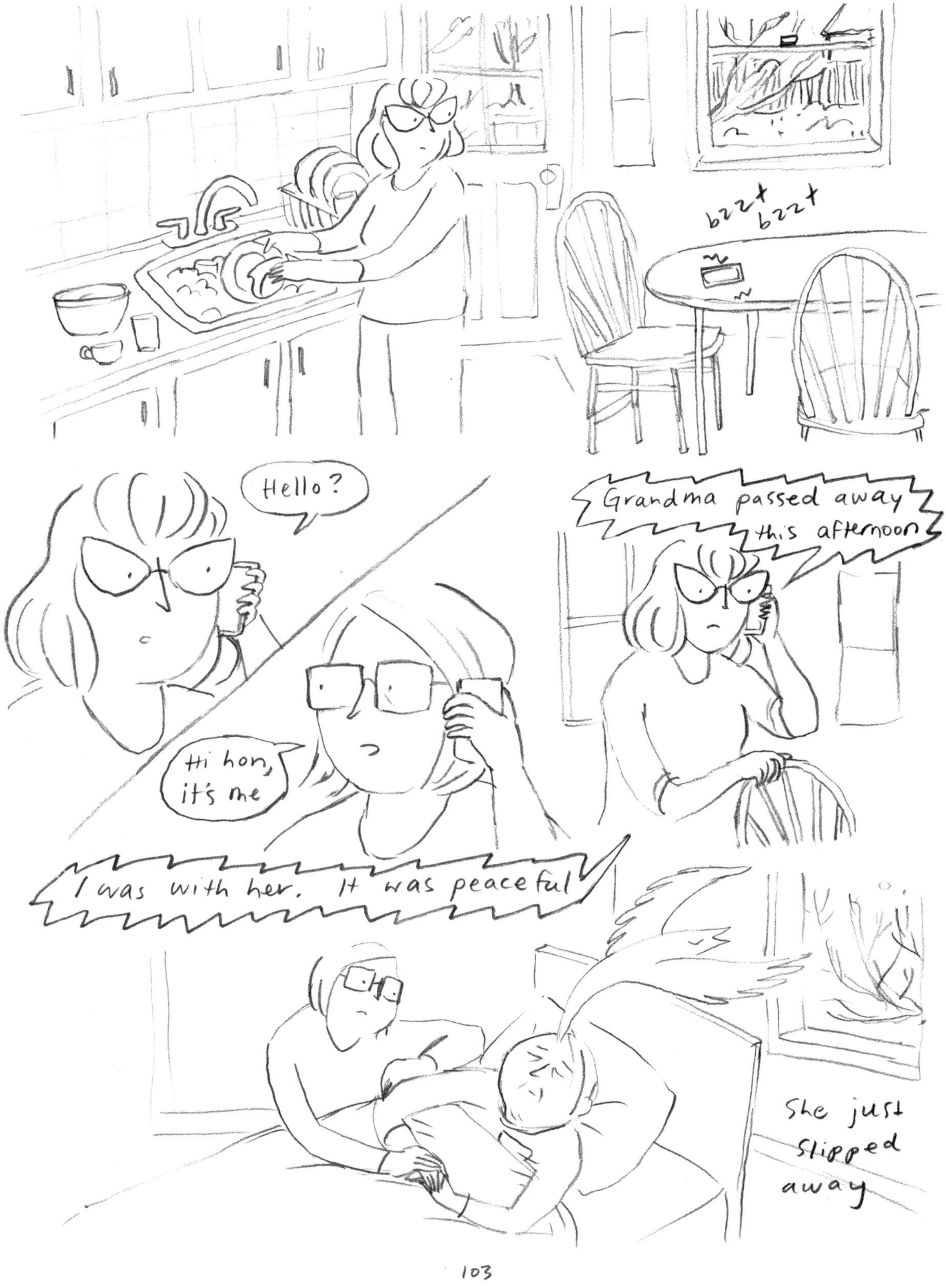
bzzt bzzt
Hello?
Hi hon, it's me
Grandma passed away this afternoon
I was with her. It was peaceful
She just slipped away

The nurses wheeled her out, singing Amazing Grace, laid rose petals on her body

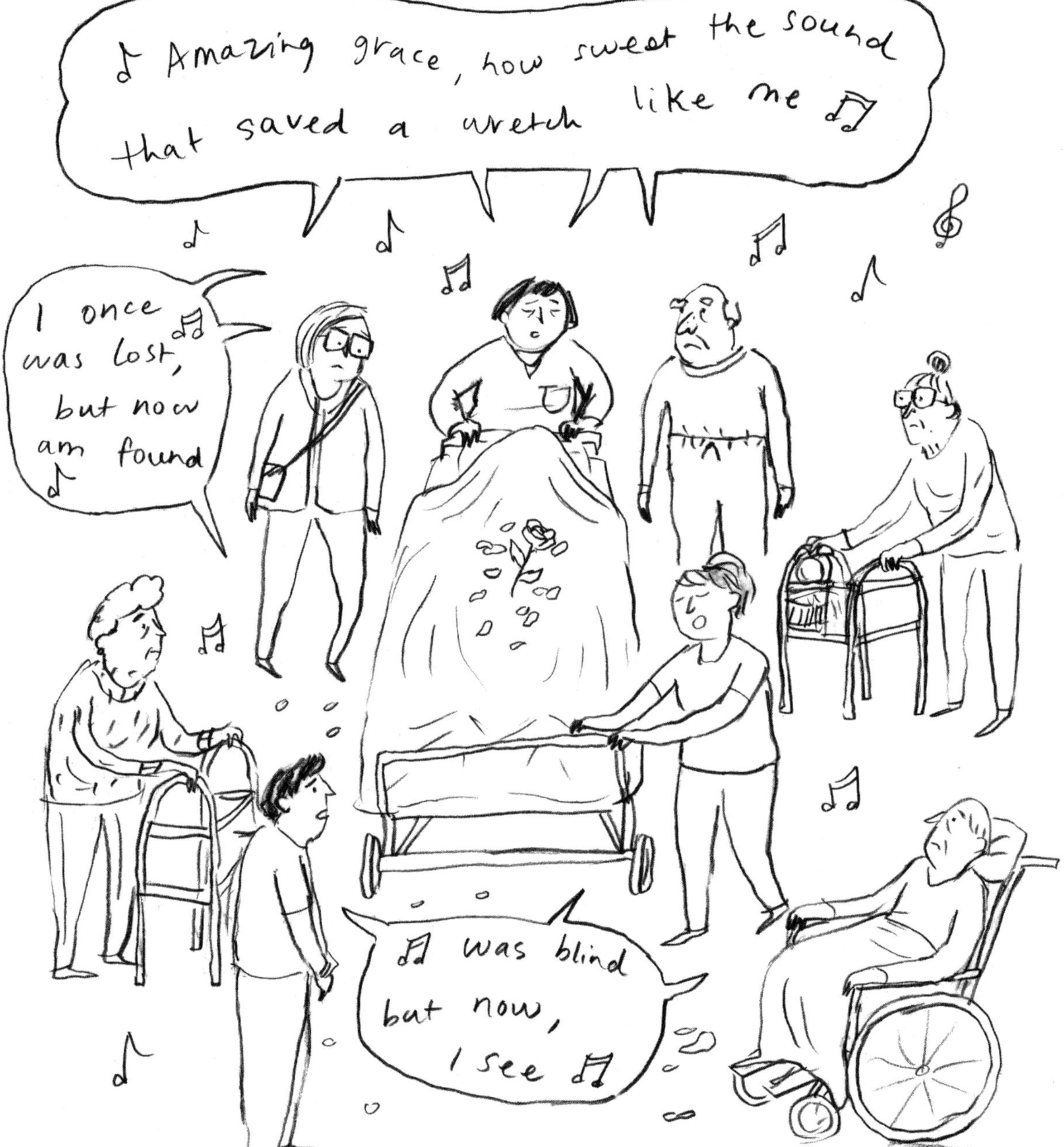
Amazing grace, how sweet the sound that saved a wretch like me
I once was lost, but now am found
was blind but now, I see

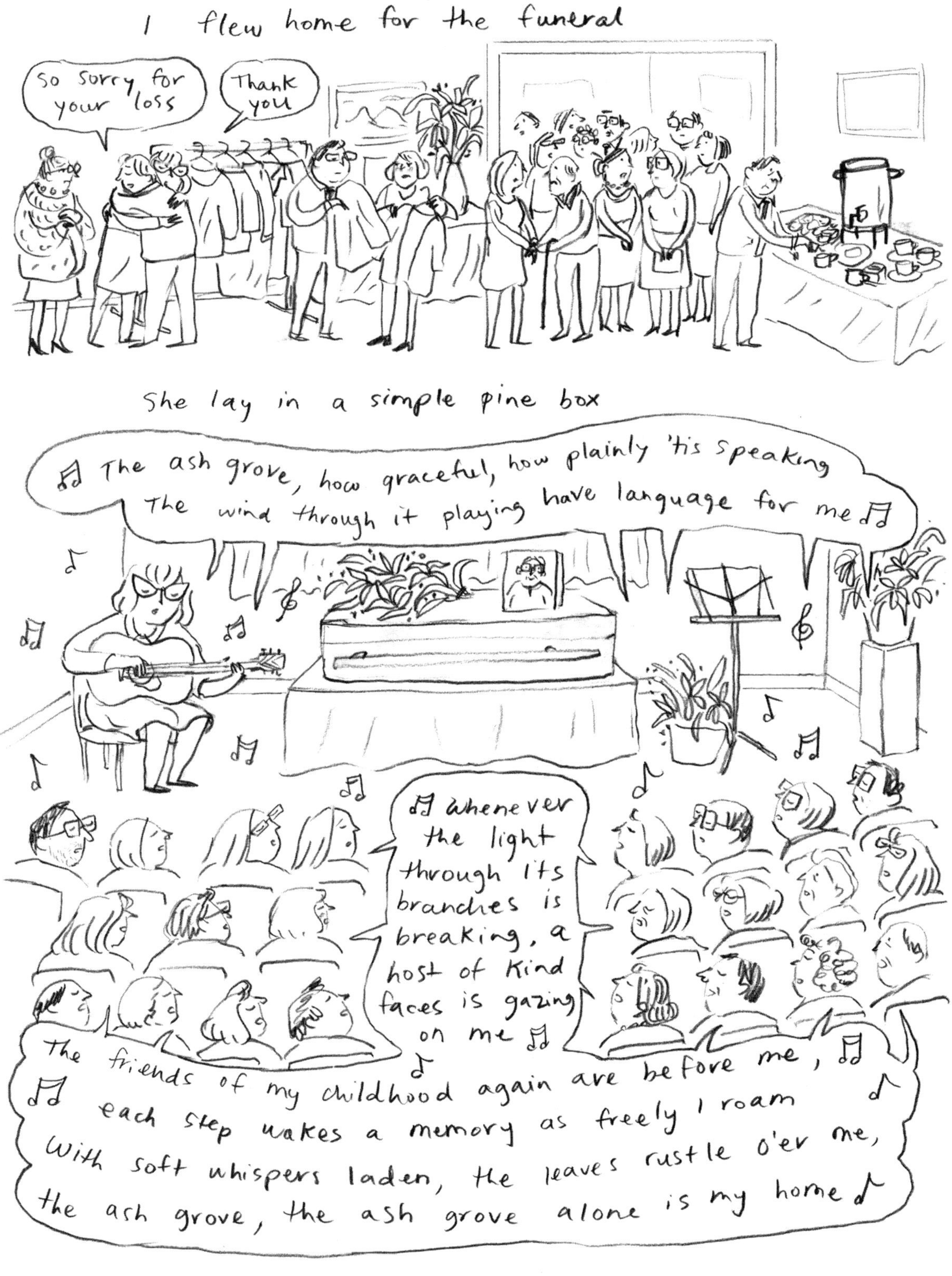
I flew home for the funeral
So sorry for your loss
Thank you
She lay in a simple pine box
The ash grove, how graceful, how plainly 'tis speaking The wind through it playing have language for me
Whenever the light through its branches is breaking, a host of kind faces is gazing on me
The friends of my childhood again are before me, each step wakes a memory as freely I roam With soft whispers laden, the leaves rustle o'er me, the ash grove, the ash grove alone is my home

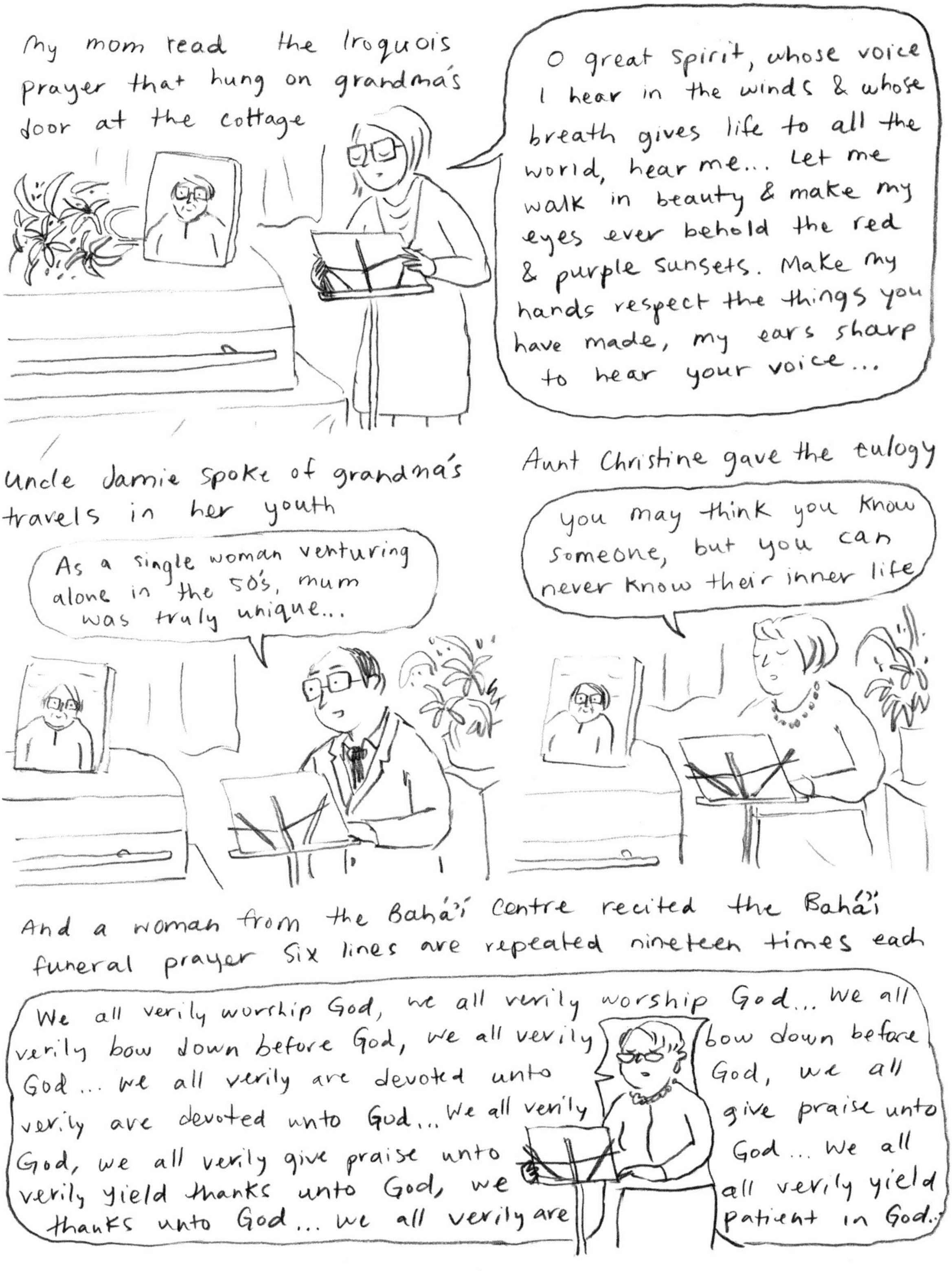
My mom read the Iroquois prayer that hung on grandma's door at the cottage
O great spirit, whose voice I hear in the winds & whose breath gives life to all the world, hear me... Let me walk in beauty & make my eyes ever behold the red & purple sunsets. Make my hands respect the things you have made, my ears sharp to hear your voice...
Uncle Jamie spoke of grandma's travels in her youth
As a single woman venturing alone in the 50's, mum was truly unique...
Aunt Christine gave the eulogy
You may think you know someone, but you can never know their inner life
And a woman from the Bahá'í Centre recited the Bahá'í funeral prayer. Six lines are repeated nineteen times each
We all verily worship God, we all verily worship God... We all verily bow down before God, we all verily bow down before God... We all verily are devoted unto God, we all verily are devoted unto God... We all verily give praise unto God, we all verily give praise unto God... We all verily yield thanks unto God, we all verily yield thanks unto God... We all verily are patient in God...

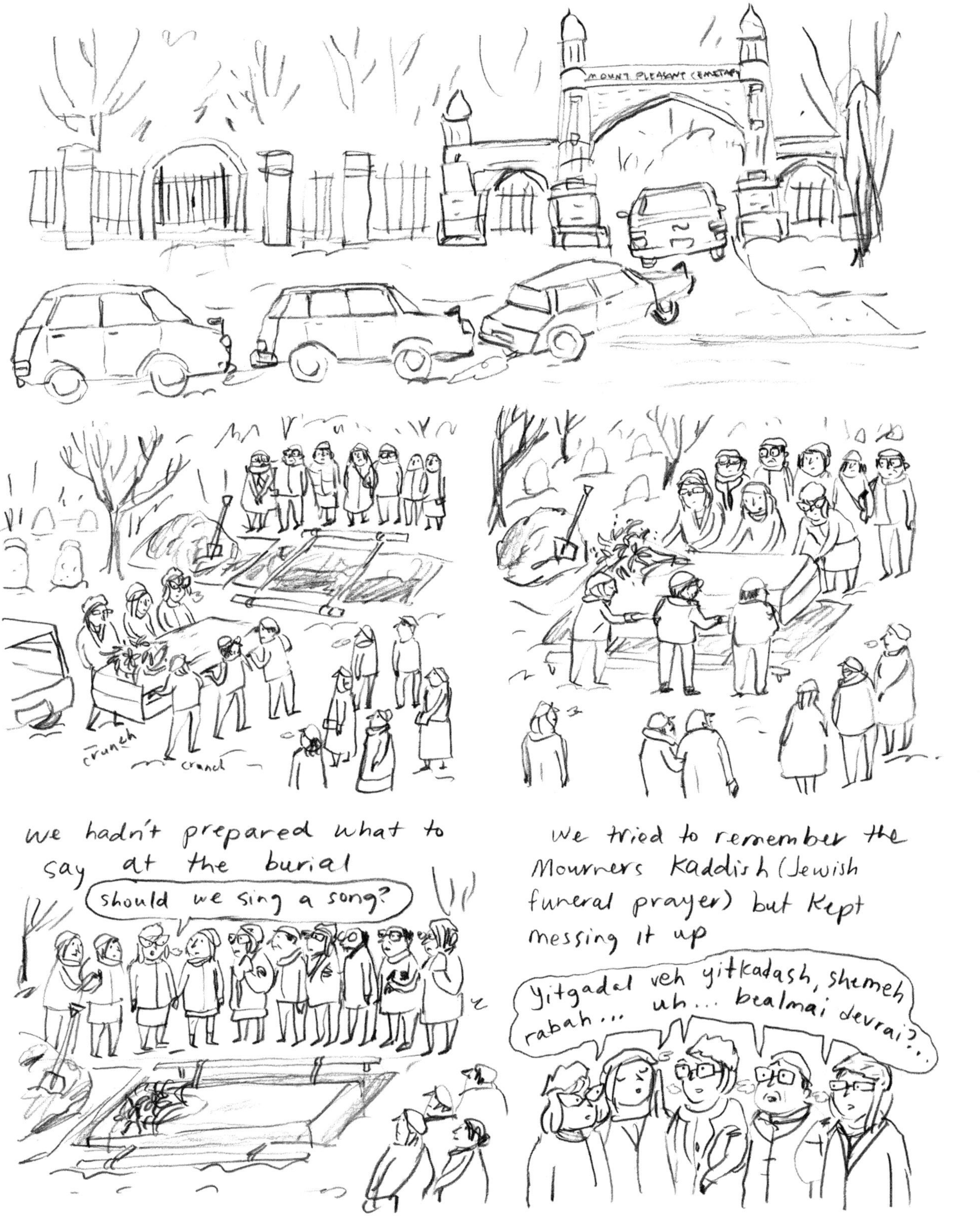
MOUNT PLEASANT CEMETARY
crunch
crunch
we hadn't prepared what to say at the burial
should we sing a song?
We tried to remember the Mourners Kaddish (Jewish funeral prayer) but kept messing it up
Yitgadal veh yitkadash, shemeh rabah... uh... bealmai devrai?...

The Bahá'í woman began to sing a beautiful Celtic Prayer

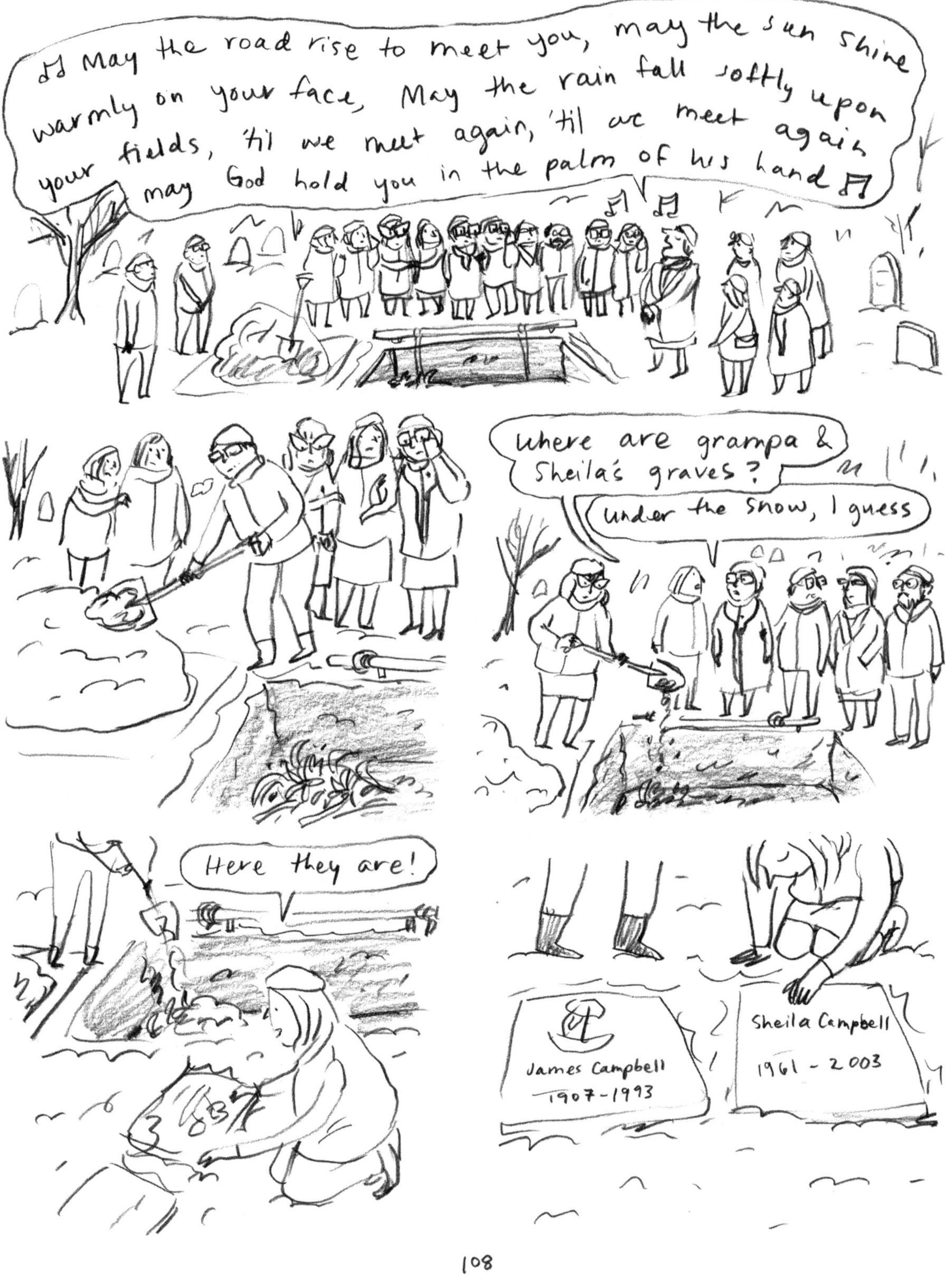
May the road rise to meet you, may the sun shine warmly on your face, May the rain fall softly upon your fields, 'til we meet again, 'til we meet again may God hold you in the palm of his hand
Where are grampa & Sheila's graves?
under the snow, I guess
Here they are!
James Campbell 1907-1993
Sheila Campbell 1961 - 2003

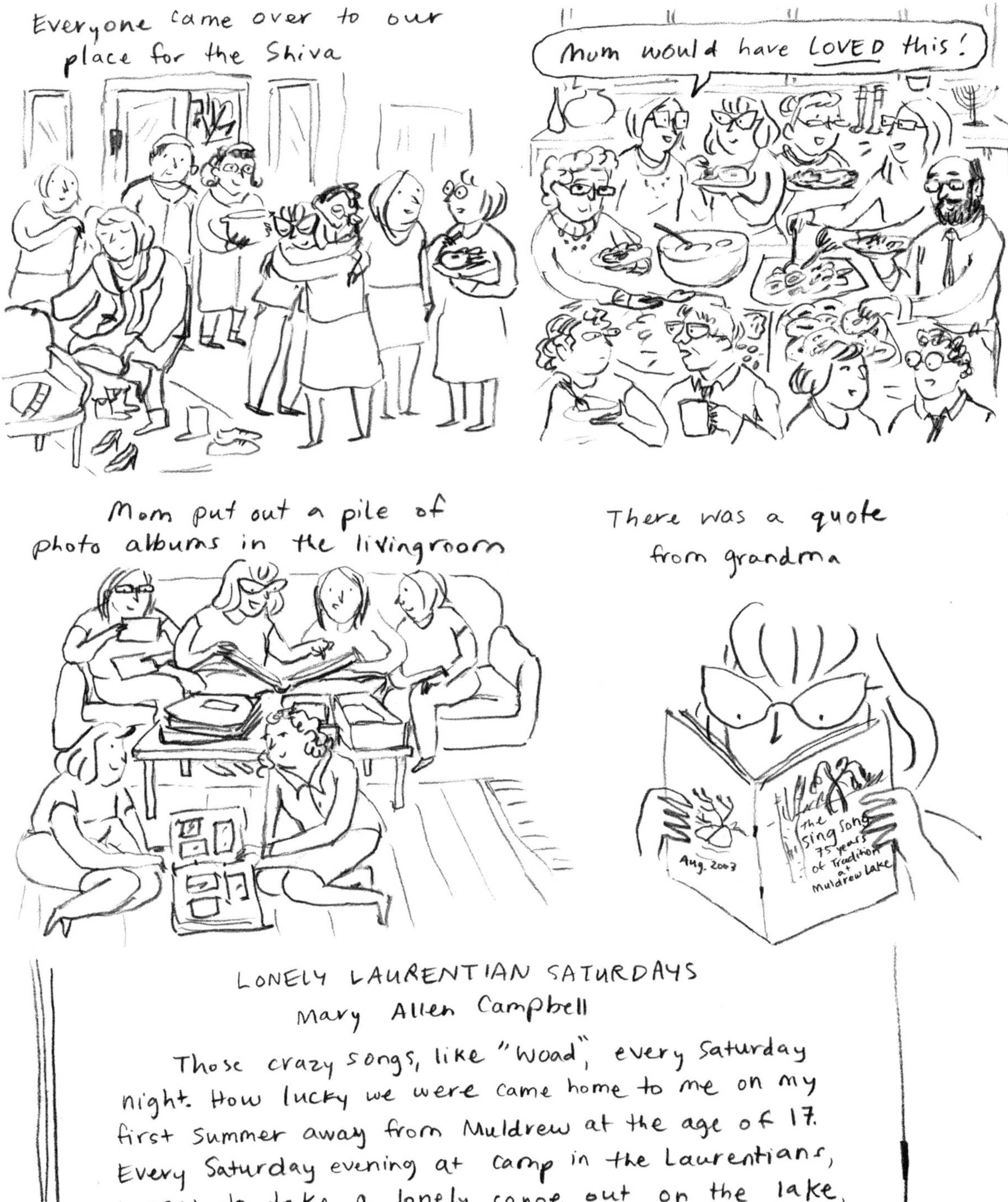
Everyone came over to our place for the Shiva
Mom would have LOVED this!
Mom put out a pile of photo albums in the livingroom
There was a quote from grandma
Aug. 2003
The Sing Song 75 years of Tradition at Muldrew Lake
LONELY LAURENTIAN SATURDAYS
Mary Allen Campbell
Those crazy songs, like "Woad", every Saturday night. How lucky we were came home to me on my first summer away from Muldrew at the age of 17. Every Saturday evening at camp in the Laurentians, I used to take a lonely canoe out on the lake, feeling deeply homesick for the Sing Song.

Rebecca Roher is a cartoonist & illustrator from Toronto
with an MFA from the Center for Cartoon Studies.
Her comic "Mom Body" was nominated for an Ignatz
Award in 2015. Rebecca currently lives on the
Toronto Island & enjoys walking other people's dogs.

02/02/15

WRAP ME UP IN MY TARPAULIN JACKET

by R. H. DAVIES

1

A tall stalwart Lancer lay dying,
  And as on his deathbed he lay
To his friends who around him were sighing,
  These last dying words he did say —

CHORUS.

Wrap me up in my (tarpaulin / old sable) jacket,
  And say a poor buffer lies low,
And six stalwart Lancers shall carry me,
  With steps, solemn, mournful, and slow,

2

Had I the wings of a little dove,
  Far, far away I would fly,
Straight to the arms of my true love,
  There I would lay me and die.
    Chorus — Wrap me up, &c.

3

Then get you two little white tombstones,
  Put them one at my head and my toe,
And get you a pen-knife and scratch there
  Here lies a poor buffer below.
    Chorus — Wrap me up, &c.

4

And get you six brandies and sodas,
  And lay them all out in a row,
And get you six jolly good fellows,
  To drink to this buffer below
    Chorus — Wrap me up, &c.

5

And then in the calm of the twilight,
  When the soft winds whispering blow,
And the darkening shadows are falling,
  Sometimes think of this buffer below.
    Chorus — Wrap me up, &c.

HBC. 2485.

Mary Louise Allen Campbell
"Grandma Wylie"
1921 - 2015